Rethinking Thailand's Southern Violence

Rethinking Thailand's Southern Violence

Edited by
Duncan McCargo

NUS PRESS
SINGAPORE

© NUS Press
National University of Singapore
AS3-01-02, 3 Arts Link
Singapore 117569

Fax: (65) 6774-0652
E-mail: nusbooks@nus.edu.sg
Website: http://www.nus.edu.sg/npu

First Edition 2007
Reprint 2007

ISBN 978-9971-69-362-6 (Paper)

National Library Board Singapore Cataloguing in Publication Data

Rethinking Thailand's southern violence / edited by Duncan McCargo. –
    Singapore : NUS Press, c2007.
        p. cm.
        Includes bibliographical references and index.
        ISBN-13 : 978-9971-69-362-6 (pbk.)

        1. Insurgency – Thailand, Southern.   2. Islam and politics – Thailand,
    Southern.   3. Muslims – Thailand, Southern – Political activity.   4. Thailand,
    Southern – Politics and government.
    I. McCargo, Duncan.

JC328.5
322.4209593 — dc22   SLS2006043767

Printed by: Vetak Services

CONTENTS

Maps, Illustrations, Figures and Tables

Maps

Illustrations

Figures

Tables

PREFACE

ANY ACADEMIC STUDY OF THE SOUTHERN THAI CONFLICT must engage with the politics of language. The debate begins over the use of place names: "Pattani" is the name of a modern Thai province, whereas "Patani" alludes to an older and larger area (roughly corresponding to the three provinces of Pattani, Narathiwat, and Yala), and may carry some Malay nationalist connotations. As Chaiwat Satha-Anand has argued, while on one level the different spellings simply reflect a minor variation between Thai and Malay, to use the term "Patani" could also be a political choice, since the word "reflects the grandeur of this Malay kingdom in the past, refuses the present administrative arrangement which, in turn, means that to some extent the possibility of change can still be thought of."[1]

By the same token, using the double "t"-ed spelling, "Pattani," could be seen as expressing support for the existing political order in the region. In this volume, contributors have exercised a free choice in such matters, using "Pattani" or "Patani" as they felt appropriate. The use of the spelling "Patani" here does not necessarily have the political implications suggested by Chaiwat; in some cases, the spelling has been employed descriptively, or simply because it seeks to invoke (rather than to commend) a wider imagined or historical region than that described by the modern administrative term "Pattani." While we need to be alive to the nuances of linguistic choices, we should also recognize that not every linguistic choice carries a loaded political meaning.

Similar considerations apply to the terms used to describe the Muslim people of the southern border provinces. Chaiwat himself prefers the term "Malay Muslims,"[2] but many more conservative Thais insist on using "Thai Muslims." After much debate, the National Reconciliation Commission (NRC) finally settled on the rather convoluted formulation: "Thai Muslims of Malay descent."[3] Most of the contributors here have followed Chaiwat in using the term "Malay Muslim," but there has been no editorial attempt to enforce consistency of terminology.

Thai transliteration is another vexed area for anyone writing about Thailand in English. Like most of my other publications, this volume employs a simplified version of the Library of Congress system, using only the twenty-six letters of the Roman alphabet, with no tone markers and no indications of vowel length. The aim is to transliterate Thai roughly as the language is pronounced, rather than as it is written.

This edited volume, which began life as a themed issue of the journal *Critical Asian Studies* (formerly the *Bulletin of Concerned Asian Scholars*), has been made possible with the support of various organizations and individuals. The nucleus of the project was a program of academic exchange on the theme of conflict resolution in the Thai South. This Higher Education Link between the University of Leeds and Prince of Songkla University — originally negotiated by Michael Connors — was funded by the British government's Department for International Development and managed by the British Council's Bangkok office from 2002 to 2006. When Thailand's southern border provinces became the focus of renewed political violence after January 2004, the rationale for a sustained critical analysis of the issues involved was clear.

At our initial workshop, held in Pattani on 26 February 2005, additional papers by Chidchanok Rahimmula and Ibrahem Narongraksakket helped shape our thinking, as did the participation of Sukree Langputeh, Worawit Baru, and other colleagues. Arlene Neher, organizer of the Ninth International Conference on Thai Studies held at Northern Illinois University, DeKalb, Ill., 3–6 April 2005, kindly gave our session "Crisis and Conflict in Thailand's Deep South" the opening slot of the conference, immediately following Chaiwat Satha-Anand's keynote address. The participation of Ukrist, Srisompob, and Wattana in the DeKalb conference was made possible through the helpful intervention of Thongchai Winichakul, with funding from the University of Wisconsin, Madison. Chaiwat Satha-Anand's participation was supported by the Asia Foundation. Panyasask and Tan-Mullins received financial assistance from the conference organizers, and McCargo from the British Academy and the University of Leeds. In editing the papers for publication, Duncan McCargo wishes to acknowledge help received from Michael Connors, Patrick Jory, Francesca Lawe-Davies, Michael Montesano, M.L.R. Smith, and Michelle Tan.

McCargo's own fieldwork in Pattani from September 2005 onwards was supported by the Economic and Social Research Council, grant number RES-000-22-1344. At Prince of Songkla University, Srisompob, Wattana, and many other colleagues provided him with an apparently inexhaustible supply of hospitality and intellectual companionship. Final editing of the book manuscript was completed while McCargo was a visiting senior research fellow at the Asia Research Institute, National University of Singapore; thanks are due to Tony Reid and Bryan Turner for their support.

Finally, this project could not have been completed without Tom Fenton, the indefatigable managing editor of *Critical Asian Studies*, who prepared the texts of both the thematic issue and the subsequent book more or less single-handedly. He also compiled the index. Tom succeeded in retaining his good humor throughout a protracted and often fraught editorial process, and really deserves some sort of medal for his service to the cause.

Duncan McCargo
August 2006

Rethinking Thailand's Southern Violence

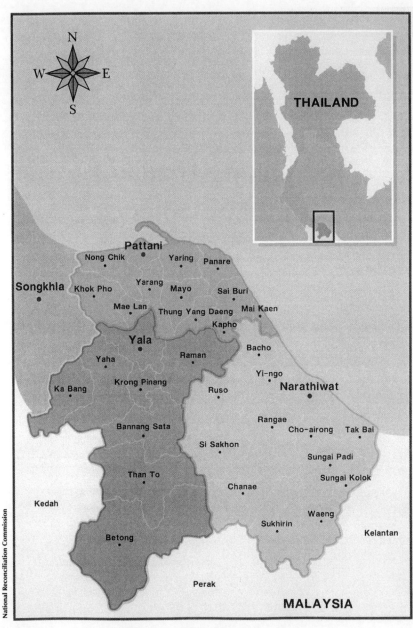

Thailand's Southern Border Provinces

INTRODUCTION

Behind the Slogans:
Unpacking Patani Merdeka

Duncan McCargo

W HAT LIES BEHIND THE RECENT VIOLENCE IN THE THAI SOUTH? This apparently simple question is surprisingly difficult to answer. The subregion that includes the three provinces of Pattani, Yala, and Narathiwat (see map, facing) was only incorporated into Siam (as the country was then known) in 1909, and roughly 80 percent of its population of around 1.8 million are Malay Muslims. Political and administrative power, however, remains firmly in the hands of a de facto Buddhist state. The area has a long history of resistance to the authority of Bangkok, and the past century has been characterized by periodic bouts of insurgency.[1] During the 1970s, this insurgency was linked to an explicit "separatist" movement. Many of the leaders of that movement surrendered under an amnesty policy announced in 1980. The Prem Tinsulanond government (1980–88) effectively brokered a kind of social contract in the area. The security forces were not too abusive, local Muslim leaders could report problems to a central agency and in exchange violence was kept to manageable levels. Nevertheless, Malay Muslims in the three provinces continued to harbor a range of grievances against the Thai state, particularly about access to educational and employment opportunities.

In February 2001, Thailand underwent a change in political direction. Whereas the 1990s had seen the decline of military influence, the institutionalization of parliamentary politics, and the promulgation of the liberal, reformist 1997 constitution, the new millennium witnessed the remarkable political rise of Thaksin Shinawatra. A billionaire telecommunications tycoon, often casually compared with Italy's Silvio Berlusconi, Thaksin was also a former police officer who was determined to subordinate Thailand to his personal control.[2] He soon set about changing the security structures in the South. By 2003, his new policies saw a growing number of extrajudicial disappearances in the three provinces, provoking a strong and hostile reaction. At the same time, local militant groups had apparently been rethinking their strategies, partly inspired by the changing geopolitics of the time. Thaksin was a staunch ally of the United States, and strongly supported the post–September 11 "war on terrorism" declared by President George W. Bush. His decision to send a token contingent of Thai troops to Iraq infuriated Thailand's Muslim population, especially in the South.

On 4 January 2004, more than a hundred assailants made a bold attack on an army camp in Narathiwat, seizing over four hundred weapons and separating out and killing four Buddhist soldiers. Thaksin responded by declaring martial law, and a new phase of violence ensued.[3] On 28 April 2004, more than a hundred lightly armed militants were killed after making simultaneous attacks on eleven security checkpoints. Thirty-two of them were shot at point-blank range inside the historic Kru-Ze mosque in Pattani.[4] Matters escalated further after a demonstration outside the Tak Bai police station on 25 October 2004, when over a thousand Muslim protestors were arrested and piled into trucks. Seventy-eight of them died en route to nearby army bases. Since Tak Bai, shootings, arson attacks, and bombings have continued on a more or less daily basis in the three provinces, with no end in sight. The conflict has created problems for Thailand's relations with neighboring Malaysia, with Indonesia, and with the Organization of Islamic Countries.

The Thai government pursued two parallel yet contradictory courses of action during 2005. In March, under pressure from the Privy Council, Thaksin set up a high-profile National Reconciliation Commission (NRC) to develop proposals for a peaceful solution to the

Duncan McCargo

"War Room" at government offices in Narathiwat Province, southern Thailand. Political and administrative power in Thailand's Muslim-dominated southern provinces "remains firmly in the hands of a de facto Buddhist state."

violence in the South. Yet, in July, the cabinet hastily approved new emergency legislation that gave the prime minister unprecedented personal powers. Despite paying lip service to ideas of reconciliation, Thaksin has demonstrated a consistent preference for policies of securitization and repression.

The chapters in this book shed light on the southern Thai conflict from a variety of perspectives. Chaiwat Satha-Anand, himself a leading member of the National Reconciliation Commission (he was responsible for drafting its report), addresses a set of themes that reflect many years of studying the political history of the region. His ostensible focus is not on the present day, but on an obscure monument that stands inside the provincial police compound in Narathiwat. The bullet-shaped monument, which has no accompanying plaque, commemorates the deaths of around thirty police officers in the "Dusun-nyor rebellion" of 1948, when the police fought pitched battles with Malay-Muslim villagers. Chaiwat suggests that the obscurity of the monument reflects a degree of collective amnesia about the events. The rather gruesome shape of the monument might be seen as glorifying the deaths of numerous Malay Muslims (estimates range from thirty to six hundred) in the violent incident. Yet in many respects the "Dusun-nyor rebellion" has important parallels with much more recent events, notably the heavy-handed actions of the Thai security forces on 28 April 2004. Ironically, it seems highly possible that Dusun-nyor was not intended as a "rebellion" at all — the intentions of the villagers may have been misunderstood by local security officials, who launched an unnecessary attack on them. Chaiwat's chapter urges his readers to pay attention to the ambiguities and nuances of local histories and sensitivities in the deep South, rather than supporting simplistic solutions driven by a preference for violence.

The next two contributions examine the Southern conflict in relation to the government of Thaksin Shinawatra. Since the two authors have coauthored a book on Thaksin,[5] it is not surprising that there are some similarities of perspective, though these chapters were written quite independently. Duncan McCargo relates the conflict in the South to a struggle for the control of Thailand more generally. In this struggle, Thaksin was initially pitted, not against separatists or the opposition Democrat Party, but against "network monarchy," a set of power structures linked to the palace. Making arguments generally avoided by Thai scholars, McCargo suggests that Thaksin has been engaged in a competition for power with the monarchical institution. He further argues that Thaksin's attempts to displace monarchical power contributed substantially to the post–January 2004 upsurge in violence. Subsequent developments, notably the creation of the National Reconciliation Commission, illustrate the attempts of "network monarchy" — led by a group of prominent members of the Privy Council — to resist Thaksin's seizure of power. Read in this way, the southern conflict is not simply about the South per se. The "liminal zone" of the border provinces has been thrust to the very center of Thailand's national politics; in this sense, "the periphery has come to town."

Ukrist Pathmanand emphasizes the way in which Thaksin has sought to exploit the South to whip up nationalist sentiment, thereby distracting public attention from his own policy shortcomings. He argues that Thaksin's hawkish approach to the South involves a deliberate "mobilization of hatred"[6] among Thai Buddhists toward the country's Malay-Muslim minority. Ukrist suggests that Thaksin has successfully manipulated Buddhist chauvinism, in conjunction with hard-line policies aimed at suppressing resistance in the South, as a means of courting electoral popularity in the rest of Thailand. Thaksin has deliberately surrounded himself with security chiefs who share his views. In any case, he has rotated his adjutants with such frequency that they are all completely subordinated to his personal dominance.

A group of men allegedly involved in militant activities surrender to the authorities at Narathiwat Provincial Hall, 15 August 2005. Most of those participating in these "surrender ceremonies" turned out to have little or no involvement in the ongoing violence; they were coerced or cajoled into turning themselves in, after their names appeared on official blacklists.

Ukrist argues that Thaksin has been playing a very dangerous political game in the South, one that could have disastrous consequences for Thailand's future. The arguments made by McCargo and Ukrist resonate with the views of many Malay Muslims in the deep South, who insist that if Thaksin were no longer prime minister, the conflict would immediately decline. This widely shared assumption remains unproven.

The next two chapters are the first extended English-language journal articles on the recent conflict by scholars who are based in the deep South, and should really be read together. In a chapter that will serve as an important reference point for everyone working on the southern conflict, Srisompob Jitpiromsri and Panyasak Sobhonvasu set out to review a considerable body of statistical material about the conflict. First, they clearly demonstrate that the escalation of violence in January 2004 was an extremely dramatic one. They go on to examine data concerning socioeconomic explanations for the southern conflict, and soon conclude that while legitimate Muslim grievances over issues such as employment and education are important, they do not begin to account for the January 2004 upsurge. Nor are historical explanations about Malay-Muslim culture and identity adequate reasons for the latest violence — this is much more than a spontaneous "peasant uprising" of the kind Thailand has often experienced. Srisompob and Panyasak report the results of two surveys of urban residents of Pattani, both of which reflect general confusion on the ground about the identity of the perpetrators of violence. However, the surveys appear to show a growing belief that militant movements are the leading perpetrators: theories implicating local officials or organized criminals were less popular in February 2005 than a year earlier. The chapter's most important findings come at the end, where the authors discuss a recent survey of more than a thousand key informants. The informants were asked to explain local understandings concerning the identities of perpetrators involved in recent violent incidents. The response — one that surprised the authors — was that more than 80 percent of the perpetrators were believed to be militants. Viewed alongside data illustrating a growing proportion of the victims of violence are Muslim — including the majority of those murdered in the first half of 2005 — the evidence suggests that Muslim-on-Muslim violence is now the fastest growing category of violent incidents in the deep South.

Srisompob's colleague Wattana Sugunnasil takes up the argument at this point, insisting that the jihadist overtones of the recent violence need to be more seriously acknowledged and analyzed. These overtones were most clearly seen in the 28 April 2005 attacks, during which young men wielding knives charged at armed soldiers and police. Though not "suicide attacks" in the commonly understood sense, these were attacks apparently undertaken by men who must have known they would not survive. Wattana finds clues concerning their thinking and motivation in a document entitled *Berjihad di Patani*, which was found in the Kru-Ze mosque after the bloody siege. Important elements in this document include injunctions to the faithful to turn their backs on their own family members in the cause of Islam, and statements that "hypocrites" (fellow Muslims who were collaborating with the enemies of religion) deserved to die. Wattana argues that such ideas, which have a long provenance in militant Islam, are important in explaining the changed tactics of the southern insurgent movement since the beginning of 2004. Focusing on militant Islam is not a popular line of interpretation in Thaksin's Thailand. The Thaksin government and the security forces prefer to believe that they are fighting "bandits" or some reconfigured version of the old separatist groups. They also tend to see the struggle in terms of territory, hence all the talk of communist–insurgency-style "red zones." By contrast, the conciliators — the NRC, and most liberal or progressive thinkers in Thailand — prefer to construct the conflict in terms of abstract principles such as truth, justice, equity, and transparency, and typically view abuses by the Thai state as the primary catalyst of the struggle. For Wattana, though, the southern Thai conflict is now becoming a struggle of ideas derived from radical readings of Islam.

In two further contributions, May Tan-Mullins and Michael Connors offer additional vantage points on the conflict. Looking from the bottom up, Tan-Mullins gathers together snippets of conversations collected during her doctoral research in Pattani in 2003 and 2004, fragments that offer insights into how ordinary people — both Buddhist and Muslim — perceive the conflict on the ground. Her contribution brings the diurnal realities of the southern Thai violence to life. Looking from the top down, Michael Connors discusses the only book in English so far published on the southern crisis, *Conflict and Terrorism in Southern Thailand*, by Rohan Gunaratna, Arabinda Acharaya, and Sabrina Chua.[7] He argues that, to date, experts on "international terrorism" have brought little of value to our understandings of the Thai conflict. Books and articles by terrorism specialists are generally under-researched, and characterized by catalogs of errors, sloppy thinking, and a preference for overly speculative explanations. Connors is deeply uneasy with the attempts of Gunaratna et al. to translate a complex, messy, and highly ambiguous conflict into a tidy narrative of political violence perpetrated by specified actors for explicit motives. He urges those working on this and similar ethnic or religious conflicts to resist the seductions of reductionist explanations.

The conflict in the Thai South clearly cannot be divorced from wider political developments in the post-9/11 world. Yet the contributors to this book are unanimous in seeing the conflict as primarily framed by Thailand's domestic political and social realities. But it would be simplistic to assume, for example, that just because the conflict has not been explicitly linked to international militant networks, it has no Islamic dimension. The essays here all challenge the reader to question conventional categories and lazy assumptions. Catchall terms such as "the Thai state," "militant groups," "Muslim communities," and "security agencies" need to be closely scrutinized, unpacked, and critically reviewed before convincing conclusions can be reached. These essays are a small start in this important direction.

❑

1 THE SILENCE OF THE BULLET MONUMENT

Violence and "Truth" Management, Dusun-nyor 1948, and Kru-Ze 2004

Chaiwat Satha-Anand

I N HIS LECTURE "QU'EST-CE QU 'UNE NATION'?" given in Paris in 1882, Ernest Renan wrote: "Forgetting, I would even go so far as to say historical error, is a crucial factor in the creation of a nation, which is why progress in historical studies often constitutes a danger for [the principle of] nationality. Indeed, historical enquiry brings to light deeds of violence which took place at the origin of all political formations."[1] If Renan is right, not only does every state need to foster a sense of sustained nationhood through the construction of imagined communities, it also needs to manage "truth" about its founding violence.[2] I am interested in how different political formations manage "truths" about violence that appeared not only at the moment when a nation was born, but also at different moments in its biography and in different sites such as in local communities remotely situated from the center of political authority.

This article is an attempt to consider the problem of violence and "truth" management from a case of violence in southern Thailand, generally known as the "Dusun-nyor rebellion," which occurred in Narathiwat Province in April 1948. Some Muslim writers maintain that this was the "most violent confrontation" ever between the police and local Muslim villagers.[3] Surin Pitsuwan considers the case of Dusun-nyor symbolically as the spirit of resistance and a continuing inspiration for various liberation movements in southern Thailand.[4] A local Malay-Muslim historian[5] calls the rebellion "the greatest tragedy in the history of the Malay struggle for justice and freedom."[6]

When I first saw a picture of the bullet-shaped Dusun-nyor monument in Narathiwat in a Muslim newsmagazine,[7] I was surprised both by the shape and form of this monument and by the fact that, as someone interested in the subject for some time, I had not been aware of its existence. The more I worked on this case, the more astonished I became because even some academics in the South were confused. Some confused this incident with another that took place in Pattani in 1947, when a police officer was shot dead in Balugasamoh. A group of police officers returned to the village, brutally interrogated some villagers, accused them of collaborating with the bandits, and burned the village to the ground. The Balugasamoh incident left some twenty-five families homeless.[8] In the course of conducting research on this subject, most of the people I talked with, police, soldiers, and academics, were not aware of the existence of this bullet-shaped monument. Both the confusion about the case and the absence of knowledge about the monument led me to try to understand the sound of silence that surrounds the case and the monument of Dusun-nyor.

Though necessary for any research, my sense of wonder is not sufficient to answer why a monument should be turned into an object of study. I will therefore begin with the importance of monuments as an embodiment of collective memories or as a "truth" management instrument, as distinctively seen in international and local academic landscapes during the last decade. Then the Dusun-nyor case will be discussed in the eyes of both Thai and Malay academics, as well as from interviews with survivors from the rebellion. The monument itself will also be analyzed in the context of how Dusun-nyor is remembered in order to understand how this, the "greatest tragedy in the history of the Malay struggle," has been managed through the silence of monument as a representation of that "truth." The place of this study in the landscape of present monument studies will be outlined. Finally, the ways in which "truth" management in the case of Dusun-nyor could be connected with more recent violence, especially the incident generally known as Kru-Ze 2004, will be suggested.

Monument Studies 101?

Monuments contain, or point to, traces of collective memory, which is a way public memory could be produced.[9] The shape, site, and official description of a monument indicate how a political society wishes to remember incidents and people(s) in the past in the process of galvanizing a sense of belonging among people in a newly created political society. One basic problem is that political societies are not monolithic. Peoples' feelings vary, especially in connection with traumatic experiences of past violence such as those in Brazil, Argentina, Chile, Uruguay, Turkey, and Israel-Palestine, among others. The problem of social memory is highly contested between those who believe that a society has to move on — and therefore the past needs to be forgotten — and those who maintain that the only way to move into the future is through remembering the pasts. After Uruguay "returned" to democracy in 1985, President Julio Maria Sanguinetti said that democracy would be badly served by a "morbid dwelling on prior history." General Augusto Pinochet of Chile put it bluntly: "It is best to remain silent and forget. It is the only thing to do: we must forget. And forgetting does not occur by opening cases, putting people in jail."[10] A "counter-hegemonic approach" calls for confronting the pasts by recalling them to mind. Recent Latin American experiences, in which countries have turned more democratic and gained greater freedom, have also raised the question of how democratic power can be shared between the people who were once victims of torture, imprisonment, and rape and those who were victimizers, without the latter's acknowledgment of the crimes so that the pasts could not be clouded as though they had never happened. Former victims of past violence believe that remembering the past is necessary not only for moral reasons, but also to strengthen democracy by holding accountable those responsible for the political crimes, and to prevent such horror from happening in the future.[11] Remembering, however, can take many forms, including truth commissions, trials of perpetrators, lustrations, confessions, art, academic research, pedagogical packages for children, archives, and the use of museums and monuments.[12]

In Chile, there are two important monuments. The Monument in the National Cemetery to the Disappeared is a huge wall where over

Anonymous

Narathiwat's newest monument commemorates a bizarre political stunt. In December 2004, Prime Minister Thaksin "sought to create a positive news bonanza by asking Thai to produce millions of origami cranes to be scattered over the South, in a gesture indicating the popular desire for peace."

twenty-five hundred names of those politically executed or made to disappear are inscribed. The second is the reclaiming of a violent space, a former torture center, Villa Grimaldi. The center has been turned into a Peace Park, a powerful space for reflection on the past. Some might regard these monuments as memory museums.[13] It could be argued that these monuments are results of political struggles in societies that have successfully moved beyond military dictatorship. As a result, reclaiming and transforming public space into a space of memory where "truths" about traumatic pasts can be confronted, has become possible.

In the past decade, there have been at least three critical works written in Thai in the area of monument studies.[14] Nidhi Aeusrivongse's *Songkhram anusawri kap rat thai* [The battle of monuments and the Thai state] situates monuments in the context of history and different traditions of monument building in Thai society.[15] Relying on symbolic, architectural, and ritualistic functions in relation to monument building, Nidhi shows the changing character of the Thai state seen from two contested streams of Thai state consciousness: the monarchist and "the nation-state," taking into account the prevalent idolatry culture in Thai society. In writing a collective history of Thai society through monuments, it seems the monarchists' monuments featuring those of King Rama I and the equestrian monument of King Rama V emerge triumphantly over the mark of 1932, which, according to Nidhi, is nothing but a pollutant at the feet of the King's monument,[16] while the Democracy Monument on Rajadamnoen Road is truly "foreign": with its ambiguous meaning, traffic-related location, and an absence of the sacred sense, it has become powerless. In fact, it is "as bland as a large pile of cement in the middle of the street."[17]

Malinee Koomsupa studies the political implications of the Democracy Monument from 1939, the year it was built, until 1997, and found that its meanings changed over time.[18] By focusing on its name, the use of space, writings, and pictures, she shows how the meanings of this monument have moved beyond its original connection with the 1932 revolution to an expanded democracy with more popular participation. Its power is constituted by a number of conditions that include its original/historical meaning, its central location, as well as its geostrategic importance, with room for gatherings of large numbers of people. More importantly, perhaps, its power lies in the fact that through time, popular participation, which has used this monument in shaping Thai political events, has transformed its meanings into a legitimate and powerful form of knowledge.[19]

While the monuments studied by Nidhi and Malinee are national, Saipin Kaew-ngarmprasert chose to study the Tao Suranaree monument, also known as Khun Ying Moe's, because it was the first "common people" and "woman monument" to appear after the 1932 revolution.[20] Saipin suggests that this monument was built as a symbol of Korat's loyalty to Bangkok, at a time when Bangkok was in need of fostering solidarity with local people in the provinces. Saipin points out that both Khun Ying Moe's heroism and her monument were constructed for political purposes, notably to foster the state's professed ideology, which can be seen from the "messages" the monument conveys about gender equality, the success of the "democratic" faction in their fight against the royalists, and strengthening the government's security through the use of nationalist sentiment among the people.[21]

Comparing monument studies in Thailand and abroad, important differences emerge. First, in societies that have recently moved beyond long-entrenched military dictatorships, the focus is on how to confront the pasts, which depends on shifting power relations, among other things. If dictatorships still existed in South Africa and Chile, there could be no Truth and Reconciliation Commission in South Africa or Monument to the Disappeared in Chile. Those who called for the building of these monuments are primarily from civil society. But in Thailand, apart from the cases of the "October 14" and "May 1992" heroes, the monuments mentioned above continue to engage in struggles for meaning, and they reflect an unending political struggle for power as well. Thus, their meanings continue to be shaped and reshaped by ongoing struggles. The Khun Ying Moe monument is different: for it depicts the heroism of a local "woman" of common origin in a national historical plot that institutionalizes the "truth" about power relations between Korat and Bangkok. It has become a powerful monument, despite its common woman origin, due to the cult of idolatry and the tales of Khun Ying Moe's heroism revealed in historical documents and public beliefs. Its sacredness, profoundly connected with the local Korat "dignity," has been formed and steely sustained.

In the context of the monument studies outlined above, where does the Dusun-nyor monument stand? I would argue that this monument is closer to Khun Ying Moe's than to others. Located in the provinces, and the product of a "rebellion," the bullet-shaped monument was built by those associated with the powerful state. Yet, the fame of the Khun Ying Moe monument has reached the four corners of the land, while the Dusun-nyor monument remains in silence. To understand the silence surrounding this monument, it is important to understand the violence that took place in Dusun-nyor village in 1948.

The Case of Dusun-nyor: Writings and Words

The 1999 Senate Special Committee report on the "southern problems" did not mention the Dusun-nyor case in particular. It simply placed this case in the context of separatist movements that include BRN (Barisan Revolution National), created in 1960, and PULO (Patani United Liberation Organization), which began in 1968. The incident that took place in Dusun-nyor in 1948 was called the "Dusun-nyor riot."[22] When Piyanat Bunnag studied government policies toward the southern Muslims, "the Dusun-nyor rebellion" was situated in the context of Field Marshal Phibun Songkram's ascension to political power on 8 April 1948. She points out that the field marshal must have realized that his earlier policy of turning the Muslims into Thais had been too aggressive. This time the government exploited a path in moderation. A Muslim was appointed deputy minister of education for the first time. Members of parliament from Yala and Narathiwat advised the government to follow the Muslims' demands because "the unrest in the area would otherwise intensify." But then there was a huge "riot" in Narathiwat on 26–27 April 1948 that took place "before the government could solve the problems." The Ministry of Interior received a telegram from Narathiwat informing them that "around 1,000 Thai Muslims attacked a police station near the Kelantan border. The fighting went on for two days and more than 100 people had died."[23] Imron Malueleem came up with a similar account of how the Phibun government "seemed to be more cautious" and had turned out some moderate policies that included a Muslim minister and the government's willingness to listen to members of parliament regarding these Muslims' suffering and demands. But "before the government could begin to solve any problem, the crisis erupted into "the Narathiwat rebellion" on 25–26 April in the same year (1948). Some one thousand Thai Muslims attacked the police near the Kelantan border and between thirty and one hundred people died. Local people in Dusun-nyor said: "The Thai police fired first."[24]

In fact, in mid-1947, before Field Marshal Phibun came to power, Haji Sulong Abdulkader, a Malay-Muslim leader from Pattani, had presented his seven-point demands to the Thai government. He was arrested on 16 January 1948.[25] Thereafter, the Thai government tended to take the Malay-Muslims' demands seriously. Syukri wrote that after Haji Sulong's arrest on 16 January, Bangkok sent a special police force to be stationed in the southern border area to prevent further troubles on 30 January 1948.[26] Nik Anuar Nik Mahmud, a Malaysian scholar, described the Dusun-nyor incident as a spontaneous "uprising" (*kebangkitan*). On 20 April 1948, he wrote, the police fired upon some villagers who were having a socio-religious gathering. Then they retreated to Tanjong Mas for fear of the villagers' revenge. But in reporting to their superiors, they claimed that a thousand Malay bandits had been preparing to stage a rebellion.[27] On 25 April 1948, sixty more police officers arrived at Tanjong Mas as reinforcements. The Dusun-nyor villagers, meanwhile, prepared to face the police force whom they believed were coming in to vanquish the Malays. On 27 April, the government dispatched an Air Force plane to fly over the village, while the Navy sent in the warship *Bang Nara* to the port, preparing to send in troops. On 28 April, in Dusun-nyor village, deadly conflicts between one thousand Malays and the police force began when the Thai police attacked the Malays, whom the government believed were preparing for a rebellion. Fighting went on for thirty-six hours. The villagers were defeated and finally surrendered. More than four hundred Malays, including women, children, and the elderly, were killed while some thirty police officers lost their lives.[28]

Mohd. Zamberi A. Malek, another Malaysian academic, came up with different details, citing Tengku Mahmoud Mahayideen's report, which claimed that the incident began when the police abruptly attacked a gathering of between sixty and eighty Dusun-nyor villagers. The villagers were dispersed and regrouped in Tanjong Mas. More than one thousand people joined forces and they declared a jihad. The villagers claimed that the police shot into their group first because they thought that the gathering was intended to resist the government. The incident worsened when others in the area joined in because of collective anger resulting from an accumulation of the abuses of their kin at the hands of the officials. Hundreds of police officers were sent in from Bangkok. The fight took place on 26 and 27 April 1948. During the struggle, three planes from the Royal Thai Air Force circled overhead, targeting the villagers. The Royal Thai Navy had reportedly brought a warship into Narathiwat harbor and the Thai forces were rumored to be intent on destroying the Malays. "The police attacks against unarmed villagers" resulted in some four hundred to six hundred deaths among the Malays. On the government side, there were thirty to one hundred casualties, including thirty police officers killed. This incident is known as "the Tok Perak Dusun-nyor War" since the leader of the Malay fighters was one Tuan Hajji Abdul Rahman, a man from the Malay state of Perak, known among the villagers as "Tok Perak."[29]

The historical data about this case are inconsistent. What was the date of this incident: 25, 26, or 28 April? Who began this deadly conflict between the villagers and the police? And how many were killed? From all the evidence I could find, the number of police deaths was confirmed at thirty. But the numbers of Malays killed vary from thirty to one hundred, according to the official report, or four hundred to six hundred, in the writings of some Malay Muslims. One Muslim source, Serajul Islam, indicated that eleven hundred Muslims were killed in the Dusun-nyor incident. Checking his source, I found that he cited W.K. Che Man for his figure. Rechecking Che Man's work, I could not find the eleven hundred number. In fact, Che Man used figures similar to most Malay writers, four hundred Malay Muslims and thirty police officers killed.[30]

Two important points arise from such discrepancies. First, the Dusun-nyor incident was termed differently by different sides. The Thai government labeled it a "rebellion" or a "riot," yet no one from the Malay sources cited above so describes it.[31] The Malay words used to describe this incident were either "uprising" (*kebangkitan*) or "war" (*perang*). Second, the official version of this incident maintained that it was planned as a struggle against the Bangkok government. Writers from Malaysia, on the other hand, all understand it as a spontaneous incident, and not an organized movement with a clear political objective from the beginning. It is interesting to ask how the villagers of Dusun-nyor themselves remember this incident, which occurred almost six decades ago.

Rattiya Salae, a Muslim writer from Songkla, reported that the villagers called this incident "Purae Dusun-nyor" or the Dusun-nyor war.[32] The incident began with a misunderstanding when the government mistook a superstitious gathering of the villagers for an organized separatist maneuver. The villagers gathered to perform a sacred bathing ritual to make their bodies impervious to weapons. They said that their leader had supernatural powers, and could fast and recite the holy Qur'an until the floor beneath him cracked open. It was said that one of his disciples could make ten others safe from weapon attacks.[33] The question, then, is why did the Dusun-nyor villagers perform this sacred oil bathing ceremony? Why did they want their bodies to be impervious to harm?

Ahmad Somboon Bualuang raised a question in his article "Was Dusun-nyor a Rebellion?" by relating the incident from the perspective of an old man whom he believed to be involved in the incident at the time. He said the attack against the villagers took place in the morning of 28 April 1948 when the people were offering their morning prayers.

Hundreds of those who were praying were killed instantly by bullets. Some were injured while many others dispersed in different directions.... They were all killed at the hands of unjust and mad rulers....We need to fight those we had no intention to. They were officials who needed to be corrected by the government. But the Chinese [Chinese Communist Party of Malaya] were foreign bandits who threatened and abused the people of the country. When the government did not solve the problems but chose to kill the people, we were in a cul-de-sac. We had to fight and declare *jihad* against all forms of enemies....We had to find all kinds of instruments we could in the community to make our weapons: bamboos and wood turned into spears and sticks. Axes, knives and swords were sharpened and inscribed with sacred words based on knowledge from before.[34]

If this account is "true," it could be said that the villagers did prepare to fight. But the purpose was to fight against the Communist Party of Malaya, which caused them trouble, while the government was unable to provide them with protection. They had to protect themselves. But different people in this case could choose to fight the Thai government for their own reasons.

Mukta Tapoo, a seventy-seven-year–old man who was himself involved in the Dusun-nyor incident[35] was in his twenties at the time. He studied at Tok Yong *pondok* in Nong Chik, Pattani. Before the incident, he had returned to his home in Dusun-nyor for many months. Chinese bandits repeatedly attacked and stole food from his village. The villagers organized to fight these bandits. One group gathered on Tue Gor Mountain, several kilometers from the village, to perform a sacred oil bathing ceremony in a cave called "ox cave," a small place that could accommodate only a few people. Mukta himself did not participate in the ritual, but saw others who did. Many dipped their hands into the (boiling?) coconut oil in the pan, which had

Two views of the "bullet monument" (here and on the facing page). Curiously, "the monument does not appear on the official list of 184 monuments built in Thailand from 1841 to 1994."

been blessed in the ceremony. They then applied the oil on their bodies, believing that bullets and other weapons could then no longer harm them. He also said that some of the villagers who gathered on the mountain were young men who had dodged the military draft. They were afraid of the hardships that came with being soldiers. More importantly, perhaps, they believed that once becoming Thai soldiers, they would be forced to pay homage to Buddha images. The officials followed them up the mountain to persuade them to come down. But they refused and chased the officials away. After that, the police went up to fire at the villagers on the mountain. The villagers fought the police down, then congregated at the mosque and at Tok Perak's house, which served as a pondok (traditional Malay religious school) in the village.

At the time of the attack in Dusun-nyor, police officers went up the mountain to fire at the villagers who had gathered there on Saturday and were chased down. If the police assault was on Saturday, then the deadly struggle took place on Monday, 26 April 1948. More than eight hundred villagers — including Mukta Tapoo — were on the mountain, along with several of their leaders (e.g., Haji Ma Karae Pageseng, Ma Lagor Hasan, Guedor Awae, and Luedor Awae Ju). The villagers fought with whatever they could find, guns, knives, swords. On the first day, three villagers and five police officers were killed. On the second day, Mukta did not go to fight the police because his brother had been shot in the shoulder. His friend told him later that the police had to retreat, leaving behind lots of

Duncan McCargo

bullet casings at Kampong Yamu, the police stronghold. Rumors had it
that the villagers' magic made the police bullets miss them. The police
were made to see swarms of bees above their heads, they shot into the
sky, enabling the villagers to escape the bullets. Mukta pointed out that
the fighting took place in a steep area. The villagers were on the mountain and the police were down below. It was thus possible that the
police missed their targets. After the incident, most of the leaders fled
to Malaysia. They walked through the forests into Kedah and
Kelantan.[36] One month after that, kamnan Muhammad of Tanjong Mas
and Mustafa, a Muslim leader from Saiburi, were arrested as leaders of
this violent incident. Both were executed without going through due
process of law.[37]

Numerous factors underlie the Dusun-nyor incident. It is important
to note that this was the fiercest fight between government forces and
the Malay-Muslim villagers in the first half of the century. Thirty police
officers were killed while far more villagers' lives were lost, according
to unofficial sources. Thousands of Malay Muslims migrated to Malaysia. The Dusun-nyor incident has since become a symbol of
Malay-Muslim uprising against the Thai state. But from at least a part of
the Thai state's perspective, the Dusun-nyor incident was memorialized in the bullet monument. A Malay-Muslim columnist once asked
why the incident was remembered in the form of a bullet monument?
Is it to mark "the victory of the government officials in successfully suppressing the people?"[38]

This question is important because if monuments are a form of
speech, as Ben Anderson suggests, then what do their specific shapes
and messages tell us?[39] Apart from this important and direct question, I
am also interested in why the Dusun-nyor monument is hardly
known? Why does this bullet monument have no sound but silence?

The Bullet Monument and Silence

Despite the fact that the Dusun-nyor monument could be photograph-
ically captured and pictured in a newsmagazine photo, it does not
appear on the official list of 184 monuments built in Thailand from
1841 to 1994.[40] When asked, the Department of Fine Arts official who
had conducted a nationwide survey of monuments in Thailand (*Monuments in Thailand*)[41] replied that he had never seen the Dusun-nyor
monument. (Nor does the monument appear in the second volume
that the Department of Fine Arts is preparing for publication.) The official suspected that the monument did not have the Department's

authorization. Quite a few monuments did not receive Department permits, yet they were built. When my research assistant checked with police officials at the provincial police station, the site of the monument itself, he was told that there were no documents relating to the monument. If documents did exist, they may have been destroyed in 1967, when local police authorities reorganized their official papers. When a retired police officer, who was serving in 1948, was asked about the monument, he said that he did not know anything about it. When I went to photograph the monument on 9 April 2002, I asked several police officers at the station about the monument, but they told me nothing more than its name and only speculated about "things" they believed were inside the bullet monument. Lieutenant Colonel Seni Nilwang, an eighty-three-year–old retired police officer, who now lives in Narathiwat, maintained that the monument was built one year after the incident at Dusun-nyor by the then commander of the provincial police force of Narathiwat. He also thought that it was Police General Pao Sriyanont, who often visited Narathiwat during the time, who ordered its construction. Seni claims that while hundreds of villagers died in the incident, only four police officers were killed, and not thirty as reported.[42]

In such silence, what can the "Dusun-nyor rebellion monument" represent? It is important to note that representation is the psychological image of perceived external reality.[43] When a monument has no other explanatory documentation, then contemplating its physical reality may help us understand its silence as representation.[44] By "physical reality" I mean the shape of the monument (a bullet, in this case), whatever may be contained inside the monument, and its site.

The Bullet That Put Down a Rebellion? And the Offerings

The Dusun-nyor monument has three tiers, on top of which sits a gold-colored bullet. In the shell of the bullet, within the 341 cm.–tall structure, is a small rectangular opening that may contain the remains of officers who died in the Dusun-nyor incident (see below). There is no name on the monument, and no description of any kind.

A weapons expert informed me that though it was difficult to identify the type of bullet from the photograph I showed him, he felt certain that it was a bullet from a rifle used during World War II, thus a weapon of war.[45] Yet, only three months after the Dusun-nyor incident, on 6 August 1948, the Ministry of Interior passed a ministerial order classifying war weapons and bullets that were not permitted in private hands. The order included the 1923 rifle and its bullets as prohibited war weapons; only the authorities could use these.[46] This order did not mention the 1945 rifle, however. It could be that this type of rifle was yet to be introduced into Thailand. Most officials at the time were using the 1923-type rifles. If the bullet monument was an exact replica of the bullet used at the time, it is less likely that it would be the bullet of a 1945 rifle but a 1923 rifle, though the two types of bullet are quite similar. If the 1945 bullets were used, they were highly likely to be used by police from Bangkok rather than by local officers.

Duncan McCargo

A close-up photograph of the bullet monument shows the enclosure where the bones of deceased police officers are reputedly stored to be honored.

Whatever the physical dimensions of the monument or questions about the type of the bullet represented in the monument the important point is to remember that the monument calls to mind the deadly fight between the police and the villagers. In fact, the monument contains the memory of violence used as symbolically reflected by the bullet. In addition, the type of bullet is one that only government authorities and not the villagers would have used. Thus, we can conclude that the bullet-shaped monument represents "truth" about the Dusun-nyor incident in the form of state violence against the Malay-Muslim villagers.

When I visited the monument, I saw white and blue plastic bowls on the highest tier at the foot of the bullet; placed alongside used incense sticks, the bowls contained liquid offerings. On the second tier were small jasmine and rose bouquets. Police officers at the station told me that these offerings were meant to honor the thirty police officers killed during the Dusun-nyor incident. But is there any other reason why the offerings were placed at the bullet monument?

Bones in the Bullet?

Nidhi once asked whether, if the Private Black monument in Nakorn Srithammarat were in the shape of a spear on the floor, "so many people [would be] coming to make offerings at the monument?" He believed that a "Thai" monument must blend in the idolatry character popular among local people by "using a respectful human image rather than an [abstract] symbol." The Thais were treating monuments as they would the idols they respect although the building of monuments is a "foreign tradition."[47] If such is indeed the case, why were there offerings at this bullet monument?

When I asked a police officer at the Dusun-nyor station about the offerings, he told me that the small window-like space in the shell of the monument contained the bones of police officers (though he didn't say for certain that these were officers killed in the Dusun-nyor struggle) and the offerings were to honor their memory.[48] When my research assistant inquired later, however, officers said the box contained the bones of officers who were killed in the Dusun-nyor incident. No other details about the owners of these bones or the number of these owners are available.[49]

The shape of a monument can symbolically reflect a past event. But when there are bones of dead people inside, the symbolic bullet assumes a sense of sacredness, although it was not built into a human image, as is the custom in this society. The "bullet" in the Dusun-nyor monument can be read as a story of the police suppression of a rebellion. In this story the officers sacrificed their lives for the nation and thus the bones inside the monument are those of "heroes" and prayers and offerings are appropriate. But if the story is so heroic, why is it so little known among most government officials and the public at large?

The Bullet at the Police Station

The Dusun-nyor rebellion monument is inside the compound of the provincial police station, town district, Narathiwat, and, significantly, not at the site of the violence in Ra-ngae district. The absence of any marker or explanatory description on the monument could account for the silence surrounding the Dusun-nyor monument. Perhaps, a

monument in the shape of a bullet that is more than likely the type the
police used against local villagers does not fit with later state narratives
about the Muslim South, narratives that promote assimilation and,
more recently, acceptance of cultural diversity in Thai society.[50] I would
argue, however, that two further reasons account for the silence. First,
the nature of the monument itself. When Benedict Anderson wrote
"Replica, Aura, and Late Nationalist Imaginings," discussing the relationship between public memorials and dead heroes, he began with a
strange quotation by Robert Musil, from his *Nachlass zu Lebzeiten*.
Musil wrote: "There is nothing in this world as invisible as a monument." Although built to be visible, Musil explained, something in the
monument itself "repels attention, causing the glance to roll right off,
like water droplets off an oilcloth, without even pausing for a moment." This is because monuments "make demands on us that run
contrary to our nature." The head of the monument cannot turn, its
eyes do not blink, nor do its fingers move in step with the music of the
time, as is now seen from mannequins' or robotic movements in some
department stores. Musil thinks that perhaps the monument sculptors
"do not…comprehend our age of noise and movement."[51] The connection between the site and the shape of the monument is also
conducive to the silence in this case. The Dusun-nyor monument is in
the police station and the shape of the monument is that of a rifle bullet. Although the 1923 bullet may symbolically reflect the heroic deeds
of dead police officers almost six decades ago, the image of a bullet in a
police station is not unusual in any sense. In a place where guns and
bullets are kept as stocks needed to defend law and order and protect
citizens' lives and properties, they are normal artifacts.[52] It is not unlike
seeing medicines and dead bodies in hospitals or machines in factories. In the shadow of normality, overlooking this bullet is easier than if
the Dusun-nyor monument had been built into some other symbolic
form.

Anderson raises another interesting question: if Musil is right and
monuments are generally invisible, why is it that they are given such
importance? At the national level, this could be the consequence of the
nationalization of the fallen. But it could also be because some of these
monuments, or graves of unnamed fallen heroes, as in Europe, are in
fact empty, without dead bodies inside. As a result, the monument
could contain the grief and private memories of those who have lost
their loved ones. When an American stands in line to pay respects in
front of the Washington monument, s/he is standing in a line of collec-

tive grief shared by strangers around him/her. But the person is acutely aware of the fact that the ceremony s/he is about to perform is also uniquely private, and cannot be repeated by others due to the private connection each mourner has with the particular fallen hero.[53]

But what happens when people come to pray or make offerings at the bullet monument? I would argue that they also engage in their own private affairs. It is not difficult to imagine a police officer paying his respects or making offerings before leaving on a mission involving the use of his gun and the risk of his life. In this sense, it matters little whether the Dusun-nyor monument is connected with a rebellion that occurred more than half a century ago. It is important, however, for officers making the offerings to connect with the fight of police officers who sacrificed their lives to protect the nation and its people. A very concrete monument in the form of a lone bullet from the past could therefore provide a broad abstract space conducive to connecting peoples of differences in the present. The absence of elaborate or distinctive information about the monument but for its name unlocks its anchor in the past and allows its meanings to float freely in connection with anyone in the present who comes to bow before it and offer individual wishes or prayers.

Second, after the 1948 incident, the Phibun government, like many governments after it, set up a committee to solve the southern problems. This committee returned from field trips to report that the Muslims in the area were deeply dissatisfied. They also predicted that mass migration by the local Malay Muslims to Malaysia was likely.[54] They reported to the government that the Dusun-nyor incident was a result of a misunderstanding that began with a ritualistic gathering of a large number of Malay Muslims to bath themselves in magic oil to make their bodies invulnerable. The police were suspicious and went to check. The villagers refused to allow the police to come up and the conflict expanded and turned deadly. The official committee concluded, "The cause of the riot was not political."[55] Thus, it agreed with the villagers: both concluded that the incident was indeed spontaneous and resulted from a misunderstanding. The villagers at the time were preparing to fight threatening Chinese bandits and not the government. The state officials' misunderstanding and fear of the villagers resulted in the villagers fighting the government forces. If this is indeed the "truth" about the Dusun-nyor incident, then the deaths of the police officers and the Malay Muslims were due to misunderstandings and mistrust. If this is the case, then how should the deaths of these police officers be remembered? Should they be loudly memorialized as the sound of the bullets used in glorious battle? Or would a bullet monument be more appropriate — a monument without any description or records, and almost unknown, an invisible monument like most in the world where people glance right past them as it sits in silence?

The Dusun-nyor Rebellion Monument and the Sound of Silence

"Truths" about the Dusun-nyor incident have been recorded in various forms. Malay-Muslim academics and writers have written about this incident from the perspective of local Pattani Muslims who were forced to connect themselves with destiny and changing governance of the Thai state in the context of the British imperial power controlling much of the Malay peninsular at the time. They remembered the incident both in their writings and memories as an "uprising" or "war" when brave Dusun-nyor villagers fought against the powerful Thai state. Victims of violence in the incident were glaringly called "Melayu," following their distinctive imagined identity. Not surprisingly, the Thai state labels this incident "a riot" or "the Dusun-nyor rebellion."

But the Dusun-nyor incident has also been given expression in the form of a lonely and silent monument: lonely because there is no other monument in the province of Narathiwat; silent because it is a monument without description, without an official name posted anywhere, with almost no one to tell its story. It has only a name, "the Dusun-nyor rebellion" (in common usage), and a shape, a rifle bullet. In analyzing monuments of fallen soldiers, Anderson writes, "at the moment when the real dead are simultaneously forgotten, replicated, sequestered, serialized, and unknown, one returns to the paradoxical question of the origins of what one can only call originlessness."[56] I believe that the Dusun-nyor rebellion monument is something like this. Most Thais are unaware of its origin and although many believe that it contains the bones of dead police officers, no one remembers their names. Yet some Malay Muslims still remember the names of the leaders of the "Dusun-nyor uprising" or the "Dusun-nyor war."

Although I have pointed out that this Dusun-nyor rebellion monument is "invisible," is the bullet monument really silent? What does this monument as "speech" say? It might be silent about the Dusun-nyor incident itself, but the bullet monument as "speech" is making two important points.

First, whatever the "truth" is about the Dusun-nyor incident, this monument is truly one-sided. The monument was built inside the provincial police station, an official institution, an office of government officials who are civil servants charged with maintaining order in Thai political society. They are also a party to the conflict in the Dusun-nyor incident. In addition, the bones of those killed in the incident are believed to be inside the monument. It matters little if the number of these bones matches the number of officers killed. It is important to note, however, that the unnamed police officers must have been Buddhists and they were therefore cremated and their bones stored in the monument. More importantly, they all died at the hands of "the rebels" from Dusun-nyor, all of them Malay Muslims. In this sense, the physical appearance of the Dusun-nyor rebellion monument does "speak" about something. It remembers parts of "truths," namely, that thirty officers were killed while performing their duties, though their names have been forgotten. The monument is blind to the facts that in the same incident, Malay Muslims were murdered by the police, and between two thousand and six thousand Malay Muslims left their homes after the incident and migrated to Malaysia. "Truths" about these people were made "invisible" at the same time. In this sense also, the Dusun-nyor rebellion monument is saying something, perhaps in a whisper. Because this incident may be something other than the heroic deeds of the police, the monument is softly speaking the state's one-sided "truth" about the Dusun-nyor incident.

Second, Pierre Bourdieu once wrote about symbolic violence in which domination is cloaked behind an enchanted relationship in the forms of personal domination or through cultural arbitrariness. For example, in a sophisticated society, the education system becomes an institution that uses symbolic violence because it renders some cultures legitimate through a hidden power that exists.[57] I would argue that although the bullet monument can be seen as a symbol used to manage "truth," what has happened in this case is not equivalent to Bourdieu's symbolic violence. Instead, the monument itself has become a symbol of violence. No matter how silent the monument is about the Dusun-nyor incident, its very shape — a bullet from a police rifle — speaks loudly in praise of violence; the shape legitimates the use of violence, especially by state authorities. A bullet cannot do anything but be shot out of the barrel of a gun with the intention of creating fear, submission, injury, or death. Although the monument is silent in almost every way, the concreteness of the bullet seems to be loudly voicing the sound of violence, in terms of the general use of state violence: it grounds the case of Dusun-nyor, the police, their institution, and the relationship between the police and the people, especially in the cultural space of Pattani, in the history of killing, in the legitimate use of state violence, and in the possibility of a seemingly unending use of violence in the South. If a political society sees it as its duty to produce "truth" and represent the "truth" produced, then the bullet monument might represent the silence of "truth" about the Dusun-nyor incident while it simultaneously sounds the tunes of the legitimation of violence.

Conclusion: "Dusun-nyor 1948" and "Kru-Ze 2004"

This discussion of the Dusun-nyor incident, which took place in 1948, is appropriate and relevant today for at least two reasons.

First, the similarities between this case and the more recent and shocking incident on 28 April 2004 are uncanny. Both involve deadly violence between Malay-Muslim villagers and Thai authorities. In both 1948 and 2004, the villagers primarily used knives as weapons in attacking government officials armed with guns, and both groups of Muslim militants reportedly exercised some forms of Islam-inspired magic to make them invulnerable to the dangers. Both events ended with a high number of deaths among the Malay Muslims and a much lower number of deaths among the authorities. On 28 April 2004, more than a hundred militants attacked eleven government locations, seven in Yala, three in Pattani, and one in Sabayoi district, Songkla. When the violence ended, one hundred and six Muslim militants had been killed, while five soldiers and police officers lost their lives.[58] After the incidents, both the Phibun and Thaksin governments set up committees to investigate them. In addition, both incidents took place around the same time in the month of April.

Second, when I was interviewed by the Thai media right after 28 April 2004,[59] I answered the question of why it occurred on that very date by pointing out the possible linkage with the Dusun-nyor "uprising" fifty-seven years ago, which according to some sources discussed above, also took place on 28 April. I added that there are two ways to understand this, either by maintaining that it was a sheer coincidence that both incidents happened on the same day, or that they are symbolically connected.

I would argue that the symbolic connection theory makes more sense. I say this, in part, because of what was found on the bodies of some dead Muslim militants, their belongings, which include Muslim prayer mats and prayer beads, and the booklet, *Berjihad di Patani* (The holy struggle for Patani), which declares in its first paragraph: "Religious warriors will rise in the land of Patani with the Light of fighting in the course of God"; their weapons of choice, primarily knives and machetes; and their willingness to use these weapons against the authorities' guns, which reflected their willingness to die fighting.[60] By symbolically linking the present with the Dusun-nyor "uprising" in the past, while showing a strong determination to commit the present to the memory of the future as the deaths of more than a hundred "martyrs," thirty-two of them killed in the ancient mosque, and the mosque itself was attacked by the Thai troops despite earlier prohibition coming directly from the deputy prime minister, the militants successfully entered the collective memory of the South as a new breed of martyrs who helped change the landscape of violence in a way that has not happened before for at least two reasons. First, their decision to attack government posts — perhaps partly informed by beliefs in their magic, yet knowing the possible consequences —suggests that their understanding of victory might not be defined by the number of people they killed, but from the ways by which they died. Second, the political significance of the 28 April incident could be assessed by the ways in which their deaths will be remembered. Most of the bodies were buried unwashed and without a prayer, as has been the religious traditions for those whose deaths were considered *shahid* (those who died at the hands of non-Muslims in the battle to defend Islam). Even in cases of those whose bodies were washed and prayers offered before burials, when a few journalists returned to the graveyards some two months after the incident, they found that the signs on their burial ground include the names of the deceased, ending with the word "shahid."[61]

On 9 May 2004, *Matichon Daily* printed a letter from a district education officer in Satun questioning the accuracy of both the date and the number of people killed in the Dusun-nyor incident as I gave them in my public interviews. As the author of a distinguished thesis on Haji Sulong, written in 1986, he pointed out that according to official sources, the Dusun-nyor incident took place on 25 April 1948 and that thirty villagers as well as five police officers were killed. He concluded his letter to the daily newspaper with a request for a verification of the information I gave because, he maintained, under the circumstances of tension and separatist thoughts in the South, the inaccuracy could lead to public misunderstanding because it is an exaggeration, an abuse of data which academics must be aware [of], and the printing press must be responsible for the possible undesirable effects. I don't want to see more emphasis put on hatred in the hearts and minds of Islamic people towards the Thai government, Thai officials and Buddhists. As things are now, the country [*baan-muang*] is already in an unbearable turbulence.[62]

In this chapter, I have already discussed "truths" about the date and number of people killed in the 1948 Dusun-nyor violence. Echoing Hannah Arendt's thought, compared with "rational truth," defined as contested philosophical opinions on society and the world, "factual truth" is much more problematic because it cannot be compromised. If one "factual truth" is right, its opposite cannot be. In this sense, "factual truth" does not possess a persuasive quality but a coercive one; it is deeply despotic.[63] This is one of the reasons why it is more important to underscore the many ways in which "truth" will be remembered by different peoples in their subtle imaginative acts, involved in the process of re-presenting violence in southern Thailand.

As has happened with the Dusun-nyor incident in 1948 — remembered as a "riot" and "rebellion," or "uprising" and "war" — it is also important to try to understand how violent events such as those in 2004 will be remembered. The 28 April 2004 incident has begun its metamorphosis into the landscape of modern memory as "Kru-Ze bloodbath,"[64] "the siege of Kru-Ze,"[65] "Kru-Ze wound,"[66] "Kru-Ze tragedy,"[67] and "martyrdom at Kru-Ze,"[68] among others. Perhaps, the comparison between the modern lightning, which struck the ancient Kru-Ze mosque in the form of five rocket-propelled grenades, with the legend of lightning that left the mosque unfinished for so long as cursed by the Chinese goddess, is not but a wild imagination.[69]

Although "factual truths" about the incident will continue to be contested,[70] I would not be surprised if the 28 April 2004 incident enters the "Thai" collective memory as the "Kru-Ze 2004 incident." Given both the political and symbolic significance and consequences embedded in the violence at Kru-Ze, it is highly likely that it will eclipse memories of violence in other places. Facts about the young average age of those soccer players-turned-militants killed in Saba Yoi, or the seventy-four other militants and two government officers killed at ten other spots elsewhere in the three provinces that day, will be clouded by the prominence of the Kru-Ze case. In other words, some of the "truths" about events that day will be mainly shaped by "truth" remembered about violence at Kru-Ze. Remembering the violent events on 28 April 2004 as "the Kru-Ze violence" is a way that Thai society manages "truth" about violence in the South, not unlike the case of the silent monument of Dusun-nyor, by revealing some elements, while concealing others.

I have argued elsewhere that due to its historical-religious-mythical significance and strategic location, standing by the main road about seven kilometers from the center of Pattani, side by side with the Chinese goddess' shrine, "Kru-Ze" is ideal as a theater for Malay Muslims to renegotiate their identities in Thai society.[71] Such negotiated lives can certainly take many forms, mainly nonviolent as in 1990,[72] or violent as in April 2004. The militants' decision to fight from within the mosque on 28 April could be seen as an astute political maneuver. If the military had backed off, the sanctity of the place would have been reaffirmed, and its religio-historical-mythical status heightened. When the military decided to attack the mosque, the sanctity of the place was violated and the political cost of such an act in the eyes of Muslims, both in Thailand and abroad, has turned out to be almost incalculable.

In the first nine months of 2005, several violent incidents affected the ways in which violence in the South was seen. Among others, the 14 July riot, which shut down Yala; the killing of a respected Imam in Narathiwat, which led to the exodus of 131 Malay Muslims to Kelantan on 30 and 31 August; the shooting at villagers of Tanyong Limo, which led to two deaths and the subsequent taking of two marines as hostages by the villagers. The marines were later killed. These events have driven a wedge between the Thai state and the Malay Muslims and left both in profound fear and mistrust.[73] But on 16 October 2005, armed men attacked Phromprasit Temple in Panare, Pattani, killing two temple boys and an elderly monk. The attackers burned the monk and also parts of the temple. This case of monk killing is different than those that took place in early 2004 because it happened inside a Buddhist temple. It is not difficult to imagine what reactions would be to the killing of a monk in the Muslim-dominated area and the profane violation of a sacred place in Thai society, especially in terms of relationships between Buddhists and Malay Muslims.

However, the highest political cost in my estimation is that when the sanctity of a religious place that should be off-limits to violence — be it a mosque, a temple, a church, or a synagogue — has been violated, some of the civility necessary for a political society is lost. Accepting that violence exists does not mean that a humane political society should set no limits to violence. The attack on the mosque, bombs thrown in, rocket-propelled grenades fired, people killed inside, is not unlike the killings of the monks that took place in January 2004 and October 2005 because these acts, committed by state officials or others, cut into the cultural ties that bind together peoples of differences in a political community. Once broken, these ties will be difficult to mend.

Perhaps, now more than ever, it is important to be able to look beyond the theater itself to see the "truths" about those fallen victims of violence and to refuse to be constrained by violence such that the possibilities of political alternatives are forgotten.

ACKNOWLEDGMENTS: This paper, a revised version of my keynote address at the Ninth International Conference on Thai Studies, Northern Illinois University, DeKalb, Ill., 3–6 April 2005, is mainly based on chapter 3 of my larger research on "Violence and 'Truth' Management: Half a Century of Pattani," supported by Thailand Research Fund under the project "'Truth' Management in Thai Society," led by Sombat Chantornvong of Thammasat University. See Chaiwat Satha-Anand, *Khwam runraeng kap kanjatkan "khwamjing": Pattani nai rop kung satawat* [Violence and "truth" management: Half a century of Pattani] (Bangkok: Thammasat University Press, forthcoming). I wish to thank Arlene Neher and Thongchai Winichakul for inviting me to give this keynote address; the Asia Foundation for funding the trip to Northern Illinois; Duncan McCargo for his decision to include this paper in this issue of *Critical Asian Studies*; Tom Fenton for his superb editorial suggestions; an anonymous reader for critical comments; and Saronee Duereh for his fine assistance in conducting this research.

❑

2 THAKSIN AND THE RESURGENCE OF VIOLENCE IN THE THAI SOUTH

Duncan McCargo

O VER A THOUSAND PEOPLE MET DEATHS attributed to political violence in Thailand's southern border provinces during 2004 and 2005.[1] Underlying the resurgence in violence was a complex combination of factors, which have not yet been clearly understood. This article seeks to address the crucial question "Why now?" by relating the explosion of southern violence to much deeper issues concerning the Thai political order. It does not purport to offer a complete explanation of the violence or its origins. Rather, it argues that the renewed violence reflects a direct challenge by Prime Minister Thaksin Shinawatra to well-established networks of power relations centered on the palace, and mediated by former premier Prem Tinsulanond.

It is tempting to relate the 2004 upsurge in violence simply to a long-standing, low-intensity conflict between the Thai security forces and militant "separatist" groups. Yet such a narrow explanation fails to account for the upsurge in political violence in recent years: the "separatists" had been largely moribund for the previous two decades. This article will explore alternative explanations for the dramatic increase in political violence close to the Thai-Malaysian border. Its core argument is that national-level political conflicts, rather than local or international factors, offer a core explanation for the upsurge in violence.

The renewed wave of violence began in the Thai South on 4 January 2004, with an attack on a Narathiwat army base (marked by four fatalities), coupled with twenty school burnings. Prime Minister Thaksin Shinawatra adopted a hard-line response, including use of martial law. The police in particular appeared to be complicit in the unexplained disappearances of numerous Malay-Muslim suspects. Another 113 men died on 28 April. These deaths resulted from eleven separate attacks on security posts in three provinces by groups of young Muslim men wearing black. A few carried guns, but most wielded nothing more than knives. In one of these incidents, security forces stormed the historic Kru-Ze mosque in Pattani, killing thirty-two lightly armed men who had barricaded themselves inside. An official investigation later found that the commander had used excessive force, a charge he denied.[2] Though less attention has been paid to the other ten attacks, there is evidence of extrajudicial killings by security forces in several places, notably at Saba Yoi

Anonymous

Thai prime minister Thaksin Shinawatra visits a Narathiwat village specially constructed to accommodate the widows of victims of the southern violence — a project under the patronage of the Queen — in August 2005. Thaksin has been widely criticized as unsympathetic to the plight of those affected by the violence.

market, where fifteen of the nineteen attackers killed had gunshot wounds to the back of the head.[3]

In October, several demonstrators were shot dead during a peaceful protest outside a police station in Tak Bai, Narathiwat. The army rounded up over a thousand men from the streets and piled them into trucks; seventy-eight apparently suffocated on the way to military camps. The Tak Bai incident had the effect of internationalizing the conflict, producing strong criticism from Malaysia and Indonesia. Murders, explosions, and other violent incidents continued throughout 2004, on an almost daily basis. Victims included a judge, a deputy governor, and numerous police and military personnel, as well as teachers and civilians.

Thaksin's response was to persist with a hard-line approach, whilst flirting with more conciliatory policies. In early April, Deputy Prime Minister Chaturon Chaisaeng proposed demilitarizing the area and working toward a political solution, but his ideas failed to win support from his boss. Thaksin's main response was repeatedly to reshuffle senior officers whom he held accountable for the worsening situation. By the end of the year, trust between the Buddhist and Muslim communities in the deep South had largely broken down. The Thai Rak Thai (Thais Love Thai) Party won a sweeping national victory in the February 2005 elections, but was trounced in the South. The party lost every one of its seats in the southern border provinces. Faced with growing criticism from the palace, Thaksin finally agreed to appoint respected former prime minister Anand Panyarachun to head a National Reconciliation Commission (NRC), aimed at restoring the region to normalcy.

The Key to the South: Network Monarchy

It will be argued here that the current upsurge of violence in the South of Thailand strongly reflects domestic political developments, including the mishandling of the security order by Thaksin personally. The South is the principal site for Thaksin's attempts to wrest control of Thailand from the old power networks that dominated the country prior to 2001. The South is unusually combustible, highly sensitive, and had developed a distinctive and precarious set of accommodations. Closely related to these political issues were competition for power and resources among the various government agencies responsible for security in the South.[4] This is not to suggest that a desire to control the lucrative smuggling trade motivated Thaksin to intervene in the South; rather, this trade supported a set of political arrangements that Thaksin found intolerable — and with good reason.

Thaksin Shinawatra has sought to lead (or perhaps, to manage) Thailand very differently from his predecessors.[5] One essential difference relates to the extra-constitutional role of the monarchy. The dominant mode of governance used in Thailand since 1980 may best be termed monarchical network governance, or network monarchy.[6] Since his success in helping to oust the Thanom-Praphas regime, Thailand's King Bhumipol has been far more than a conventional constitutional monarch. Rather, he has sought to institutionalize a range of extra-constitutional political powers. Occasionally, he makes open, personal interventions in the political process. The most well-known example was following the violent demonstrations of May 1992, when he called in Prime Minister Suchinda Kraprayoon and protest leader Chamlong Srimuang for a public, televised dressing-down. Much more commonly, the monarchy operates through proxies, led by former prime minister and Privy Council president Prem Tinsulanond, dubbed by Chai-Anan Samudavanija Thailand's "surrogate strongman."[7] Prem exerted considerable control over military and bureaucratic appointments, and intervened in the formation of government coalitions in 1994 and 1997. During the 1990s, Prem worked through a series of weak coalition governments to help preserve royal prerogatives and influence. It seems highly possible that Prem helped Thaksin escape conviction by the Constitutional Court in August 2001, when he faced charges of assets declaration violations.[8] As prime minister, Thaksin's aim was to displace network monarchy, and to replace it with a much more centralized form of political control. The crisis in the South that began in 2004 was simply the most blatant manifestation of this political project.

The Rise of Thaksin

The economic crisis and the new constitution of 1997 paved the way for the rise of Thaksin Shinawatra. In the January 2001 general elections, the Democrats were roundly defeated by the recently formed Thai Rak Thai (TRT) Party led by the super-wealthy telecommunications magnate Thaksin Shinawatra. Thaksin campaigned as a new look "CEO" leader, capable of addressing national problems swiftly and effectively. TRT deployed a range of populist policies — such as a subsidized health-care scheme — to attract rural voters. Their campaign was also backed up by old-style big spending, buying in electable candidates and dispersing sizeable funds for vote buying. Thaksin epitomized new political forces unhappy with the residual influence of network monarchy. Knowing full well that other prime ministers who lacked palace support — such as Banharn Silpa-archa and Cha-valit Yongchaiyudh — had been quickly ousted, Thaksin set about systematically challenging Prem's political networks, ruthlessly install-ing his own relatives and associates in key positions. Thaksin was seeking to dismantle network monarchy, and to replace it with a much more familiar political economy network of the kind based on inside connections and business arrangements.[9] As Ockey observes, "Since the revival of the monarchy under Sarit, political leadership has been overshadowed by symbolic leadership. Not until Thaksin has any leader managed to consistently gain such a share of the limelight."[10] Thaksin was the first popularly chosen Thai prime minister to chal-lenge the palace for the leadership of the country. He sought to combine political and symbolic leadership, supported by overwhelm-ing electoral legitimacy. His entry to Government House marked the beginning of a new form of Thai politics: instead of operating through loose alliances, Thaksin was intent on securing control of the entire country through tightly managed personal networks.

Prem, Network Governance, and the South

The South was Prem's backyard: although he never served in the Fourth Army Region, he came from Songkla, and was very familiar with the border provinces. His strategy there was to replicate the work he had done to combat the anticommunist insurgency in Isan. His princi-pal adjutant for both projects was Harn Leenanond, whom he appointed Fourth Army commander. Harn was one of the architects of the Southern Border Provinces Administrative Centre (SBPAC), estab-lished on 20 January 1981 by Prime Minister's Office Order 8/1981. Using a policy known as "Tai rom yen" (South in the cool shade), Harn used a mixture of development projects and public relations initiatives to calm local tensions.

As a Southerner, Prem understood the mindset of the Democrat Party. As the architect of an uneasy truce in the southern border prov-inces, he understood the importance of this subregion: it was an enclave of military power and privilege, supported by local govern-ment officials who were overwhelmingly loyal to the Democrats. The governance network in the border provinces was centered on Prem: it was a working microcosm of the national-level political networks that

ที่อ่านหนังสือพิมพ์
ประจำหมู่บ้าน

PATANI
MERDEKA

Duncan McCargo

A "Free Patani" (Patani Merdeka) slogan painted on a wall inside a small *sala* in a village in Narathiwat Province. The upsurge in violence in southern Thailand since January 2004 is often narrowly understood simply as part of "a long-standing low-intensity conflict between the Thai security forces and militant 'separatist' groups."

he masterminded for over twenty years, which involved a complex mixture of monarchism, moralism, and structural corruption. Right up until 2001, Prem was often able personally to determine who was selected to serve as provincial governors, senior military commanders, and other key administrative posts in Pattani, Yala, and Narathiwat. This was all part of the deal.

Other elements in the deal included: promoting local Muslims to positions in the bureaucracy, notably as district officers; giving local military commanders carte blanche to "secure" and oversee the Malaysian border (in effect, a license to coax or to extort rents and commissions from those engaged in illegal border trade); providing "development" funds and projects to the subregion, managed by the military, and so permitting the creation of local patronage networks; and cultivating a grassroots network of informers who would tip off the military about actual or potential "separatist" activity. At the same time, local Muslims were encouraged to enter politics, contesting parliamentary seats and gaining ministerial posts under the auspices of the Democrat Party and later the New Aspiration Party.[11] Administratively, this deal was managed via bodies such as the SBPAC, under the oversight of the Interior Ministry.

The SBPAC was seen as a liberal enclave within Thailand's security apparatus, and had worked hard to build trust with Muslim leaders and their communities. The SBPAC received large numbers of complaints about abuses committed by government officials in the area — 1,354 complaints about 1,322 individuals between January 1998 and December 2000, resulting in fifty-one officials being transferred.[12] The Centre coordinated preparations for the annual hajj pilgrimage in the deep South, and had tried (albeit ineptly) to broker a compromise over the issue of headscarf-wearing in government educational institutions.[13] The Centre also intervened in the appointment of provincial governors in the area. Prominent Pattani Muslim Worawit Baru argued that "You can't just look at the surface of the SBPAC" — it was more than just a formal institution.[14] Rather, the Centre was a beacon for ideas of administrative justice, symbolizing the Thai state's sincerity and goodwill.

Institutional Culture and Tacit Understandings

For many years, there had been widespread skepticism in Bangkok about the extent to which "separatist violence" in the deep South was really orchestrated by any political movement. Some estimates placed the strength of the movement at "no more than 120 leaders, 200 armed men, and 30 to 40 armed bandits who sometimes worked with the militants."[15] As Croissant argues, "it would be naïve to assume that criminals and terrorists can be clearly distinguished... there is a grey zone of greed and grievance in which there is no clear threshold between 'entrepreneurs of violence' and 'warriors of convenience.'"[16]

Separatist groups were accused by one source of hiring teenagers to cause trouble, paying them between five thousand and ten thousand baht each.[17] SBPAC intelligence sources reported that of twenty-seven incidents between October 2000 and July 2001, sixteen were based on benefits-related conflicts, two from personal conflicts, and three could not be accounted for. The four remaining were believed to be the work of bandits linked to the separatist movement — in other words, one in seven of the total.[18] In 1998 SBPAC chief Palakorn Suwannarat told the *Bangkok Post* that 70 percent of all sabotage attacks in the South were the work of bandits; the rest were "ordinary" criminal acts, some of them committed by officials themselves. By 2001, Palakorn was quoted as saying that only 20 to 30 percent of violent incidents in the deep South were the work of terrorists — the others arose from personal and business conflicts.[19]

Increasingly, the Thai government began to believe that violent incidents in the South were no longer fundamentally political, but reflected a complex pattern of criminal activity. Chidchanok has suggested that prior to 2002, roughly 80 percent of "separatist" incidents in the deep South were essentially fake.[20] Practically every local resident in the border provinces had stories to tell about the fabrication of terrorist incidents, generally referred to as *sang sathanakan*. When the discourse of incident fabrication became ubiquitous — and people began to believe that everything they saw and heard about was fake — it was dangerously easy to assume that the underlying political problems of the border region had simply gone away. "Thus people resort to assumptions, which mainly center on the conspiracy theory: a conspiracy of lies and official thievery."[21]

Arson attacks were particularly suspicious — burning down schools in the middle of the night made alarming national headlines, but left no one hurt, and meant an additional budget allocation for their reconstruction. Coordinated arson attacks on thirty-four schools on 1 August 1993 were highly suspicious.[22] The major beneficiaries of the long-standing conflict in the South were the officers of the Fourth Army Region: the supposed insurgency provided the justification for their budget allocations, special allowances that boosted their pay, their extensive "development" projects, and their jurisdiction over the border (for which read, control of smuggling). Although the army practiced a degree of rotation in the assignment of officers, most officers had a core assignment with one of the four major army regions for their entire careers. The Fourth Army had a particularly clannish culture, excluding outsiders from senior positions, based on the belief that only those who spent their whole careers in the South were qualified to manage the complex problems of the border region. In other words, the Fourth Army saw itself as an untouchable enclave within an already highly privileged military institution. A 2002 Philippine government study found that "the military also initiate dialogues with armed units of separatist groups, not for surrender, but to find out their needs."[23] In other words, the Fourth Army had a very good idea of who the militants were, and how to contact them.

Thaksin and the South: Ripe for CEO Intervention

Thaksin's first term as prime minister clearly demonstrated his standard approach to problems. First, he viewed existing bureaucratic and administrative arrangements with distrust, believing that officials and the security services were too slow, unreliable, and inefficient to handle difficult issues. Second, he believed that structures had been created to serve the purposes of the old system of network governance: in other words, he suspected officials (especially in the South) of holding a primary loyalty to the Democrats, Prem, and the palace, rather than to him and his government. Third, he believed that simply by "thinking new and acting new" he could find creative ways of resolving issues that had plagued the Thai state and society for decades or even generations. Fourth, he believed that he could make the right decision very quickly indeed, so long as he was well advised by one or more of his most trusted associates. Fifth, he believed that transferring officials was the key to solving problems: put the right man in the right job (it was nearly always a man), and a difficult problem could be solved in a matter of weeks, or even days. Sixth, as a former police officer, he regarded complex social and political problems — ranging from drug abuse to low-intensity conflict — as manifestations of criminality, which could be solved by firm law enforcement.

Thaksin's approach to the South follows logically from these principles. His strategy was to send in some of his own people to report on the issues, identify the key representatives of the old power group, transfer them out of the region, then quickly move to dismantle the existing power structures, put in new officials loyal to himself, and give the police an enhanced role in a new power structure. The objective was twofold: to break the power of Prem's governance network in the deep South and (incidentally) to bring the low-intensity conflict to a complete halt. Unfortunately, the first task was less easy than he appreciated, and the second task was completely beyond him. Thaksin was not really interested in the South, except insofar as it constituted an unacceptable zone of liminality, an area of Thailand he could not yet control on his own terms. Emboldened by his success in seeing off the 2001 assets declaration case, Thaksin decided to challenge Prem's authority in his own backyard, by unraveling the political and security arrangements that Prem had created in the southern border provinces. In so doing, Thaksin aimed to undermine the mode of network governance that Prem had forged there. The key elements in this governance network were Prem's own central position in determining appointments and setting policy, the dominant role of the military, a prominent role for the palace, and the importance of bureaucrats loyal to the Democrat Party.

Thaksin began putting pressure on the existing security structures very soon after becoming prime minister, making it clear that he expected quick results. After nine separate bomb incidents on 18 and 19 June 2001, Thaksin berated the shortcomings of authorities in the South, and warned of a shake-up to come. He declared, "Transfers will be ordered for those who are inefficient and I am looking for a place to keep them. They won't be around here."[24] He announced an investigation into reports that some recent attacks had been orchestrated by police officers seeking money to purchase positions in the forthcoming reshuffle, saying, "It definitely has something to do with the positions." Thaksin rejected the idea that these attacks had any political foundation. The clear implication was that the SBPAC was failing properly to oversee security problems in the region.

Preemptive Strike: Palakorn's Elevation

In July 2001, SBPAC chief Palakorn Suwannarat abruptly resigned in very unusual circumstances: he became a member of the Privy Council on the day of his departure. For one of the Interior Ministry's most senior officials, a deputy permanent secretary with seven years remaining until retirement, it was an extraordinary exit. Only three months earlier, Palakorn had been widely tipped to assume the powerful post of director-general of the Local Administration Department.[25] Anonymous leaflets distributed the following day at the Interior Ministry criticized Interior Minister Purachai Piemsomboon's treatment of Palakorn. They alleged that Purachai had briefed the press against Palakorn, telling the media that he was being transferred from his post for failing to contain terrorist violence in the South.[26] Palakorn declined to elaborate on the reasons for his resignation, saying only that he was very gratified by his appointment to the Privy Council, and would serve the country and the monarchy honestly. Purachai refused to comment on Palakorn's performance at the SBPAC, but admitted that he had reprimanded him on occasion. Religious and business leaders expressed disappointment at his resignation. Some pointed out that the SBPAC was not charged with fighting terrorism, and had no authority to issue orders to the army or police.

The implications of Palakorn's forced departure were interesting. Palakorn was a key figure in the old power network that had long controlled the southern border provinces, and was closely linked to Prem and to the palace. He had made a name for himself as a very liberal governor of Pattani in the early 1990s, once declaring that "tens of thousands of Southern Muslims will rise in protest if police throw the wrong people in jail."[27] Second, by resigning just before Purachai could oust him, and by leaving on his own terms for a seat on the Privy Council, Palakorn demonstrated that he had the full backing of the monarchy. Third, this pyrrhic victory exposed the government's heavy-handedness, and clearly indicated the real politics underlying the battle for the South. Incensed by media coverage of the affair, Thaksin declared that "it was inappropriate to criticise the issue since such an act could affect the power of his Majesty the King."[28] In effect, Thaksin was seeking to shelter behind the lèse-majesté laws to discourage discussion of his own political meddling. Finally, the elevation of Palakorn can be seen as network monarchy's first challenge to Thaksin's strategy for the South.

Thaksin Restructures Power in the South

With Palakorn out of the way, discussions about the future of the Centre could proceed unchallenged. Thaksin decided to send in his own people to work on the southern problem. He assigned Major General Songkitti Chakkabhatra to study the situation and report back. Songkitti had an unusual international profile, having served as deputy commander of Interfet, the East Timor international peacekeeping force. But more importantly, Songkitti was one of Thaksin's classmates from the military pre-cadet school, Class 10: the two men had known each other for thirty years.[29] Thaksin appointed Songkitti deputy commander of the Fourth Army in October 2001, despite the fact that he had never previously served in the South. His appointment was criticized as politically motivated.[30] Songkitti reportedly studied the southern situation for several months before making a detailed report to Thaksin early in 2002.[31] He argued there was no real insurgency in the South, and that Thaksin should normalize the security situation there. As Wasanna Nanuam writes:

> Lt-Gen Songkitti's theory convinced Mr Thaksin, who mocked the southern attackers as nothing more than "common bandits." He subsequently ordered the paramilitary ranger divisions 41 and 43

Duncan McCargo

Anti-Thaksin graffiti on a billboard in Narathiwat Province, southern Thailand. "For Thaksin, the southern conflict was a personal challenge to his authority. This personalization reached its height during the Tak Bai incident in October 2004."

and the marine corps out of the trouble spots in Pattani, Yala and Narathiwat provinces, and back to their barracks and based in Nakhon Si Thammarat, well away from the violence. There was growing disgruntlement from the military….The military could do nothing to stop the pullout, of course. Officers rationalised that Mr Thaksin, a former police lieutenant colonel, would naturally rather listen to fellow police than the military.[32]

Purachai elaborated the government's thinking following a series of fatal attacks on the police in March 2002. "These groups tried to make it look like the work of [Muslim] separatists, but it's not. These people were dissatisfied after they were demoted, or did not get promotions, or saw their interests affected."[33] Ironically, the strongest supporters of conspiracy theories about the southern violence fell into two mutually supportive groups: Muslims in the border provinces, and the prime minister's own closest advisors. Such theories were fueled by intelligence reports that related almost every violent incident in the southern border provinces to elaborate domestic plots. A ninety-seven–page Thai-language document evidently compiled by someone with access to intelligence sources gives a flavor of these views.[34] Apparently produced around March 2004 on Thaksin's orders, the undated document catalogued those allegedly behind dozens of incidents in the deep South, listing different political, military, and police factions, as well as separatist and Islamist organizations. The thrust of the report was that the overwhelming majority of violent incidents were orchestrated by politicians — notably a Democrat politician nicknamed "Thepthuek" (apparently a pseudonym for veteran Surat Thani politician Suthep Thueksuban), and Pattani senator Den Tohmeena — or by police and army commanders in the region. Thaksin's comments on developments in the South throughout the 2001 to 2004 period suggest that he was fed a constant diet of similar reading.[35] The report has strong echoes of conspiracy theories widely supported by local Muslims.

Thaksin's main assault on the Prem-centered governance network came when he abolished the SBPAC on 1 May 2002, some sixteen months after becoming prime minister. He thereby removed the only venue where "soldiers, police, Muslim leaders and religious teachers, and local officials met to exchange views and compare notes."[36] Officially, the Centre was closed because the National Security Council (NSC) argued that security problems in the area were caused by "conflicts among interest groups"[37] rather than genuine political grievances. At the same time, Centre 43 — the 43rd joint civilian, police, and military task force, an operational agency — was also dissolved. Thaksin saw these agencies as having been captured by Democrats and possessing close ties to Prem; this view undoubtedly underpinned his decision to abolish the Centre, reflecting his determination to stamp the force of his administration upon the entire country. The demise of SBPAC was widely criticized: the Centre had offered an important channel of communication between the government, and the leadership of the Muslim community. The abolition was carried out hastily, based on a prime ministerial order issued on 30 April 2002, which came into effect the following day. The ISOC (Internal Security Operation Command) Command Area 4, second detachment, remained in place in the southern border provinces, however, providing some continuity in military intelligence and psychological warfare.[38] Pattani governor Somporn Chibangyan told visiting Philippine officials that provincial governors in the South would continue to carry out the NSC policy for the southern border provinces on their own, despite the abolition of the SBPAC.[39] But this proved a short-lived aspiration, and Somporn himself — a Prem protégé — was transferred the following year to the governorship of neighboring Songkla.

Yet the government began backpedaling very soon after abolishing the SBPAC; in July 2002, the NSC announced that it was creating a Southern Coordination Administration comprising military, police, and civilians to help unify security operations.[40] Following the dramatic escalation of violence in 2004, that April the government created a new agency, the Southern Border Provinces Peace-Building Command (SBPPC), which assumed some of the functions of the SBPAC. However, the new agency had a much lower profile and status. Crucially, it lacked direct contacts with Muslim leaders, the primary strength of the SBPAC. Muslim residents told a government peace envoy that they wanted to see the command abolished.[41]

It is striking that very few commentators have supported the decision to dissolve the SBPAC. Chulalongkorn University military specialist Surachart Bumrungsuk, a security advisor to the Thaksin government, has written that the police way of viewing the southern conflict from a "denial perspective" was very problematic.[42] Similarly, Dr. Rung Kaewdaeng, another Thaksin advisor, argued in his book on the South that the police proposal to close the SBPAC and Centre 43 coincided with the wishes of the insurgents themselves, and the thinking of some local politicians. Thaksin failed to investigate deeply, and so did not catch the hidden agendas that underpinned the proposal.[43] He sent people to look into the matter, but they did not give him all the information — or they fell victim to surreptitious ploys.[44] Rung views this as a serious mistake on the part of the government, providing an ideal opportunity for the separatists to re-emerge rapidly.

When the closure of these agencies was followed by a new wave of violent incidents, senior figures offered a range of contradictory and incoherent explanations. Thaksin again claimed that the incidents were the work of bandits; Chavalit suggested that large-scale terrorist groups were in operation in the South; and police chief Sant Sarutanond declared that everything was down to internal conflicts among security officials. It seemed abundantly clear that no one in power really understood what was happening around the southern border. Srisompob Jitpiromsri of Prince of Songkla University later argued that the dissolution of the two agencies in May 2002 marked a turning point, precipitating a great upsurge in political violence.[45]

Thaksin responded to the deteriorating situation by dispatching a team of fifty-three generals to the region to gather intelligence and report back.[46] When this initiative yielded no answers, Thaksin became increasingly determined to put his own man in direct charge.

In April 2003, Songkitti was promoted to lieutenant general and Fourth Army commander. As *The Nation* noted, "Songkitti's taking control of the southern forces is viewed by critics as showing the Thai Rak Thai Party's determination to strengthen its position in the Democrat Party's stronghold ahead of the next general election."[47] Yet despite — or because of — Thaksin's personal backing, Songkitti faced entrenched resistance from fellow officers, and was moved to another post in October 2003. Pongsak Ekbannasingha one of Songkitti's earlier rivals for the post, was brought back to head the Fourth Army Division — but his reign was to prove short-lived after he was held responsible for the deteriorating security situation the following March. The same applied to Pongsak's successor, Pisan Wattanawongkiri, who took the blame for the Tak Bai incident in October 2004.

The security situation in the South deteriorated gradually during Songkitti's two-year tenure as Thaksin's man in the region. His unwelcome assignments had provoked intense conflict within the Fourth Army, generating considerable infighting and exacerbating a difficult situation.[48] Meanwhile, Thaksin continued to view the Fourth Army with suspicion and even hostility, and senior officers from the Division found their promotion prospects sharply curtailed. As Liow argues, Thaksin's excessive enthusiasm for reshuffling military commanders "no doubt affected the operational readiness of security forces in the South and contributed to their unprepared state in the face of sweeping offensives since January 2004."[49] Thaksin also changed defense ministers with increasing frequency. Thaksin's principal point man on the South at police headquarters was his close associate Police Lieutenant General Wongkot Maneerin, commissioner at the Central Investigation Bureau, and husband of Deputy Education Minister Sirikul Maneerin. Thaksin relied on Wongkot for advice on security matters in the South.

Dismantling Network Governance

Thaksin took office determined to replace what he saw as a lumbering set of Prem-based power networks with a much more effective and decisive political order of his own devising. Seeing control of the southern border provinces as an example of the kind of governance network he despised, he set out to disrupt it through a series of moves. First, in May 2002 he abolished the Southern Border Provinces Administrative Centre. Second, by dissolving the joint security force that same month, he handed over responsibility for security in the area to the police, thereby breaking the control of the military commanders and also reducing Prem's influence.

Third, in May 2002 he appointed Wan Muhammad Nor Matha, a Muslim, leader of the Wadah faction, and senior NAP (New Aspiration Party) politician from Yala, to the post of interior minister. Wan Nor has been courted by New Aspiration leader Chavalit Yongchaiyudh, and had played an important role in legitimating Chavalit's brief rise to the premiership in 1996–97. Chavalit had brought in Wan Nor and his Wadah faction as a means of consolidating his power base in the deep South. Thaksin assumed that Wan Nor would be able to wrest control of the administration of the subregion from Democrat officials whom he believed to be in Prem's pocket. As the only faction of non-Democrat MPs in the Thai South, Wan Nor's Wadah clique was the obvious starting point for Thaksin to begin his attempts to penetrate the region politically.[50] Bringing on board Wan Nor and his supporters was one of the aims behind Thaksin's incorporation of the NAP into TRT. But after being appointed interior minister, Wan Nor proved a broken reed who had lost the trust of many of his fellow Muslims and lacked the ability to manage the complex problems of the subregion. His oversight of the police brutality associated with the breakup of a demonstration against the Malaysian gas pipeline in Hat Yai on 20 December 2002 did much to undermine his position. As one irate protestor, Areeya Maedee of the Ban Nai Rai village, put it: "How could [Interior Minister] Wan Nor order the police to beat us? He is also a Muslim. Does he realize what he has done to his people?"[51]

Good intelligence about the situation on the ground dried up, and all manner of political and other tensions that had been artfully suppressed by the old Prem-brokered benefit-sharing arrangements quickly emerged into the open. Violence swiftly followed. After failing to control the security situation in the South, Wan Nor was unceremoniously ousted from the Interior Ministry in March 2004. Within days, members of the Wadah faction were actually implicated as possible suspects behind the 4 January 2004 raid on an army base.

Fourth, the war on drugs that Thaksin declared in February 2003 gave the police carte blanche to target selected locals for extrajudicial execution. Among those killed were long-standing informers with

Anonymous

Checking a motorcycle near Sungai Padi, August 2006. Thai security forces have made extensive use of roadblocks to check suspicious vehicles. Malay Muslims in the area complain that these checks are intrusive, and almost never lead to any arrests.

close ties to the military. The result was, literally, insurrection: the police and the army fought bitter turf wars over the control of smuggling and other illegal activities.

Fifth, by putting in Songkitti to head the Fourth Army, Thaksin tried to undermine the prevailing institutional culture of the military in the South, setting out to subvert local commanders' privileged sense of entitlement.

At its core, Thaksin's main approach to dealing with the South was tactical, rather than strategic: the deliberate rotation of senior officials. Army commanders-in-chief, Fourth Army commanders, defense ministers, provincial governors, national police commanders, deputy prime ministers, senior police officers, interior ministers — men in all these categories were subject to an increasingly arbitrary pattern of transfers, and punished for their supposed failures and shortcomings. Yet with one or two exceptions they were all hard-liners, with near-identical approaches to the border region's problems. In this elaborate game of musical chairs — which allowed Thaksin endless opportunities for public grandstanding and displays of dramatic action — the only beneficiary was Thaksin himself, who increasingly bypassed existing structures for managing the security situation. As *The Nation* argued, even Thaksin's cousin Chaisit was unable to exercise any effective control while army commander. "[He] took firm action for about a week before fading from the scene," believing that the army was being bypassed and that Thaksin favored the police. Relying on security adviser Surachart Bumrungsuk[52] and chief adviser Pansak Vinyaratn, Thaksin adopted a hands-on approach to the conflict, delegating the NSC to a subordinate role: "Armed with a weekly intelligence briefing from Jumpol [Intelligence Chief Jumpol Manmai], Thaksin directly supervises police operations in the South, pushing the Army — constitutionally empowered to enforce martial law — into the background."[53]

A source familiar with Thaksin's intelligence-gathering capabilities argued that the prime minister lacked accurate information and analysis of developments in the South. By early 2004, the government had virtually no reliable human intelligence from the ground, and Thaksin was surrounded by security analysts and military officers who still believed that they were fighting a cold war–style insurgency with a communist enemy. To make matters worse, intelligence gathering was in the hands of too many overlapping agencies, most of them dysfunctional. Matters were not helped by the fact that Thaksin rarely read anything longer than a two-page briefing document, and was thus over-reliant on the ability of his officials and advisors to distill information accurately and concisely.[54]

For Thaksin, the southern conflict was a personal challenge to his authority. This personalization reached its height during the Tak Bai incident in October 2004, when Thaksin declared that he had taken direct control of handling the demonstration. "Thaksin said he had personally supervised Monday's anti-riot operation from 11 a.m. 'I commend the anti-riot forces for adhering to my instructions,' he said."[55]

This declaration is very hard to reconcile with the findings of the Tak Bai inquiry, chaired by Pichet Soonthornpipit:

> The inquiry chairman said security officials ran the entire crowd dispersal operation. Thaksin, he said, had no direct involvement in the operation, citing statements by General Samphan Boonyanant, defence minister, and General Sirichai Thanyasiri.[56]

As a basic operating principle, Thaksin prevented his subordinates from carrying out their formal duties. He did not rely on traditional methods of network governance: he was unwilling to put structures and officials in place and give them months or years to become effective. Indeed, he demonstrated contempt for the weaknesses of individual government officials, declaring that soldiers who failed to defend themselves "deserve to die,"[57] and commending insurgents for their boldness.

Santhiphap nai plaew phleung [Peace in flames], a book on the southern violence written by two *Nation* reporters, Supalak Ganjanakhundee and Don Pathan, offers a succinct analysis of the problem. They argue that the SBPAC achieved considerable successes, and that the fourth National Security Policy for the Southern Border Provinces (1999–2003)[58] — based on extensive community consultation — received widespread support.[59] In the three years prior to the Centre's dissolution, 114 former insurgents surrendered to the authorities. All this changed under Thaksin.

> However, the Thaksin government had received proposals from the police, then under the leadership of former police chief General Sant Saturanont. Sant argued that the conditions in the South had returned to normal. Although there had been violent incidents on a monthly basis since the mass school burnings of 1993, these were a normal state of affairs in the South. Under these circumstances, it was appropriate for the region to be subject to normal modes of governance, according to which the police would be made responsible for general security, and the Interior Ministry would oversee development activities. The Army should withdraw from these spheres, and concentrate on their basic duties of guarding the border. Right after the election, a police officer close to Thaksin despatched a considerable number of associates to work in the border area. They hoped to change the SBPAC's hitherto biased political relations, because they believed that the old structure was closely related to the Democrat Party.[60]

But the intervention of Bangkok-based police officers in the micro-politics of the southern border proved an unmitigated disaster. They pursued a policy of illegal arrest (known as "*um*"), extrajudicially killing individuals whom they suspected to be part of the movement. Many of those they killed were actually former separatists, who had long since served as informers for military intelligence.[61] Some had previously taken up amnesty offers in the belief that they would be safe. Many had not been active in the movement for decades. By killing them, the police were being provocative, stirring up resentment in Muslim communities. At the same time, they were also curtailing the flow of grassroots intelligence information on which the security forces had long relied. Three disappearances in Narathiwat in October 2003 were especially provocative. The relatives of these men were convinced the police were responsible, since on 19 October the men had been taken to a police station for questioning and were never seen again. All three men were former separatists, who had given themselves up in 1981 when the amnesty policy was first announced. Since then, they were said to have been sources for military intelligence.

Similar disappearances took place no fewer than twenty times during 2002 and 2003.[62] Indeed, Muslim residents of the southern border provinces complained to a government envoy in March 2005 that around fifty people had disappeared to date.[63] Military intelligence strongly believed that these disappearances were a very important factor in fueling the discontent that erupted from 4 January 2004 onwards. Though hard to prove, it seems highly possible that the targeting of military informers was a deliberate policy by the police, intended to eradicate the long-standing networks of the Fourth Army and to strengthen their own power in the area.

Wassana Nanuam argues that friction between the police and army commanders reached extraordinary levels after January 2004, especially over a leaked police inquiry report on the 4 January incident. The report concluded that "weapons from the army development unit 4 had been stolen by army insiders who concocted the insurgent robbery story to cover their tracks."[64] Army commander Chaisit Shinawatra made a series of extraordinary public responses to the report, challenging the credibility of the police inquiry, calling on soldiers not to be provoked by the report, and urging the police to desist from spreading groundless rumors that could undermine the reputation of the army. As the intra-security forces blame game grew increasingly acrimonious, the violence continued to escalate.

Chaturon and the Liberal Turn

In March 2004, Deputy Prime Minister Chaturon Chaisaeng was assigned to develop proposals to ease the conflict. A former student leader with leftist, activist credentials, Chaturon was arguably the most sympathetic member of the government toward Muslims. He met more than a thousand local people, canvassing their views and listening carefully to them. The outcome was a set of seven proposals for addressing the situation. The most important proposals were an end to state killings; the immediate transfer of Bangkok-based police officers back to the capital; and an amnesty for everyone involved in the conflict who had not committed criminal offenses.[65] One of Chaturon's media statements is worth quoting at length:

> This proposal is based on listening to the voices of local people, and comes from the police, military, governors, district officers and all sides. The point on which there is the greatest agreement, the point which will really demonstrate the sincerity and determination of the government, is that the extra-judicial killings and torture must stop. Some other measures follow on from this: the withdrawal from the area of forces sent from police headquarters has been requested by the Fourth Army, governors, and district officers, along with local police commanders, who are all of the same view. It is not just my opinion, because the people are most afraid of them.[66]

Yet despite his attempts to argue that his proposals represented a mainstream position, widely supported even among the security forces, Chaturon was branded a soft liberal whose pacifist views were both unworkable and dangerous. His critics were led by General Chetta Thanajaro, who took over as defense minister in March 2004. Chaturon's proposals went nowhere; Thaksin kicked his ideas into touch by asking him to do further work on them. Chaiwat argues that the rejection of the Chaturon proposals was highly predictable, since the "insecurity industry" reaped considerable benefits from the conflict. Furthermore, the consultative approach used by Chaturon meant that his proposals were too radical to gain support.[67] Meanwhile, Chavalit was given notional responsibility for the security situation in the South.

The violent events of 28 April saw a resurgence of hard-line stances. Army Commander Chaisit Shinawatra denounced the Muslim youths who had attacked army and police posts as "inhumanly courageous" and "bloody crazy."[68] Faced with what they chose to construct as a fanatical and irrational other, the security chiefs of the Thai state convinced themselves that only forceful repression could bring the situation under control. Confronted with this enemy, forces on the ground ignored Chavalit's instructions not to storm the historic

Kru-Ze mosque, which instead became the scene of an appalling episode of extrajudicial killing. The idea that Chavalit was in charge of the
situation was exposed as a fallacy: a politician in Bangkok, even a former army commander, had no effective jurisdiction over troops in the
field. The very approach that Chaturon had most explicitly disavowed
became the basic instrument of state policy only a few days later. The
police did not have a monopoly on extrajudicial killing: it was also
standard practice for the army. Nor was it a response that met with general condemnation from the wider society: as Chaiwat observes, there
was general public approval for the Thaksin government's handling of
events at both Kru-Ze and later Tak Bai, approval that echoed popular
support for the 2003 war on drugs.[69]

Supalak and Don see the Chaturon proposals as clear evidence of
the government's incoherent and fragmented approach to the southern conflict, and Thaksin's inability to adopt a consistent and unified
policy. The government was not even clear about what was going on in
the South, let alone how to address the problem.[70]

Network Monarchy Responds: Ticking Off Thaksin

Thaksin's relations with the palace have long been complex. The
King's December 2001 birthday speech appeared to criticize Thaksin,
while in the same month Prem made a major speech urging people to
face up to reality, and refrain from admiring rich people who were not
worthy of respect.[71] Early in 2002, a short item in the *Far Eastern Economic Review* hinting at tensions between Thaksin and the palace
provoked uproar, and two *Review* correspondents were almost ex-
pelled from the country.[72]

The royal family has been closely involved in the mode of network
governance promoted in the southern border provinces. Since 1973,
they have visited the South regularly, often spending several weeks at a
time at their Taksin Rachaniwes Palace in Narathiwat. The Queen has
taken a particular interest in the region, providing moral support to
the military units stationed there, and sponsoring local handicrafts
production. This concerted activity by the royal family reflects part of a
long-term project to secure the legitimacy of the Thai state in this border region. By implication, acts of "separatist" violence could be
construed and constructed not just as challenges to political authority
but as slights directed toward the palace itself. The involvement of the
royal family in the area serves to raise the stakes of any conflict: violent
actions directed at the state may be seen as acts of disloyalty toward the

crown, and potentially even as acts of treason. This was most graphically seen in 1977, when a bomb attack on Yala station involved attempted regicide. In 1982, Muslim separatists tried to disrupt the Bangkok bicentennial celebrations (also the bicentennial of the Chakri dynasty) by placing a series of bombs around the capital.[73] Retired general and Thaksin advisor General Kitti Rattanachaya has repeatedly argued that separatist groups have a "seven-step plan" to seize the border provinces in a thousand days.[74] In an extreme version of this argument, Defense Minister Thammarak Issarangkura na Ayudhaya raised the specter of a direct threat to the monarchy: he announced live on television that militants in the South planned to capture Taksin Rachaniwes Palace within a thousand days, raising their flag over it as a prelude to declaring an independent state.[75]

On 24 February 2004, Thaksin was summoned to the palace. The King urged him to deal with the southern crisis by using the principles of accessibility, understanding, and development.[76] This royal intervention may have partly inspired Thaksin's decision to ask Chaturon Chaisaeng to develop proposals for addressing the crisis, but Chaturon's was a short-lived initiative. In a very similar move, the King called in Thaksin again on 1 November, advising him to handle the troubled region "with care." The King also urged Thaksin to allow the participation of local people in resolving problems. In addition, he asked Fourth Army commander Lieutenant General Pisan Wattanawongkiri to give him a report on the Tak Bai incident.[77] Both the February and November audiences were private meetings, and the King made no public statement.

The Queen was more outspoken. On 13 October, two officials who were in the South to help block roads for the Queen were shot dead while purchasing *longkong* fruit in Narathiwat.[78] The men, a retired police captain and a mechanic, were working for the Highway Police Department. The incident received little detailed coverage in the Thai press, but a news agency reported that the men had been driving a palace Land Rover, and were actually buying the fruits for the Queen.[79]

Addressing an audience of more than a thousand people at Chitrlada Palace, the Queen said what she had experienced during her long two-month visit to the South forced her to speak out.[80] The scale and format of the event were unprecedented, with an audience including representatives of community organizations, nongovernmental organizations (NGOs), the media, and members of the Cabinet, including the prime minister.[81] In her speech, broadcast nationwide, she described Muslims "she had never known" as the brutal murderers of many ordinary citizens and government officials. Every member of the audience received a card containing a poem entitled "The Ultimate Dream," written by the Queen herself, and declaring the willingness of the Thai people to die for their compatriots. She urged the three hundred thousand Thai Buddhists in the region to remain the area and not be intimidated. "Even at the age of seventy-two, I will learn how to shoot guns without using my glasses," she declared, urging Thais in the three provinces to take shooting lessons. Her statements represented a significant raising of the political temperature in the South, supporting a policy of firm securitization. Thaksin was swift to respond: "We will not have our Queen use a gun to defend the country, but she has shown she is ready to defend the country. All Thais can't sit idly by." The Queen's comments were followed by a rally of some twenty thousand members of the infamous Village Scouts at Bangkok's Sanam Luang on 21 November, at which they called for "separatist enemies" to be driven out of Thailand.[82] It was the largest Village Scout rally since 1976. Meanwhile, the education minister announced plans to step up the use of nationalism in the school curriculum.[83] This was not the sort of royal intervention liberals had hoped for.

The following day, in a speech also broadcast on radio, the King addressed 510 newly promoted police and army officers. He declared that greater unity and cooperation between the police and the army could have avoided some of the "unrest and disorder" Queen Sirikrit had witnessed during her stay in the South.[84] The King's statement contained a more subtle message, making it clear that he viewed the security forces themselves as a major part of the problem in the troubled border region. This public speech was less explicit than his private admonitions to Thaksin on 24 February and 1 November, but the direction of his comments was much the same.

Faced with Thaksin's apparently intractable hard-line stance on the South, some public intellectuals — both Buddhist and Muslim — began to hope that that the King might make an extra-constitutional intervention to address the growing crisis, perhaps even by creating a caretaker government of national unity like the one formed after May 1992, when Anand Panyarachun was asked to return as interim prime minister following mass demonstrations that culminated in bloodshed and the resignation of the Suchinda Kraprayoon government. In the aftermath of Tak Bai, the *Bangkok Post* carried a front-page story headlined "Muslims to Ask King to Change Govt."[85] Dato Nideh Waba, chairman of the private religious school association in the southern border provinces, as well as deputy chairman of the Islamic Council, had proposed an appeal to the King to establish a royally appointed government. This was a remarkable volte-face, since Dato Nideh "had been regarded for decades by local security officials as 'our man.'"[86] He had stated: "We have no alternative apart from asking our beloved King, who is our father, to give us a royal government to tackle problems down here." Dato Nideh recognized that the move had no constitutional basis, but it was designed to put increased pressure on the Thaksin government. He claimed that in informal discussions, fellow Muslim leaders had supported petitioning the King as a last resort. "In a critical time like this, who could we turn to if not our fatherly King who is our sole hope since all Muslims down here regard him with the utmost respect."[87] Political scientist Somkiat Pongpaiboon was quoted in the same story as calling for Prem and Chavalit, former architects of the successful struggle against communism, to develop strategies for the South that respected cultural and religious differences. His statement could be read as a coded plea for intervention by Prem.

The following day, however, other Muslim leaders denied supporting Dato Nideh's plans for a petition. Paisan Promyong, deputy secretary general of the Central Islamic Committee of Thailand, suggested that the idea came from Dato Nideh alone.[88] Unbowed, Dato Nideh repeated his intention to appeal to the King, though acknowledging it would be a "symbolic gesture"; he was also planning a rally of sixty thousand Muslims to protest about Tak Bai.[89] Despite public denials by Nideh's fellow leaders, both Muslims and Buddhists continued to talk privately about the desirability of a royal intervention. On 12 March 2005, the Hong Kong-based human rights group Asian Human Rights Commission petitioned the King to "express concern" about the unsolved disappearance of prominent Muslim lawyer Somchai Neelapaijit.[90]

A persistent rumor in Bangkok was that former army commander (and privy councilor) Surayud Chulanont was planning to stage a military coup, with tacit approval from the palace, aimed at ousting Thaksin. Surayud spent the 2004 rainy season ordained as a monk in Nong Khai Province. While there was no evidence to support the coup rumor, it indicated the desire felt by some Thais for a reassertion of network monarchy. Surayud began speaking out on the South right af-

ter leaving the monkhood. On 2 November he gave an interview to the
Thai Post newspaper in the wake of Tak Bai, emphasizing the importance of building trust with Muslim community leaders. Surayud
declared, "To regard others as the opposite side or as enemies won't
bring about a good result. We are all Thais and we can talk to each
other with no need to pick up guns and fight."[91] Speaking at a seminar
on 16 November, Surayud shared a platform with Anand Panyarachun.
Both men used the occasion to state that crowd control and the dispersal of protestors were not proper tasks for the army. Lamenting the
way in which "history repeated itself," Surayud called for the creation
of a special unit to deal with such situations.[92] In a January 2004 newspaper interview, he urged the authorities to reach out to local Muslims
in the South, in order to build sufficient understanding with them.[93]
Early in 2005, prominent Muslims in the South still privately argued
that action was needed from a source "higher up" than the Thaksin
government.[94]

Thaksin Re-emboldened: Paper Cranes and Ballot Papers

As *The Independent* put it, "The prospect of a gun-toting Queen has
galvanised the nation into a frenzy of origami-folding."[95] Thaksin
sought to create a positive news bonanza by asking Thais to produce
millions of origami cranes to be scattered over the South, in a gesture
indicating the popular desire for peace.[96] Thaksin's initial response to
the royal admonitions of November 2004 was a piece of pure political
theater. While derided by his critics, the plan did strike a popular
chord with many Thais, especially in other parts of the country. It allowed Thaksin to make a grand gesture of peace, while continuing to
militarize the situation on the ground. The terrible Indian Ocean tsu-
nami of 26 December eclipsed news of the southern unrest for a
couple of weeks, allowing Thaksin to launch his election campaign
with renewed energy in early January 2005.

Following his landslide election victory in February 2005, Thaksin
Shinawatra seemed re-emboldened to tackle the woes of the deep
South — where TRT was decisively rejected by the voters, and the
Wadah faction was humiliated. Thaksin immediately announced that
he was sending twelve thousand more troops to the southern border
provinces.[97] Three other initiatives followed in quick succession. The
first was a proposal to divide the three provinces into colored zones
based on their degree of loyalty to the Thai state, depriving the 358 vil-

lages designated "red zones" of government development funds. The second proposal, partly in response to the outcry of dissent over the zoning plan, was a plan to send twenty-five TRT ministers and MPs down to the South to assess the situation and report back. The third proposal, closely linked to the second and announced at the same time, was a decision to allow a rarely convened joint session of the Senate and Lower House to debate the crisis in the South on 30 and 31 March. But these three moves were not enough to satisfy Thaksin's growing critics.

The Privy Council Speaks Out

After the first anniversary of the King's 24 February 2004 admonition to Thaksin, three members of the Privy Council made strong public statements. On 24 February, Surayud told a group of reporters that urgent action was needed to treat the wound in the South, which could otherwise become a malignant tumor.[98] He compared the southern unrest with the communist insurgency, an insurgency that emerged because villagers were treated unjustly. Surayud reported during the Crown Prince's recent visit to the region, Muslims in the South had given accounts of the injustice they had experienced. Religious teachers had been arrested on suspicion of masterminding attacks, while none of those responsible for the deaths of protestors at Tak Bai had been arrested. They had also raised the case of Somchai Neelaphaijit. Surayud argued that the justice system needed to treat people from both sides with equal fairness. He was also uneasy about the zoning plan, suggesting that it could inflame feelings of hostility. These were very detailed and highly critical comments on government policies, practically unprecedented for a member of the Privy Council. It is difficult to believe that Surayud would have made such remarks if they were not on some level sanctioned by the palace, or at least by Prem.

On 28 February, Prem made a remarkable public speech at the Chulabhorn Research Institute in Bangkok, in which he suggested that Thaksin accept advice from the King and Queen, and should adopt a peaceful and cautious approach to the problems of the South, rather than using military force hastily and without a deep understanding of the issues. Prem was speaking at a seminar entitled "Joining forces in solving problems in Southern provinces based on royal speeches," and referred back to the 24 February 2004 royal speech advocating accessibility (*khao thueng*), understanding (*khao jai*), and development (*pattana*). Thaksin had been present at the original speech, but the clear implication was that he had failed to take on board the King's words. Prem explained that everyone, ranging from community leaders to state officials, academics, and NGOs, should study the royal advice and adopt the same language. Prem stressed that Muslims with Thai citizenship must not be treated as second-class citizens.[99] Privy Councilor Kasem Wattanachai spoke at the same seminar, praising the wisdom of the King and Queen, and quoting the King's speeches for most of his presentation.[100] Kasem stressed the unity and equality of all Thais, and commended the King's "principles of thought" as the basis for addressing the country's problems.[101] Ten of his eleven slides feature quotations from the King, and only one from the Queen.

Creating the National Reconciliation Commission

Thaksin clearly got the message, going to see Prem the next day for private discussions. He immediately announced his fourth initiative on the South since the election, a plan to establish a National Reconciliation Commission headed by former prime minister Anand Panyarachun.[102] The idea of creating such a body had been mooted earlier by academics such as Chulalongkorn University sociologist Surichai Wungaeo, and had been in Thaksin's mind before the Prem speech. The choice of Anand, the King's personal choice as prime minister after May 1992 and the leading figure in drafting the 1997 constitution, spoke volumes. Anand had been a vocal critic of the government during Thaksin's first term. An anonymous Government House source declared that Thaksin had told Anand during a two-hour meeting "the government can no longer handle the southern violence alone."[103] The controversial zoning plan was abruptly dropped,[104] though the idea of "red" and "yellow" zones persisted in the thinking and vocabulary of local officials and residents.

The setting up of the NRC demonstrated that Thailand was torn between two major political directions. One view saw Thaksin and his TRT as the primary engine of dynamism in the country, and argued that by concentrating power in his hands, Thailand would be able to overcome problems such as weak coordination and decision-making to move forward according to a clear strategic vision. The second view held that Thaksin was not capable of managing complex social issues, as exemplified by the delicate situation in the South. According to this reading, Thailand needed to draw upon the wisdom of liberal elder statesmen such as Anand, who in the 1990s crafted a project of political reform that culminated in the passage of the 1997 constitution. In this sense, the NRC's creation implied a shift back to the more pluralistic and consensual politics of the 1990s.

Yet by bringing in new emergency legislation on 16 July 2005, Thaksin essentially blew the NRC out of the water, assuming personal powers completely unprecedented for a civilian Thai prime minister.[105] These included powers to declare a state of emergency and impose curfews anywhere in the country, and to ban public gatherings, censor news and ban media circulation, close premises, order evacuations, detain suspects without charge, confiscate property, intercept telecommunications, and order wiretaps. While some of these powers were not made immediately effective, they could be implemented at any time. What made this assumption of additional powers so extraordinary was that Thaksin had acted without consulting or even informing Anand and other members of the Commission — thereby preempting their special role to find a solution for the crisis, even before they had produced a report. Some NRC members openly complained that the legislation had made their task irrelevant, and many threatened to resign. Anand had to work hard to talk them out of it.

Assuming that Thaksin wanted to signal his displeasure with the NRC, which he clearly viewed with growing irritation and suspicion, he chose a particularly crude form of action in relation to such a sensitive issue. TRT had an absolute majority in Parliament, and the prime minister could have railroaded the emergency legislation through effortlessly — something he finally did on 29 August. The irony was that despite his own successful career in electoral politics — and his wealth derived from the modern sphere of telecommunications — Thaksin appeared to prefer the old

Thai police officers in Narathiwat Province, southern Thailand, practice handling guns, 15 June 2004. As alarm spread among state officials following the rise in violence, training in the use of weapons became a priority. Even the Queen declared that she planned to learn to shoot.

politics of exploiting state power, ruling by executive decree, and ig-
noring the voices of fellow MPs (even from his own party), critical
journalists and academics, and wise elders.

A televised conversation between Thaksin and Anand, broadcast
from Government House on 28 July 2005, clearly illustrated the gap
between the government and the NRC.[106] Billed as a demonstration
that the two sides were working together, the program actually revealed the intellectual and moral gulf between them. Anand stressed
the need to recognize Thailand's ethnic diversity and establish basic
principles of justice; Thaksin talked about combating terrorists, finding masterminds, and the problem of bad teaching in Islamic schools.
Supported by a patently pro-government "moderator," Thaksin —
who sat, presidentially, in the center of the room — repeatedly inter-
rupted Anand. Anand appeared, in effect, an alternative prime
minister, offering a different set of approaches and policies to the Thai
public. In the broadcast he took on the role of the underdog —
sidelined and harried — yet his greater moral authority shone
through. In a very real sense, the NRC was becoming an alternative to
the Thaksin government. When Thais talked about other people who
could replace Thaksin as premier, the names most readily on their lips
were those of Anand, and Privy councilors such as Surayud or
Palakorn. The NRC had become the de facto opposition, representing
a set of values and ideas comprehensively opposed by the Thaksin government. While the formal membership of the NRC included a
number of bureaucrats and Thaksin associates, by October 2005 most
of the core participants were people aligned with the NGO sector.[107]

Conclusion: The Periphery
Comes to Town

Thaksin Shinawatra has established a new mode of Thai leadership for
the twenty-first century, associated with the creation of a quasi-profes-
sional political party and new alliances between political actors and
the forces of big business.[108] Most importantly, Thaksin did not take his
cues from lines scripted by the palace: this prime minister was answer-
able only to himself. Nowhere was this new mode of premiership
demonstrated more clearly than in Prem's backyard, the southern border provinces, which Thaksin sought to make a test case for the
superiority of executive management, rather than loose network governance. The terrible upsurge in violence during 2004, TRT's

disastrous performance in the February 2005 parliamentary elections in the three border provinces, and Thaksin's constant flip-flopping and inept handling of the growing crisis, all suggested that he was failing to prove his point. Yet the southern crisis also succeeded in smoking out Prem, and exposing the workings of network monarchy as never before. Thaksin's refusal to listen to private royal admonitions or coded signs of displeasure meant that Prem had to make an extraordinary public intervention on 28 February 2005, using a major public speech to rebuke the government and reject its policies.

Also evident was the way in which Privy Council appointments had been politicized during the Thaksin government. Three senior officials who had problems with Thaksin were fast-tracked to Privy councilor status: Kasem Wattanachai, Thaksin's first education minister, Palakorn Suwannarat, director of the SBPAC, and Surayud Chulanont, former army commander and supreme commander. Two of them were actively deployed to question Thaksin's policies toward the South, backing up Prem with language scripted directly by the palace. Thaksin's powerful political position demanded a fresh strategy by network monarchy. Following the February 2005 elections, Thaksin's control of Thailand was formidable. Thaksin may have been believed that his super mandate from voters trumped the residual super mandate cherished by network monarchy. Yet the election also revealed Thaksin's weakness: his popular support did not extend to the South, and his MPs had been decisively rejected in the deep South. It was here that the old power networks chose to stage their struggle to regain the political initiative. This national power struggle was one core meaning of the renewed political violence in Pattani, Yala, and Narithiwat since January 2004.

Thaksin had set out to transform Thailand's deep South from a zone of liminality that resisted and undermined his authority, to a zone of conformity that he could dominate and control. Yet his misguided handling of this sensitive region seriously backfired. Far from being subordinated to the will of the center, the deep South began to undermine Thaksin's personal authority. Things fell apart, and the center could not hold. A small area containing less than 2 million people, one thousand kilometers from Bangkok, became a principal focus of news and public attention. In a highly centralized country such as Thailand, this was previously unthinkable: the provinces had no right to challenge the capital city in such a fashion.

Having told Anand in February 2005 that his government could not handle the South alone, Thaksin now seemed to believe that he could manage the growing crisis personally. As the violence continued unabated, there seemed scant evidence for this view: instead, Thaksin increasingly resorted to the mobilization of hatred, denouncing the killers of two marines in a Narathiwat village as "beasts." Following the violent murder of a monk in Pattani, the provincial Sangha Committee called for the abolition of the NRC; a Pattani abbot gave an interview in which he accused the NRC of sympathizing with terrorists, and declared that the Muslim and Buddhist communities had been divided for a long time.[109] Anand, having earlier declined to criticize Thaksin publicly, became less and less coded in his dissatisfaction with the government. He told a conference in Hat Yai in September 2005 that the government showed little willingness to apologize for past mistakes, or to accept the viewpoints of others.[110] On the first day of 2006, deputy premier Chidchai Vanasatidya asserted that the southern violence was now on the decline: over 190 suspected insurgents had been captured, and local people were cooperating much more with the authorities.[111] He anticipated that by April, the situation would be largely under control. Chidchai's remarks appeared to trigger a new wave of violent incidents. His attempts to claim that the government's security policies were succeeding provoked a swift reaction from Prem Tinsulanond, who visited the southern border provinces for the first time since the January 2004 escalation. Speaking to over two thousand representatives of ninety-three civic groups and organizations in Pattani on 7 January, Prem repeated the royal mantras about the importance of understanding, access, and development as keys to resolving the conflict. He urged the government to listen to his advice, and expressed the concerns of the King and Queen over the continuing violence.[112] This exchange by leading proxies of Thaksin and the palace illustrated the continuing gulf between the two sides.

Faced with an invigorated parliamentary opposition under new Democrat leader Abhisit Vejjajiva, and undermined by persistent allegations of corruption and cronyism surrounding projects such as Bangkok's new airport, as well as rising oil prices and other economic problems, Thaksin was now on a downward spiral.[113] Related issues included Thaksin's attempts to bypass royal approval for the annual military promotions list, the launch of a book on "royal powers" by renegade TRT MP Pramuan Ruchanaseri,[114] and the removal of outspoken Thaksin critic Sondhi Limthongkul from his popular Channel 9 television program. Indirectly, the NRC served as a rallying point for much of this political dissent, by opening up greater political space for reformists and friends of the palace.[115] Thaksin was able to manipulate and to capitalize upon public skepticism about the NRC's "soft" approach to the southern violence. Yet the NRC had provided Thaksin's enemies with an opportunity to regroup. Network monarchy might not possess the solutions to Thailand's political problems, but it could mobilize formidable moral resources to harass and discredit the Thaksin government.

Why did violence flare up in Thailand's deep South early in 2004? Though not a complete explanation, one important answer is that Thaksin Shinawatra had chosen the region as the battleground for his fight to wrest control of Thailand from the palace, the Privy Council, and from network monarchy. Thaksin and the forces he commanded were not directly responsible for all — or even most — of the violent incidents that erupted in the South from January 2004 onwards. Nor was this violence directly initiated or inspired by Prem, or by forces loyal to network monarchy. Rather, national-level tensions between the competing networks of Thaksin and the palace provided a context and background for the renewed southern violence, creating a space in which other forces could emerge and operate. Yet, Thaksin provoked a remarkable backlash from a wide range of groups and individuals who had come to oppose his rule. He retained such formidable wealth and power that he would not be readily ousted from Bangkok's Government House. Instead, he seemed destined gradually to become a gesture politician, reduced to endless grandstanding as complex problems such as the intractable southern conflict moved beyond his ability to control. The South had come to symbolize all the problems faced by Thaksin and his government, and all the deficiencies of his authoritarian mode of leadership. "The South" was no longer about the South: it was about the legitimacy of the Thaksin government, and of the Thai state itself.

ACKNOWLEDGMENTS: The author would like to thank the many people who have commented on these issues, or raised questions following earlier presentations of this material in Pattani, DeKalb, and Australia during 2005. Special thanks to Kavi Chongkittavorn, Michael Connors, John Funston, Kevin Hewison, Michael Montesano, Michelle Tan, and Thongchai Winichakul for their encouragement, help, and suggestions. I gratefully acknowledge the British Academy conference grant that enabled me to present an earlier version of this paper at the Ninth International Conference on Thai Studies, Northern Illinois University, DeKalb, Ill., 3–6 April 2005.

❑

3 THAKSIN'S ACHILLES' HEEL

The Failure of Hawkish Approaches in the Thai South

Ukrist Pathmanand

PRIME MINISTER THAKSIN SHINAWATRA'S MISHANDLING of the conflict in Thailand's Muslim South during 2004 and 2005 had serious consequences both at home and abroad. By exacerbating the violence, he hurt Thailand's domestic security as well as its relationships with neighboring Malaysia, the Association of Southeast Asian Nations (Asean) and the broader Muslim world. While in March 2005 it appeared that Thaksin was changing tack with the creation of the National Reconciliation Commission (NRC), in fact the government was persisting with populist and confrontational policies that increase the threat of a broad-based secessionist movement.

During his first couple of years in office, Thaksin scored popular successes in his handling of the Cambodian Embassy crisis and the controversial war on drugs. In both cases, success was based on an image of quick and decisive action. However, Thaksin's approach was less successful when he subsequently faced more complex problems that resisted simple, shoot-from-the-hip solutions. The first of these was the outbreak of the bird flu epidemic, a natural problem somewhat beyond human control, putting both major and minor poultry farmers into great peril.[1] An even more insoluble issue was the violence in the South, a multidimensional problem rooted in long history and cultural differences.[2]

Since the beginning of 2004, more than one thousand people have died in political violence in the three predominantly Muslim provinces of Yala, Narathiwat, and Pattani, on Thailand's border with Malaysia.[3] In January 2004, insurgents had looted weapons from the Fourth Development Battalion of the Royal Thai Army in Narathiwat's Jo Airong district. This was followed by arson attacks on twenty schools. On 28 April, simultaneous attacks on security checkpoints by lightly armed militants saw 113 people killed, 32 of them in an assault by the Thai military on the historic Kru-Ze mosque in Pattani. The most infamous incident took place on 25 October 2004, when over a thousand Muslim protestors were arrested outside Tak Bai police station. Transported in tightly packed trucks to a detention center some 130 kilometers away, seventy-eight people died from suffocation or dehydration.

In addition to these major events, other violent incidents have occurred on an almost daily basis. Victims have included a judge, a deputy provincial governor, government officials, police and military officers, as well as monks, teachers, and ordinary residents. In July 2005, an attack by insurgents in the town of Yala left two police officers dead and twenty-two people injured. Thaksin reacted by introducing a host of draconian new legislative measures by emergency cabinet decree. These included some that allow the detention of suspects without charge and the banning of newspapers and other publications that are deemed a threat to national security.[4]

How did Thailand find itself in this predicament? From the start of his first term in 2001, Prime Minister Thaksin, an extremely wealthy telecommunications magnate, never paid much attention to simmering dissatisfaction in the South. His initial reaction to the eruption of violence following the looting of army weapons on 4 January 2004 was to quell the uprising quickly and decisively. In this, Thaksin has been advised by a group of close associates who will be termed here the "hawkish faction," which has persistently advocated using state violence to suppress militant activity in the South. Nevertheless, Thaksin security advisors are not unified, but are often in conflict with one another. Thus the conflict in the southern border provinces should not be seen simply as a local affair, but as a mirror and an extension of conflicts within Thailand's security and political elites. Some commentators have stressed Thaksin's credentials as a businessman-turned-politician, modeling his political strategies on approaches borrowed from the business world.[5] But his handling of the South reveals another side of Thaksin's character, his preference for the use of violence to tackle problems, and his disdain for "softer" methods such as discussion and negotiations.

The State's Initial Response toward Unrest in the South

In the aftermath of the terrorist bombings in Bali, Indonesia, on 12 October 2002, the Thaksin Shinawatra government vigorously campaigned to convince both foreign tourists and their governments to believe Thailand was safe, and not by any means a haven for terrorist movements.[6] Thaksin rejected a claim in Simon Elegant's *Time* article, dated 11 November 2002, that some international terrorist groups had been trained in southern Thailand in the previous year.[7] From then on, the government persisted in claiming that Thailand was not a target of terrorism and that the country remained a tranquil tourist destination.

Following the January 2004 arms seizure, in which four soldiers were killed, Thaksin initially dubbed the suspects "common bandits," while announcing that they would all be arrested within seven days. In fact, Thaksin was preparing to resort to violence: on 5 January, Fourth Army chief Lieutenant General Pongsak Ekbannasingha declared martial law in every Narathiwat district except the town area, supposedly to prevent the transportation of the stolen weapons. Thaksin also summoned all units involved in security for a meeting on 5 January and reprimanded those in charge of the area — including Interior Minister Wan Muhammad Nor Matha and army commander General Chaisit Shinawatra — because no forewarning had been given. In fact, Thaksin was even more furious with the police department, when it emerged that the police had been warned both of the planned robbery and the strewing of spikes on the road to deter pursuit, yet had failed to notify the military.[8]

When the incident was followed by the violent clashes of 28 April, the Bangkok public tended to understand events in the deep South in terms of two theories: either separatists were behind the violence, or groups of "influential people" linked to organized crime were involved.[9] The first view was that insurgent groups had been consolidating their forces and training militia under an administrative

Billboard in Pattani, picturing Prime Minister Thaksin; the writing is in Yawi script. Since the bombings in Indonesia in fall 2002 the Thaksin government has "vigorously campaigned to convince both foreign tourists and their governments to believe Thailand was safe, and not by any means a haven for terrorist movements."

and military structure up to the district level. According to Thammarak, the insurgents were prepared to embark on a seven-step plan, leading ultimately to the overthrow of the Thai state in the area. The 28 April operation was believed to be the first of the seven steps, aimed at providing a psychological boost to the radical cause, and unnerving the Thai authorities. According to some versions of this explanation, the insurgent movement was thus operating in coordination with terrorist movements outside the kingdom and was also linked to Jemaah Islamiah (JI).

For the most part, police and military officers involved in security units — including some senior retired generals, e.g., Defence Minister Chetta Thanajaro; Deputy Director of the Internal Security Operation Command (ISOC) Pallop Pinmanee; and Kitti Rattanachaya, specialist advisor on security affairs to the prime minister — subscribed to this view. Kitti warned in one interview that the situation in the South now looked more serious: insurgent separatists were believed to possess fifteen hundred firearms that had not yet been used.[10]

An alternative theory to explain the violence was advanced by such high-profile figures as Prime Minister Thaksin Shinawatra and former army chief General Chaisit Shinawatra, Thaksin's cousin. According to this theory, the violence was the work of obscure "influential groups," a Thai euphemism for organized criminals. Thaksin suggested that those involved in the 28 April attacks were linked with the suspects who took part in the looting of army weapons on 4 January, judging from their similar outfits. These covert operations had been masterminded by "dark influences" involved in drug trafficking. According to Thaksin, the unrest was about internal conflicts, and was not connected either with international terrorism or religious factors. Many of the youths involved were only teenagers, some around fourteen or fifteen. The fact that one group of ten teenagers who had been arrested earlier included some Buddhist youths illustrated the fact the causes of the violence cut across the religious divide. Also, since both Muslims and Buddhists were targets of the attacks, the violence could not be explained in Islamist terms.[11] Chaisit echoed Thaksin's views in another interview.[12]

The Tak Bai Tragedy and Thaksin's Explanatory Turn

On 25 October 2004, Lieutenant-General Pisan Wattanawongkiri, Fourth Army commander, Police-General Manote Kaiwong, commissioner of Provincial Police Bureau 9, and Deputy Permanent Secretary of the Interior Ministry Siva Saengmanee decided to use a force of three hundred riot suppression police officers, one thousand soldiers, and three hundred marines from Chulabhorn military camp to disperse a thousands-strong crowd encircling the Tak Bai police station in Narathiwat. The demonstrators had demanded to see a group of suspects, who had been arrested on charges that they had falsely claimed they had been robbed of six official weapons issued to their village security unit. Six demonstrators were killed during the ensuing clashes, while a further seventy-eight died in transit, apparently having been suffocated after being piled into army trucks.[13]

Initially, state officials concurred with Prime Minister Thaksin Shinawatra in explaining that the mass deaths were an accident caused by technical errors. They claimed that the fatalities resulted from a clumsy transfer operation during which some protestors, already exhausted after fasting all day, died of suffocation.[14] However, he eventually revealed that the decision to opt for violence in dispersing the Tak Bai protestors was motivated by a belief that the demonstration had been masterminded by terrorist groups, which had been in operation since the 4 January firearms haul.[15]

Several statements made by Thaksin during the 27 October Senate meeting and his live nationwide television broadcast on 29 October were contradictory. For example, he referred to poverty and problems in religious teaching methods that lacked any of the elementary education necessary for secular employment, and insisted the violence was not caused by religious conflict. However, at other points Thaksin seemed to be convinced that the violence was based on an organized movement, declaring:

> There are actions similar to a direct sales strategy, that is, there's a leader narrating accounts of the Pattani state while urging youths to return home, invite more friends to join them and donate 50 baht each. They are false Islamic religious teachers or ustaz. The kids were made to return again the day after. It seemed they were so impetuous they encircled the Tak Bai police station. We discovered 76 pick-up trucks and 185 motorcycles.[16]

Thaksin's nationwide television broadcast concerning the Tak Bai violence, which can be considered an official announcement, not only revealed his point of view on problems in the South as an act of terrorism, but also illustrated his attempts to assert his own legitimacy. For example, Thaksin mentioned that he had learned about poverty in the deep South while accompanying Her Majesty the Queen on her royal visits to the rural areas. He was able to invoke the need to defend the integrity of the kingdom and the sovereignty of the nation as an underlying rationale for his actions.[17] By summoning up the idea of a separatist insurgency, Thaksin sought to justify and legitimate his use of state force in the South. Thaksin's newfound belief in terrorist movements as the true root of unrest in the South was also echoed in reports issued by the National Security Council (NSC) and military units.[18] It was unusual for these documents, together with meetings of high-ranking state officials, to be disclosed to the public and publicized through the media.

Thaksin's Emergence as a "Big Hawk"

The evolution of Prime Minister Thaksin's interpretation of the problems in the South, from blaming "common bandits" to identifying a nascent terrorist movement, was not a change of views based on new information. Instead, it illustrated his hawkish approach toward problem-solving in the three southern border provinces. Other ministers and state officials working on the southern violence are simply acting on his orders and are essentially interchangeable, hence Thaksin's constant reshuffling of his security team since January 2004.

The eighth Thaksin cabinet reshuffle in March 2004 (Thaksin made an unprecedented ten reshuffles during his first term) saw transfers of ministers previously in charge of security affairs and problems on the southern borders. Defense Minister General Thammarak Issarangkura na Ayudhaya and Interior Minister Wan Muhammad Nor Matha were transferred to deputy prime minister posts, while General Chetta Thanajaro and Dr. Bhokin Bhalakula assumed the defense minister and interior minister posts respectively. It is important to note that none of these ministers advocated an alternative, more dovish policy approach in the South: they were all indistinguishable in their blind loyalty to Thaksin's orders. General Thammarak had worked closely with Thaksin, once declaring dramatically in the middle of the live broadcast of a cabinet meeting, that he was convinced the outbreak of violence in the South was the work of terrorist groups whose plan also includes the replacement of the flag at the Thaksin Ratchanives Palace in Narathiwat.[19]

In replacing Thammarak and Wan Nor, Thaksin hardly seemed inclined to pick men with the experience and expertise to assume these difficult posts. Rather, he selected people who were likely to accept his own lead in southern issues, reflecting his tendency to micro-manage complex problems. General Chetta's appointment to the post of defense minister came as a surprise.[20] Though regarded as a Thai-Burmese relations expert, he had long since retired from security affairs (his final role was as army commander-in-chief up to September 1998), and had since focused on sports-related activities. Lacking his own strong perspective on southern issues, Chetta was greatly influenced by the hawkish faction. Dr. Bhokin Bhalakula's role as interior minister was not much different. Having worked closely with Thaksin during the Chavalit Yongchaiyudh government (November 1996 to November 1997) prior to the 1997 economic crisis, he was a law expert with hardly any experience in administration and government, and no detailed knowledge of the southern region.

The new Fourth Army commander, Lieutenant-General Pisan, was also very close to Thaksin, and unlikely to dissent from his preference for hard-line measures. Pisan was a student of the Armed Forces Academy Preparatory School (AFAPS) Class 9 (one year above Thaksin

Anonymous

An anguished-looking Thaksin Shinawatra on a rare visit to the South in 2005. Despite his constant bluster and repeated reshuffles of ministers, military commanders, and other officials, Thaksin was conspicuously unable to deal with the violence in Thailand's border provinces, which became his Achilles' heel.

himself) and Chulachomklao Royal Military Academy Class 20.[21] With his knowledge of problems in the South, he was assigned by the prime minister to assist General Chaisit Shinawatra, to oversee the situation there, as well as coordinating with local religious leaders. His determination to use violence to disperse the Tak Bai demonstrators and his televised statement branding the crowd "rioters,"[22] as well as the resulting eighty-five deaths, showed that Lieutenant-General Pisan was prone to using violence and inclined to respond favorably to the prime minister's orders, not a man who would argue with Thaksin or be inclined toward a policy of compromise.

Other security agencies were also acting upon the prime minister's orders and were dominated by the hawkish faction. General Pallop Pinmanee had long believed the problems of the South were part of a terrorist movement. It was General Pallop who ordered the attack on the machete-armed assailants taking refuge inside the Kru-Ze mosque. Thaksin also had two close relatives working on his security team. The first was General Chaisit Shinawatra. Though serving in the South for ten years as an engineer before being propelled to the army chief post by Thaksin,[23] General Chaisit could boast few achievements. During his term as army commander, he made various moves to please Thaksin, such as coordinating peace talks with Burma and ordering army radio stations to make favorable broadcasts about the government's achievements. His involvement in southern operations had led to an earlier dispute with local religious leaders.[24] Thaksin's other relative was assistant deputy national police chief Police Lieutenant General Priewphan Damaphong who was specially appointed to lead a special investigation team looking into a series of killings in the deep South.[25] Priewphan resembled Chaisit in the way he acted to please Thaksin, but lacked any great competence or finesse. He was also one of the key players in the government's controversial 2003 crackdown on drugs, which allegedly led to almost three thousand extrajudicial killings.[26]

When all players in the security agencies are close and loyal associates of the prime minister, they tend to curry favor and obey orders instead of arguing or suggesting a different view, let alone proposing a peaceful approach. Since most of Thaksin's trusted security associates are military men, they tend to believe all information provided by the state without suspicion or exception. Like General Pallop Pinmanee, General Kitti Rattanachaya was convinced that terrorist movements were responsible for the problems in the South,[27] a view shared by former defense minister General Thammarak. Even General Chetta, who served in his post for less than two months believed that a separatist movement existed and that a force of four hundred men was operating in the South. Believing such claims, all these security staff consequently acted in response to the quick-thinking, quick-acting prime minister to swiftly achieve their goals. This was even more true of close relatives of Thaksin's such as Priewphan Damaphong and Chaisit Shinawatra, who owed their positions largely to the patronage of Prime Minister Thaksin Shinawatra. The new defense minister, General Samphan Boonyanant, and Deputy Education Minister Aree Wongaraya (appointed in Thaksin's tenth cabinet reshuffle, on 6 October 2004) were also the prime minister's close associates, and served their terms to repay the benefits granted to them by Thaksin.

In April 2004 Thaksin set up the Southern Border Provinces Peacebuilding Command (SBPPC), operating directly under the prime minister, doubtless intending to heal the well-publicized rifts between different agencies working to restore law and order. However, the conflicts between his associates persisted. Lieutenant General Wongkot Maneerin, assistant national police commissioner, was appointed deputy director of the Songkla-based Southern Police Operations Centre. Not only was Wongkot a classmate of Thaksin's from their cadet school days, and an officer whose preference for hard-line tactics perfectly corresponds to the government's policies, but his wife had also served as a deputy minister.[28] However, as of December 2004, Wongkot had not attended a single meeting at the SBPPC office,[29] a clear indication that his operations in the South were directly under the prime minister, and he felt no obligation to liaise with the army.

Rifts existed as well within military units. Though Fourth Army commander Pisan was very close to Thaksin,[30] he was seen as a political soldier, better deployed at official receptions than commanding troops in a conflict situation. Army commander-in-chief General Pravit Wongsuwan was said to have wanted him transferred even before Tak Bai.[31] High-ranking military officers commented that the killings at Tak Bai could have been avoided had someone with maturity, experience, and competence been in charge. Senior officers believed the Tak Bai crackdown had a hugely negative impact on the army's reputation worldwide.[32]

No matter how many ministers and security chiefs were rotated, and despite the establishment of the SBPPC, reports of almost daily killings alarmed the public and undermined Thaksin's reputation for efficiency and crisis management. As the government's popularity began to slide, Thaksin decided to play the Thai nationalist card, calculated to please both the country's Buddhist majority and the security establishment. On the night he departed for Tak Bai, he reiterated he would never sacrifice a single square inch of Thai territory.[33]

Alienating Friends

After his rise to Thailand's top political post, Thaksin initiated economic policies that, coupled with his regional diplomatic achievements and his official visits to several powerful countries, strengthened his chance of becoming a leading Asian statesman. The economic policies he developed to pull Thailand out of the 1997 crisis — focusing on domestic growth and the expansion of wealth to the grassroots level — were approvingly mentioned by other Asian leaders as a possible new economic model for the region. Thailand's hosting of the Asian Cooperation Dialogue and the APEC summit in Bangkok also increased Thaksin's stature. However, his mishandling of the southern unrest dramatically changed the tenor of relations with Malaysia and Indonesia. Instead of becoming Asia's senior statesman, Prime Minister Thaksin was increasingly seen as the troublemaker of the region.[34]

When violence in the South escalated, former Malaysian prime minister Dr. Mahathir Mohamad advised the Thai government that provinces in the predominantly Muslim South of Thailand should be granted autonomy. In a conciliatory fashion, Mahathir stressed that Thaksin was a tolerant man who would listen to the requests of his country's Muslims.[35] Mahathir also stressed the importance of holding talks and listening to the plight of southern Thai Muslims. He reminded Thailand not to allow the military to take the lead in solving the conflict in the South as that would only worsen the problem. Thaksin, however, hit back at the claim immediately, dismissing the advice as unconstructive. In his efforts to maximize votes in the February 2005 general election, he sacrificed relations with Thailand's neighbors.

In a nationally broadcast address to the governors of all seventy-six provinces in December 2004, the prime minister indicated that the Malaysian forests harbored combat training grounds for Thai terrorist movements, and that Indonesian universities were spreading the fundamentalist ideology behind the terrorist movements operating in Thailand.[36] Although Thaksin's claims concerning a connection between the terrorist movement and Malaysia and Indonesia were censured by both the Malaysian and Indonesian leaders,[37] his disclosure of the information was deliberate, aiming to justify his own measures in tackling the problems in the South and to restore his government's political popularity. Initially at least, Thaksin's claim about militia training sites seemed plausible. When suspicions concerning the combat training claim intensified, Deputy Education Minister Sutham Saengprathum came out in an attempt to restore the prime minister's popularity by indicating he had photographic evidence of the militia training in his possession.[38]

In December 2004, Malaysia's current prime minister, Abdullah Ahmad Badawi, vehemently denied Thaksin's allegation and demanded that Thailand show proof.[39] The Malaysian leader further complained that if evidence were really available, diplomatic means should have been used to inform other parties in private instead of making such accusations public, and he suggested that the coming election might have been the real motivation behind Thaksin's remarks. But instead of patching up relations, Thaksin continued to maintain a frosty distance from his Muslim neighbors to the South. This tone had been heard previously, when Thaksin threatened to walk out of the 2004 Asean summit in Vientiane if the Tak Bai incident was raised by Malaysia or Indonesia.

Rejecting Reconciliation

Throughout 2004, several proposals emerged for addressing the southern conflict by peaceful means, including the arguments of Prawase Wasi,[40] ideas advanced by a group of 144 scholars and academics,[41] a proposal submitted by the Human Rights Commission,[42] and several reports by members of Senate. However, these were all ignored by the prime minister and his hawkish team. The most obvious case is the rejection of the seven-point peace proposals advanced by Deputy Prime Minister Chaturon Chaisaeng and his team.[43] Chaturon's core proposal was that the three southern border provinces should be made a special administrative zone. Other major principles included an amnesty for political suspects held before the 4 January 2004 theft of army weapons (excluding criminal offense suspects); removal of Bangkok-based police and military officers of all units who are not southerners from operations in the area; and the lifting of martial law in certain areas.[44] Such ideas were clearly unacceptable to the hawkish faction. Even though the proposal-drafting team insisted that the guidelines truly reflected the need of people in various sectors in the three southern border provinces,[45] the hawks viewed the proposals from a cold war perspective, seeing them as creating space for separatist movements to operate and so threaten national security.

Thaksin claimed that the Chaturon proposal was based solely on information gathered from one group of Muslims,[46] and ensured that it was not discussed at the 5 April 2004 Cabinet meeting. Deputy Prime Minister General Chavalit Yongchaiyudh then ordered an additional seven thousand police and military officers into the area. Defence Minister Chetta Thanajaro made it clear in an interview that martial law should not be lifted, claiming that locals were happy to be under military protection. Chaisit Shinawatra questioned whether Chaturon's proposals really reflected the needs of the people, and insisted that the lifting of martial law was not a majority demand. Police General Sunthorn Saikwan, acting national police chief, expressed his dissatisfaction with the proposals.[47]

Armed police at a Buddhist temple in Sungai Padi, Narathiwat, 4 February 2006. The Thaksin government's hardline policies in the South looked likely to exacerbate tensions between the two main religious communities.

Military hostility to the plan resulted in Chaturon being removed from responsibility for southern affairs.[48] A backlash against the plan, which could be seen on popular internet bulletin boards such as panthip.com, revealed the extent to which many Buddhist Thais were pleased by the government's use of repressive violence in the South, and were willing to express their latent distrust or even hatred toward southern Muslims.[49] Opinion polls also showed public approval of the violent measures used in the South.[50] Thaksin and his advisors proved unable to resist the temptation to exploit nationalist sentiments to restore the popularity of the ruling TRT Party. As the 6 February 2005 general elections approached, Thaksin became increasingly cautious about the publication of reports compiled by the Kru-Ze mosque inquiry commission and the reports of the Tak Bai inquiry team.

When Thanin Jaisamut, an opposition Democrat parliamentarian, distributed CDs about the Tak Bai tragedy during his election campaign in Satun, Thaksin criticized the Democrats for having chosen political advantage over the national interest.[51] Thanin's subsequent win was later invalidated by the Election Commission on the grounds that he had slandered a rival candidate; not only did he lose his parliamentary seat, but he was banned from running in the resulting by-election. Thaksin ensured that the reports of the inquiry commission for both the Tak Bai and Kru-Ze incidents were not officially published, despite warnings that delaying publication could cause public confusion.[52] In the end, both suggest that the Kru-Ze and Tak Bai inquiries actually offered only mild criticisms of the military.[53] The Tak Bai report largely concurred with government claims that procedures had been followed correctly.[54]

The overall effect of the reports was to support the actions of security officials and the Thaksin government, which has been at pains not to antagonize the military. Thaksin has used various tactics to boost his popularity among the military, including ensuring fast-track promotions for thirty-eight of his own AFAPS 10 classmates.[55] Those commanders implicated in the Kru-Ze and Tak Bai incidents were also treated leniently. General Pallop Pinmanee's case was a highly irregular one. Pallop could have faced trial for the deaths he caused at Kru-Ze, but he was simply temporarily transferred out of the South. Yet Pallop was actually a political appointee, a retired military officer who had no business commanding troops at all. Pallop subsequently published a book entitled *Was I Wrong to Storm Kru-Ze?*[56] a sensationalized account of his supposed boldness during the Vietnam War and the communist crackdown. The book became a best-seller, reflecting public sentiment supportive of Pallop's hard-line approach, and it helped him become a symbol of tough military action in the South. His public profile made him virtually untouchable by the Thaksin government. Similarly, the Tak Bai investigative commission ascribed the deaths of seventy-eight people to mistakes by three military officers, who left the handling of the prisoners to their subordinates.[57] The report simply suggests that the defense minister should reprimand the officers involved, and hold a disciplinary inquiry into their actions. If found guilty of any criminal offenses, they should be dealt with by a military court.[58] Like Pallop, these officers became both a symbol of the military as a whole, and representatives of Thai patriotism, cherished in some quarters for their aggressive and violent retaliation against southern Muslims.

The Electoral Response: Thailand vs. the South

Following the results of the 6 February election, it became clear that the South really was Thaksin's Achilles' heel. Nationwide, TRT won a landslide victory with 377 seats while the Democrats gained 96. But in Yala, Narathiwat, and Pattani, the turnout was around 70 percent, with overwhelming support for Democrat candidates. The three provinces returned ten Democrat and one Chart Thai MPs. TRT failed to win a single seat, despite the fact that the region had previously been the stronghold of Wan Nor's Wadah faction, all of whose candidates lost their seats.[59] Veteran southern Muslim politicians running under the TRT banner found themselves ousted, sometimes by candidates who were virtually unknown. The policies of the Thaksin government, admired elsewhere in the country, were completely rejected in the deep South.

Immediately following the election results, Thaksin's response was to classify the border provinces into different zones, and cut the government budget in supposedly disloyal "red zones." He was quoted as saying: "What should I do? Should I give them [southern insurgents] money to buy more bombs?"[60] The zoning proposal generated massive public criticism, which Thaksin initially ignored, inviting all the military chiefs to play golf with him and TRT's senior members at the Lake Wood golf club on 20 February.[61] He made outspoken attacks on senior figures and academics who criticized the zoning plan.[62] But the zoning policy soon went beyond a war of words between Thaksin and his regular critics, becoming the focus of disagreements between the prime minister and the Privy Council, one of Thailand's most revered political institutions. The Privy Council consisted of eighteen wise men chosen by King Bhumibol Adulyadej as his personal advisors. Their suggestions, especially in times of crisis — such as during the "Bloody May" period of political violence in 1992, and on the self-subsistence economic projects initiated after the Asian financial crisis in 1997 — are often interpreted as reflections of the King's thoughts.

Privy councilor General Surayud Chulanont declared that during HRH Crown Prince Maha Vajiralongkorn's recent visit to the far South, several Muslims had complained to him about what they perceived as injustice on the part of authorities.[63] He emphasized the importance of impartial justice, and the need to ensure fair treatment of both sides, to avoid perceptions of inequity and oppression. For example, local Muslims were uneasy about cases where religious teachers were arrested for their suspected connections with violent attacks. By contrast, no arrests were made for those responsible for the deaths of scores of Muslim protesters in Tak Bai, or for the mysterious disappearance of Muslim lawyer Somchai Neelaphaijit, who had defended Muslims suspected of involvement in the campaign of terror.[64]

Surayud's statements were soon overshadowed by a rare intervention by former prime minister and Privy Council president General
Prem Tinsulanond, who did not mince words in his opening speech
during a workshop held in Bangkok on 28 February 2005 on using
royal ideas to solve problems. He urged the government to adopt the
royal approach to the South, emphasizing peaceful and develop-
ment-oriented means,[65] and reminded the government that before
trying to resolve a problem, it was important to understand it correctly.[66] Both Surayudh and Prem commanded considerable respect
among both the public and the military, so their voices could not
lightly be ignored. But the real bombshell came from General Prem,
who was highly respected as a national leader and is now the embodiment of honesty in many people's eyes.[67] Both figures expressed
disappointment over state injustice and the lack of rule of law.

At the beginning of March 2005, the southern crisis seemed to have
come to a positive turning point. Respected former prime minister
Anand Panyarachun accepted Thaksin's invitation to chair a National
Reconciliation Commission (NRC), which had been established to
propose solutions to the problems of Thailand's southern region.
Thaksin's initiative was a direct response to criticism by Prem and
other senior figures. In a rather surprised tone, Anand told Thais that
he had detected a positive change in the prime minister's thinking.
Even though the two leaders had opposing views on certain issues, apparently they had agreed on a final goal, namely, resolution of the
conflict by peaceful means. Anand was given the authority to hand-
pick the forty-eight members in the commission with the
understanding that it would work independently from the government. The commission comprised a variety of members from civil
society, political parties, and the public sector. Many members of the
NRC were known to have had significant disagreements with Thaksin
and the government, but all parties put aside their differences to
work together.

Initially, some of the proposals presented by the NRC met with a
positive response from the government, such as the public release of
the inquiry panel's reports on the Kru-Ze mosque massacre and the
dispersal of the Tak Bai demonstrators. The two reports — censored,
according to Anand, to protect witnesses and promote reconciliation
— were subsequently released by the NRC, rather than by the government itself.[68] Two other proposals — to drop the charges against
fifty-eight suspects in the Tak Bai police station case, and the lifting of

martial law — were also considered. The government's first responses toward the idea of lifting martial law seemed quite positive. Thaksin agreed with the NRC's observation that the term "martial law" created an unfavorable impression internationally, and said that he would consider a legal replacement. However, this produced a backlash from the military. The Supreme Command issued a statement saying that, in effect, martial law was practiced only partially, and that the Supreme Command needed a legal basis to send combat troops into any area for an operation unrelated to war. Then army chief Pravit Wongsuwan[69] insisted in an interview that the military had been protecting innocent people from offenses and providing security for people in all areas.[70] Besides, he told the reporter, he disagreed with the reduction in the number of troops operating in the South. In July, Thaksin announced new emergency legislation — enacted by Cabinet decree without any parliamentary discussion or consultation with the NRC — that was in many respects far more draconian than the martial law provisions. The new legislation even indemnified security and state officials from prosecution. In effect, the NRC's call for the ending of martial law backfired.

The government encouraged a gradual crescendo in public objections to the NRC's proposals, and also used radio programs to attack the NRC's operations. Some programs and reports criticized individual members of the NRC, and even accused them of belonging to the insurgent movements. Other programs instigated patriotic outrage toward Muslim Thais in the South. Much of the most vocal criticism of the NRC was broadcast on popular programs co-hosted by former Bangkok governor Samak Sundaravej and Dusit Siriwan, including their breakfast television show *Chao ni thi prathet thai* [This morning in Thailand], on army-owned TV Channel 5. In September 2005, Anand himself complained bitterly that distorted coverage of the NRC by the media was a way of destroying him personally.[71] Provoked by this hostile media coverage, public sentiment increasingly favored extreme solutions to address the problems of the South.

On the other side, the NRC grew impatient with the government's withdrawal of support. Surichai Wungaeo, a key member of the commission, said after a June 6 meeting that the main agenda of the meeting was to call for all units, both inside and outside the government, to strictly support peaceful means in solving unrest in the South.[72] The statement referred directly to Thaksin, indicating that the prime minister must also boost the efficiency of all agencies involved in tracking the southern unrest and build up unity among them.

"At the beginning of March 2005, the southern crisis seemed to have come to a positive turning point. Respected former prime minister Anand Panyarachun [pictured here at a village meeting] accepted Thaksin's invitation to chair a National Reconciliation Commission (NRC), which had been established to propose solutions to the problems of Thailand's southern region."

Surichai urged the prime minister to be decisive in dealing with anyone who opposed or undermined efforts to return peace to the deep South through nonviolent means, whether they were politicians, members of the cabinet, government officials, or media practitioners. Yet the government continued to allow military and security units freely to oppose the NRC's proposals and permitted criticism by some conservative radio programs to go unchecked.

In short, the government had backed away from the reconciliation process and instead was pandering to a rather crude form of Thai patriotism. Talking tough on the South offered one way for Thaksin to run away from his many political problems, including conflicts within his TRT Party, an economic slowdown as the result of high oil prices, and pressure from voters to fulfill extravagant election promises. As a result, Malay Muslims' distrust of the state continued to rise. In the medium term, the divisions among majority Buddhists and minority Muslims looked likely to become more explicit. Racism, hatred, and killing among the groups will likely continue to escalate as a consequence. The violence will continue, and the risk of secession by the three Muslim provinces is a real one.

Not since defeating the communist insurgency in the early 1980s has Thailand been confronted by such a complicated and violent conflict. Unfortunately, the government and mainstream society were partly responsible for exacerbating the conflict. Cultural and religious conflicts required time and understanding from society if they were to stand any chance of resolution. Even if the prime minister were determined to stay this course, there were no guarantees: the southern crisis required balancing cultural and religious differences, Thai patriotism and the sensitivity of the military. For a leader like Thaksin, who was not known for listening to other voices, this was an especially big challenge.

Conclusion

Leading Thai commentators[73] have explained the recent upsurge of violence in the South in terms of several factors, ranging from terrorist movements, regional and international terrorist organizations, criminal activity in the area, or even political conflicts at both community and national levels between the two major parties. All of the above reasons could be causes of violence. Yet why then has the problem intensified so greatly only since Thaksin came to power? The common denominator underlying the renewed levels of violence is Thaksin himself: his thinking, his approach, and his strategies for boosting the popularity of the TRT government.

The government has opted primarily to use violent measures in tackling the problems, based on the hawkish stance of the prime minister and his close associates. The hawkish approach corresponds to Thaksin's preference for quick thinking and quick action. All the heads of the security agencies are too close to Thaksin personally, and work primarily to please the prime minister, who consistently demands the quickest possible outcome. This ensures that no one proposes a different view. The Thaksin government has always courted popularity, and has found that many majority Thai Buddhists are readily influenced by waves of patriotism, and are willing unabashedly to project their hatred toward the Thai Malay-Muslim minority, thus creating a new form of Thai nationalism. The government has decided to ride on the waves of patriotism, by projecting to the public an image of strong decisive leadership, using all manner of military methods to defend the sovereignty and integrity of the kingdom.

The government's popularity in relation to the southern problems is also very sensitive to the feelings of the military. The government has been particularly cautious about the punishment of the military officers who ordered the Kru-Ze and Tak Bai crackdowns, because punishment of these officers would suggest that the government was acknowledging its own mistakes. Admitting fault would contradict the patriotic sentiment of the public. At the same time, the government feels the need to maintain and cherish its good relationship with the military, which is a very sensitive issue and could pose political problems. Thaksin's cosy handling of the military was nicely illustrated by the promotion of former Fourth Army commander Pisan to the rank of full general on 1 October 2005 — despite the fact that Pisan was ultimately responsible for the deaths of the Tak Bai protestors.

However, the decisive anti-TRT vote in the 2005 general election was a clear rebuke by southern voters to the government's attempts to retain the approval of both the military and the public. By responding with an aggressive proposal to "zone" the southern border provinces, Thaksin smoked out opposition from two senior retired generals, who serve as members of the revered Privy Council. These surprising interventions by Surayud and Prem were just one illustration that the far South remained Thaksin's Achilles' heel. Thaksin must now decide whether to persist with his inept securitization approach, which is conspicuously failing to mitigate the violence, or to adopt the more conciliatory path advocated by the Privy Council and the NRC. Neither route offers any easy solutions.

ACKNOWLEDGMENT: Some elements of this paper appeared in an earlier form in Ukrist 2005.

❑

4 UNPACKING THAILAND'S SOUTHERN CONFLICT

The Poverty of Structural Explanations

Srisompob Jitpiromsri, with Panyasak Sobhonvasu

"Our Southern Muslims now are living like immigrants in their own homeland. They don't have any influence over the current situation, are too frightened to confront the authorities, while too nervous to tell the extremists to quit conducting insurgencies." — Abdul Rahman Abdul Shamad, chairman of the Provincial Islamic Committee of Narathiwat (*Matichon*, 1 December 2004)

IN RECENT YEARS, violence in Thailand's deep South has escalated to a critical stage. Accounting for this trend is fraught with difficulty, given the lack of consensus that exists about both the underlying and immediate causes of violent incidents. Many observers, both from the media and from the academic community, have characterized patterns of apparently domestic, small-scale local incidents as part of a wider pattern of relatively large-scale, coordinated, and systematic attacks on government officials, public installations, as well as the people in general. The changing patterns of violence have often been invoked in support of a broad argument: long-standing separatism and subregional strife in the deep South are being gradually radicalized, internationalized, and perhaps Islamicized. Yet in reality, the explanations for the violence remain contested, and interpretations opaque. People from different backgrounds and perspectives are looking at the same situation, yet seeing different things. The empirical analysis of primary and secondary field data is essential to substantiate any argument and solutions to this conflict-torn region, otherwise opinions will be ascendant over facts. The purposes of this article are, first, to present and elaborate an analysis of research data recently gathered on the conflict and, second, to draw out some conceptual arguments about the structural root causes and ideological elements of problems in the Thai South.

Southern Violence: An Overview

Tensions and conflicts in Thailand's deep South can be traced back more than a hundred years. Levels of violence were quite high in the 1970s, when the separatist movement peaked for a time, only to decline sharply before reaching new heights early in 2004. Research data show that during the ten years from 1993 to 2004, there were 2,593 incidents of politically related violence.[1] Of these, only 750, or 29 percent, occurred between 1993 and 2003, while a remarkable 71 percent, or 1,843, took place in 2004 (including January of 2005). Eighteen percent of incidents occurred from 1993 to 2000, while 82 percent of incidents took place from 2001 to 2004 (including January of 2005). Among the three southern border provinces, Narathiwat Province saw the highest level of violence, followed by Pattani and Yala.

That most incidents took place from 2001 onwards is noteworthy, since February 2001 saw the creation of a new government led by Thaksin Shinawatra. Thaksin's Thai Rak Thai (TRT) Party had an unprecedented level of dominance over parliamentary politics. In addition, 2001 was the year of the 9/11 attacks — the onset of the U.S.-led "war on terror." This convergence of domestic and international factors clearly influenced the changing security situation in the Thai South: but which factors were most important?

Out of 2,032 victims of violence in 2004 and the first half of 2005 (January to June), 1,335 were injured and 697 died. If the 28 April 2004 attacks and the Tak Bai incident are added, the total number of

Fig. 1 Escalation of violence in the deep South of Thailand from 1993 to 2004. Number of incidents.

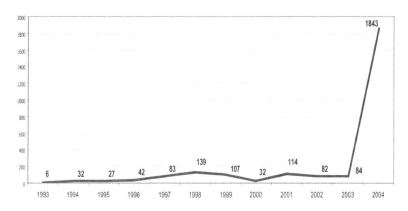

Source for figures (unless noted otherwise): Srisompob Southern Violence Database

Fig. 2. Comparing ten years of violence by province.

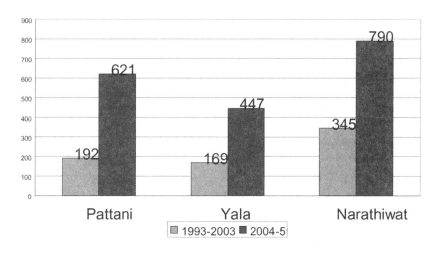

deaths for this period is 884. It is striking that significant numbers of both Muslims and Buddhists were targets of these attacks. Most of the victims, however, were Thai Buddhists and, perhaps surprisingly, most of them were ordinary people rather than members of the security services. From January 2004 to June 2005, out of the 2,032 identifiable victims, 705 were civilians, 335 were police officers, and 168 were soldiers. Moreover, employees or lower-class workers of public and

Fig. 3. Main occupations of victims, January to June 2005.

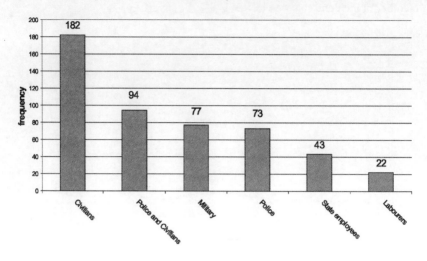

Fig. 4. Casualties of violence, January to June 2005.

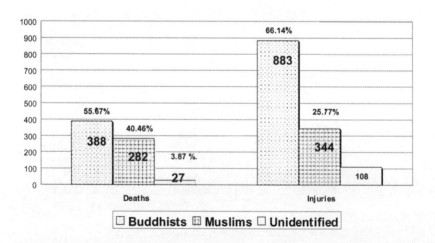

private organizations have become leading targets, with 131 victims. Village headmen and assistant headmen were also conspicuous targets of attacks, comprising ninety-five of the victims; a further forty-nine victims were government officials, and thirty-eight were teachers.[2]

The increasing number of civilian casualties suggests that the southern violence was no longer confined to "traditional" targets:

Fig. 5. Incidents of violence by province and category,
January 2004 to January 2005.

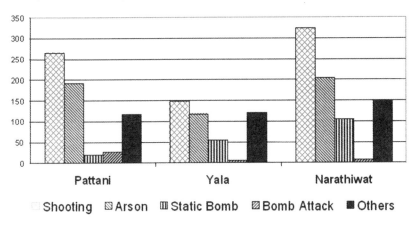

state personnel and public installations. Looking at the patterns and tactics of the almost daily attacks, it is noticeable that the most frequently used tactics were assassinations and shootings, followed by bombings and arson attacks. During the period from January 2004 to January 2005, Narathiwat was the most frequent place of violent incidents, with 790 cases, while Pattani had 621 cases, and Yala, 447. Narathiwat also saw the largest numbers of shootings (324 cases), arsons (204 cases), and bomb attacks (112 cases). Strikingly, Muang district of Pattani (the urban provincial capital) has been particularly hard hit by shootings, followed by Ra-ngae district in Narathiwat, the Yarang district of Pattani, and the Sugai Padi district of Narathiwat. Most of the attacks have occurred along urban and suburban roads, signifying the urban-based pattern of insurgencies. The 2004 data show that almost every district of Narathiwat had a relatively high frequency rate of violent incidents in 2004,[3] with an average of 61 cases per district, while Pattani Province had an average of 52 cases per district,[4] and Yala averaged 56 cases per district.[5]

During the period 1993 to 2003, the average number of violent incidents per year in the three southern provinces was around sixty-eight cases. As violent episodes surged in 2004, their frequency increased by up to twenty-seven times the average rate at which similar violent incidents took place during the previous decade. Thus the deep South quite abruptly became a much more dangerous world.

Fig. 6. Perceptions of Pattani residents concerning the perpetrators of violence, March 2004 and February 2005.

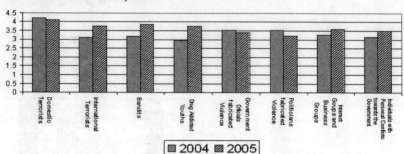

Source: Department of Political Science, Prince of Songkla University, Pattani

Worldviews and Perceptions of Threats

Although very little is known about the real perpetrators of the southern disorder, perceptions and interpretations of the situation differ widely. People with a variety of socioeconomic backgrounds and experiences seem to be looking at the same circumstances, but seeing different things. Whereas many local people do not understand what is happening, ascribed causes range from the acts of separatist movements,[6] international terrorist attacks,[7] a resurgence of historical consciousness on the part of local Malay Muslims,[8] the outcomes of the government's mishandling of the southern problems, to long-standing grievances related to poverty, unemployment, lack of educational opportunities, drug abuse, vice, crime, and social deprivation. Conspiratorial accounts also abound. Domestic versions of these theories often attribute the violence to "influential people" (a Thai euphemism for prominent criminals), to drug dealers, smugglers, and gangsters, or to personal conflicts and revenge. A variation on these domestic conspiracy theories is the belief that government officials, the military, and the police have actually orchestrated much of the violence for their own purposes. Some people subscribe to international versions of these conspiracy theories, believing that the CIA and other foreign intelligence agencies have been playing the role of agent provocateurs in the deep South.[9]

In general, local people view the situation differently from the government; the government has tended to depict the violence as actions by a minority of extremists, whereas locals favor other explanations.

Fig. 7. Attitudes of people in the three southern border provinces toward separatist movements in the South.

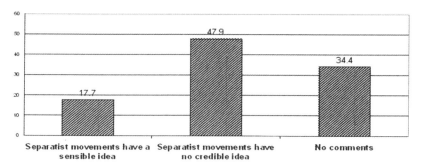

Source: ABAC Poll, Assumption University; Center for Humanities and Social Sciences Research, Prince of Songkla University, March 2005

However, recent survey data show that people are now becoming more inclined to attribute the violence to the activities of militants and extremists, acting in the name of separatist or similar movements. Attitude survey research conducted twice among Pattani residents, in March 2004 and March 2005, reveals that people considered domestic militant groups to be a major cause of the violence.[10] International militants, however, were not perceived as prime suspects. According to the March 2005 survey, "bandits" were the second most popular instigators of the conflict, followed by young drug addicts. It is striking that in the 2005 survey, the view that government officials (in the Thai context, this includes military and police officers) themselves created the violence was only the fourth-ranked explanation. One year earlier, it was the second most chosen explanation. Yet the survey also illustrates that locals advance a wide range of explanations, and no one explanation appears dominant.

On the other hand, people's specific attitudes toward the separatist movements were clearly mixed. In another attitude survey conducted by the Assumption University and Prince of Songkla University, Pattani, in early March 2005, 34.1 percent of those surveyed from the three southern border provinces acknowledged that they had some personal knowledge of the separatist movements. Moreover, 17.7 percent thought that separatism was a sensible idea, while 47.7 percent believed it was far-fetched, and 34.4 percent had no comment. When asked directly whether they would support the removal of the three southern border provinces from Thai sovereignty, only 8 percent agreed. Most people (54.8 percent), however, were confident that the conflict could be resolved by peaceful means, while 32.8 percent were not convinced that nonviolent means would succeed, and 12.8 percent had no comment.[11]

Faced with almost daily killings, local people manifest somewhat whimsical attitudes and responses. Both academics and experts from government agencies tend to believe that there are no clear explanations about the perpetrators of violence in Thailand's deep South. The 2004 edition of *Country Reports on Terrorism,* produced by the Office of the Coordinator for Counterterrorism of the U.S. Department of State, released in 2005, affirmed that "there is no evidence of a direct connection between militants in southern Thailand and international terrorist organizations." While attributing the violence to some local, home-grown insurgency groups, the report indicated that there is still no clear, direct evidence substantiating the fact that these groups "are actively organizing the violence."[12] Some observers prefer to describe the situation as a "conspiracy of silence."[13] The central questions unresolved, practically and academically, revolve around who is actually behind the surge of violence and what future courses the violence might take. Among the panoply of competing explanations, all boil down to two basic versions: structural explanations, attributing the violence to "root causes," and ideological explanations, focusing on politically motivated "movements." This article seeks to review the utility of structural explanations in the light of the available evidence.

Structural Dimensions of the Conflict

According to the National Statistics Office (NSO), the populations of the three southern border provinces (Pattani, Yala, and Narathiwat) in 2003 amounted to about 1,803,306.[14] Of the total population, 21.8 percent are Buddhists and 78.2 percent Muslims. A survey conducted in nine districts of the three southern provinces identifies various problems that local Muslim communities face. These include poverty, unemployment, lack of education, substandard infrastructure, inadequate supplies of land and capital, low quality of living standards, and other economic-related problems.[15]

The performance of the deep South's economy has improved markedly in the past few decades. Between 1983 and 2003, for example, the gross provincial products (GPP) for Pattani rose from 7,840 million baht to 33,300 million baht, while those of Yala and Narathiwat increased from 6,745 million baht and 8,737 million baht to 24,437

Table 1. Gross Provincial Products of Southern Border Provinces, 1983–2003 (Unit: 1 Million Baht)

	total	%	total	%	total	%
Pattani	7,840	5.4	28,275	6.8	33,300	5.6
Yala	6,745	4.6	17,502	4.2	24,437	4.1
Narathiwat	8,737	6.0	19,840	4.8	28,646	4.8
Songkla	26,084	17.8	86,818	21.0	120,678	20.3
Southern Region	146,537	100.0	414,272	100.0	594,657	100.0

Source: National Economic and Social Development Board (NESDB)

Table 2. Average per Capita Income of Southern Border Provinces, 1983–2003 (Unit: Baht)

Provinces\Years	1983	1995	2003
Pattani	9,340	48,499	57,621
Yala	14,987	45,107	52,737
Narathiwat	10,340	31,948	38,553
Songkla	17,287	70,184	92,614
Southern Region	16,020	52,747	69,450

Source: NESDB

million baht and 28,646 million baht, respectively. During the same period, the average per capita income of Pattani grew from 9,340 baht to 57,621 baht, while that of Yala and Narathiwat also increased from 14,987 baht and 10,340 baht to 52,737 baht and 38,553 baht, respectively.

Notwithstanding these positive developments, the region fared poorly compared either with neighboring Malaysia, or with Songkla Province, the thriving commercial and industrial center of the Thai South. In 2000, for example, the GDP per capita of Malaysia was RM 14,582 (more than 140,000 baht) and that of Kelantan, its poorest state, was RM 6,137 (over 60,000 baht). The proportion of GPP contribution of the deep South provinces to the overall GPP of the southern region during the past two decades remained substantially small or stagnant as compared to that of Songkla.

The poverty picture is a complicated one. In terms of average household income, none of the three southern border provinces is particularly poor. According to official figures for 2000, Narathiwat, the poorest of the three, ranked twenty-first from the bottom, while Pattani and Yala were in the middle group of Thailand's seventy-six provinces.[16] Many northeastern provinces and some northern ones had significantly lower average household incomes. However, nearly half of the Southerners officially living below the poverty line — 47.05 percent of them — reside in Pattani, Yala, and Narathiwat.[17] Another set of figures from a 1998 National Economic and Social Development Board (NESDB) report showed that 152,777 Yala people, or approximately 37 percent of the total population, had incomes below the provincial poverty line of 845 baht per month.[18] The same report also points to a large number of Muslims in the other two border provinces still living in poverty, ranking Narathiwat as the poorest province in southern Thailand with 46 percent of the total population, or more than 193,000 persons, living below the poverty line (808 baht a month) compared to 20.7 percent or about 125,440 people in Pattani (818 baht per month). In other words, of approximately 1.3 million Muslims in the three provinces, about 470,000 or 36 percent were living below the poverty line.[19] Overall, people in the southern border provinces are poorer than people elsewhere in the South, but their income levels are broadly comparable with Thais in many other parts of the country. Though an important objective correlative, this observation offers little comfort to Muslims in the three provinces, who are wont to compare their economic circumstances with those of fellow Malays in Malaysia, or of Buddhist Thais in Songkla and other more affluent parts of the South.

The official data also indicate that most Muslim people in the three border provinces lack educational and employment opportunities. Muslims in the deep South are more disadvantaged than their Buddhist counterparts in educational attainment, despite their status as the majority population in the region, and their strong background in religious education.

NSO data from the national census of populations and housing in 2000 reveal that, in terms of the highest level of educational attainment, 69.80 percent of the Muslim population in Pattani, Yala, and Narathiwat provinces have only a primary school education, compared with 49.6 percent of Buddhists.[20] However, levels of participation by Muslims decline strongly at the higher levels. For instance, 9.20 percent of Muslims have completed secondary education, compared to 13.20 percent of Buddhists. At this time, the NSO figures did not distinguish between government secondary schools and the private Islamic

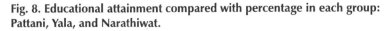

Fig. 8. Educational attainment compared with percentage in each group: Pattani, Yala, and Narathiwat.

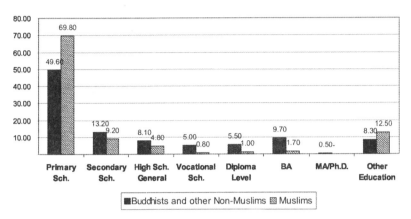

Source: National Statistics Office, the Census of Populations and Housing in 2000. Muslims comprise 1,309,109 people and Buddhists 364,767 people.

schools, which enroll large numbers of local Muslims. Nevertheless, the picture becomes even clearer at the tertiary level: only 1.70 percent of the Muslim population have a bachelor's degree, while 9.70 percent of Buddhists hold undergraduate degrees. Despite being the majority population in the three provinces, Muslims are seriously underrepresented in educational attainment.

Furthermore, attempts to implement a variety of programs of socioeconomic growth and development seem to have made much improvement at the macro-level and in service and public sectors, but this has not translated into jobs nor substantially improved standards of living for the great majority of the Muslim population. Figures for 2000 indicate that of all the 766,000 working residents in the three border provinces, only 6.6 percent were employed as government officials. Muslim government officials comprised only 2.4 percent of all working Muslims in the region, compared with 19.2 percent of all working Buddhists. In addition, the 2000 national census also reports a rather high rate of illiteracy (30.4 percent) among the local Muslim population. While Thai government statistics assert that unemployment is very low in the three southern provinces, many local Muslims view serious unemployment, underemployment, or the need for seasonal migration across the border to neighboring Malaysia as ever-present realities.[21] In Yala, for example, official figures in 2004 in-

Fig. 9. Occupations of Buddhists and Muslims in the three southern border provinces.

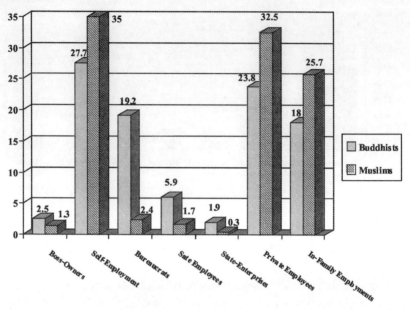

dicate that only 1,843 people were unemployed. Data on employment also show that the status of southern Muslims is significantly lower than that of Buddhists in the job market. Many Muslims, 35 percent, are self-employed, working largely in the informal sectors in occupations such as street vendors, tea shop owners, and secondhand clothing dealers. A sizable proportion of them, 32.5 percent, work in the private sector, notably in rubber plantations, farming, and factories. About a quarter of Muslims, 25 percent, were employed in their own families, many of them only seasonally. Notably, the proportions of Muslims working in the government bureaucracy and public enterprises differed greatly from the proportion of Buddhists. While only 2.5 percent of Muslims in the three southern border provinces had bureaucratic jobs, 19.2 percent of Buddhists had positions in the bureaucracy. This covers many forms of prestigious and middle-class employment, since in Thailand, teachers, doctors, nurses, and most other public sector workers are formally civil servants. Structurally, then, Muslims in the three provinces clearly have legitimate grievances against the existing political system.

Drugs and Social Problems

The difficult socioeconomic conditions for Muslims in the deep South are a contributory factor in the emergence of a significant drug problem in the region. This is potentially important for at least three reasons. First, at a general level, problems of drug abuse undermine the morale of communities and make them more likely to foster enclaves of crime and violence. Second, the government has repeatedly argued that much of the violence in the deep South is related to organized crime linked with the drugs trade, rather than with separatist or militant movements. Third, politicians and security officials have often claimed that individuals taking part in events such as the 28 April 2004 attacks or the 25 October 2004 Tak Bai demonstration were acting under the influence of drugs. Do the facts support the popular notion of a drug abuse epidemic in the deep South?

Enforcement statistics from the Office of Narcotics Control Board (ONCB) show that the numbers of indictments for supplying and abusing drugs in the three southern border provinces have dramatically increased in recent years. In particular, usage of marijuana (*ganja*) and codeine (cough mixture) among southern Muslim youths has increased greatly.[22] Because Muslims youths are not supposed to drink alcohol for religious reasons, some resort to the use of homemade stimulants, typically combining a cough mixture (which contains codeine) with drinks such as Coke or coffee. These stimulants produce a mild "high," and cause some concern among Muslim community leaders, but are not a form of drug abuse likely to lead to violent behavior. Official statistics from 2000 to 2004 indicate that prosecutions in marijuana cases in Narathiwat Province were highest among Thailand's three predominantly Muslim provinces, and higher than in Songkla — the large southern Buddhist-dominated province. The use of psychotropic drugs in this Muslim-dominated province has increased drastically compared with other parts of the country. Enforcement data demonstrate that indictments for the possession of codeine (cough mixture) or psychotropic drugs in the three border provinces have increased exponentially; Narathiwat, again, has been the focal point for emerging cases of psychotropic drug use. The level of prosecutions in marijuana cases went down to some extent as a result of the Thaksin's government's controversial "war on drugs," which began on 1 April 2003. By contrast, the number of cases involv-

Fig. 10. Indictments for marijuana possession, 2000 to 2004.

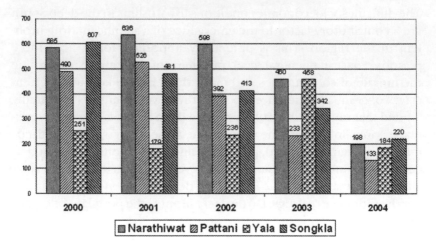

ing psychotropic drugs apparently increased after the war on drugs operations got underway.

It is striking that seizures of cough mixture and psychotropic drugs and prosecutions for possessing them in the southern provinces from 2000–2004 are among the highest in the country. For instance, prosecutions for possession of psychotropic drugs increased from 83 cases in 2000 to 126 cases in 2003, the highest levels outside Bangkok. However, they dropped back to 86 in 2004. Cough mixture cases are also rising, increasing from 247 cases in 2000 to a peak of 581 in 2003, falling back to 334 cases in 2004. More importantly, the usage and supply of cough mixture in the three southern provinces have reached a high point, indisputably much higher than in Bangkok.[23]

Structural Problems and Incidents of Violence

That drug and substance abuse was increasing in the South just as violence was escalating led the government to assume a connection between drug abuse and incidents of violence. On some occasions, such as in the Tak Bai incident on 25 October 2004, the authorities claimed that the young Muslims who allegedly instigated violent actions were apparently intoxicated.[24] However, the relationship between drug abuse and political violence remains unclear and unproven. In the Tak Bai case, of the 1,093 subjects detained at the Ingkayuth military camp, only thirteen tested positive for drugs. Of the

Fig. 11. Indictments for codeine possession, 2000 to 2004.

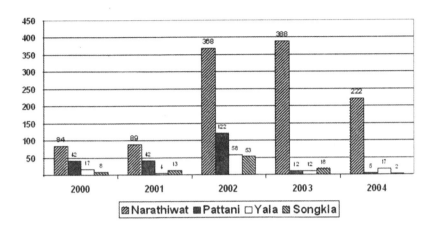

Fig. 12. Indictments for psychotropic drug possession, 2000 to 2004.

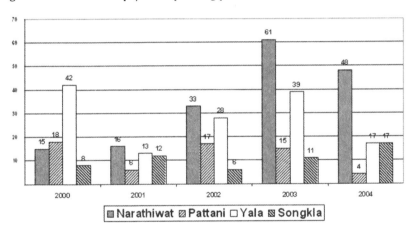

seventy-eight detainees who died, forty were tested for drugs, and only two of these tested positive.[25] Clearly, drug abuse was not a major factor underpinning the Tak Bai demonstration. Similarly, the bodies of all the militants killed inside the Kru-Ze mosque were tested for drugs, but no traces of any illegal substances were found.[26] During October and August of 2004, the ONCB investigated the cases of youths suspected for engaging in violent activities and found that, out of 1,295 cases, only 34 suspects (2.6 percent) were proven to be under the in-

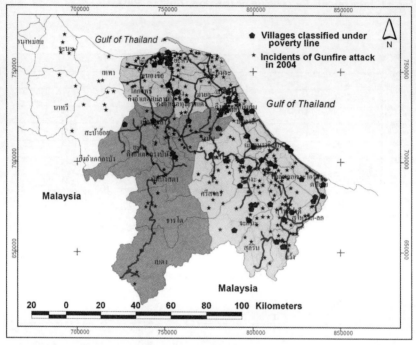

Map showing correlation between shooting incidents and poverty in the three southern border provinces.

fluence of drugs.[27] While drug abuse undoubtedly contributes to wider social problems in the deep South, there seems to be no evidence at all that the recent upsurge of violence is a direct result of drug abuse by young militants.

The relationship between poverty and violence in the three provinces is also unclear. In terms of the location of attacks, there is no evidence that poverty and incidents of violence are related. As becomes clear from the use of Geographic Information System (GIS) data, only a small proportion of the eighty-five communities officially classified as below the poverty line experienced violent incidents during the twelve months of 2004.[28] The pattern of violence bore no obvious relationship to locations of poor communities. The widely dispersed locations of violence suggest that the perpetrators operate network organizations, with the ability to instigate violence right across the three border provinces.

To cap it all, the escalation of southern violence in recent years illustrates patterns of target-oriented and well-planned attacks. This was dramatically demonstrated on the night of 26 October 2005, when militants staged coordinated attacks in sixty-three locations across the three provinces, killing four men, derailing a train, and seizing ninety-two weapons.[29] Changes of tactics, weapons, and targets are also apparent. Most of the attacks occurred along urban and suburban roads. So far, no known separatist organizations have accepted responsibility for the violence. A sizable number of people in the three provinces, as shown in the survey data, are sympathetic toward the separatist movement. On balance, however, it seems fair to deduce that the socioeconomic grievances and drug abuse may serve as necessary conditions underpinning the violence, but the decisive factors behind the recent upsurge of violence must lie elsewhere.

Distinct Discourses and Contesting Identities

Many Thai scholars view political explanations for violence in southern predominantly Muslim provinces as highly persuasive. A Thai leading political scientist, Chaiwat Satha-Anand, argues that historical accounts of the Patani people have long involved rebellions and uprisings aimed at securing independence.[30] This argument is supported by many other scholars, who believe that historical factors are critical for the people of the southernmost provinces.[31] Nidhi Auesrivongse, arguably Thailand's leading historian, considers that a better theoretical explanation for the southern movements should focus on the large numbers of ordinary, underprivileged people taking part in those operations. Nidhi has characterized the ongoing movements as peasant rebellions, twenty-first-century millenarian movements with no clear and specific purposes or targets. He believes that they have no substantive ideology, relying only on popular religion and beliefs.[32]

Chaiwat's emphasis on how the relationships between "reality" and violence have become a significant factor over the years of Pattani's struggle for independence helps account for developments prior to the 2004 upsurge in violence. Nevertheless, the dramatic change in the position from January 2004 has set in motion a debate about how one can explain the new complexity, a set of realities that involves more and more complex and compounded elements, influenced simultaneously by both internal and external factors. More than one set of realities now needs to be understood and explained.

Another group of arguments about southern violence has concentrated on the community's capacity building, local wisdom, and virtues. Dr. Prawase Wasi, a leading Thai social critic and public intellectual, has publicly raised issues concerning conflict, power, and ethics. He argues that the conflict in the South cannot be resolved through the exercise of power, since this will not bring about the necessary process of social learning. Instead, a community approach should be adopted, using religious ethics to cope with the crisis. He argues that making use of religious virtues (whatever the religion) and ethics in developmental processes creates connections, offering a basis for reconciliation.[33] This communitarian discourse is pertinent to the interpretations of many local religious and community leaders who repeatedly state that Islam is a peaceful religion. Thus, the argument goes, Muslim society in the three southern border provinces has long held a strong cultural power, highly embedded in religious beliefs.[34] The principal cause of southern violence is therefore the use of forceful means to solve the problems by the government.[35] Ethical and communitarian explanations are persuasive to many people. Muslim victims of violence, particularly in the 28 April incident at the Kru-Ze mosque in Pattani and in the Tak Bai suffocations on 25 October 2004, were widely referred to locally as "those who died under the same heavens" (*khon thi tai tai fa diao kan*). The clear implication was that violent repression by the Thai state had backfired, creating a new sense of solidarity and a heightened feeling of struggle on the part of southern Muslim communities.

On the other hand, arguments explaining the southern conflict and violence as the inevitable outcomes of underdevelopment, poverty, and scarcity are also often well received. The Thaksin government showed its attachment to this sort of explanation when it dumped a vast amount of additional funds into the southern Muslim majority areas following the January 2004 upsurge of violence, assuming that this would solve the problem of southern poverty within two years.[36] Thaksin's "CEO governor" policy, which led to a strategic plan for the provincial cluster of southern border areas, including the creation of a *halal* food industrial complex in Pattani, was strongly influenced by this developmental discourse.[37] Thaksin's nationwide television address after the Tak Bai tragedy underscored the fact that the government identified the poverty problem as a major cause of violence.[38] Yet empirical analysis has shown that the direct relationships between incidents of poverty and violence are still ambiguous. It would be a mistake to view the conflict as simply a result of the failures of local economic development.

Fig. 13. Classification of violent incidents in the three southern provinces, January 2004 - June 2005.

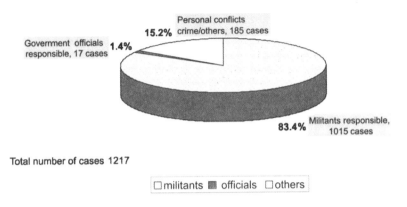

Total number of cases 1217

In the process, the rather simplistic "historical consciousness" discourse has been further developed to become a more complicated explanation about the unique identity of southern Muslims. The salience of Malay-Muslim identity is thus underscored, based on historical backgrounds, unique language, and religiosity. This discourse about the distinct characteristics of southern Muslims involves identity politics, which are based on the meanings and concepts of power. When it comes to the escalation of violence in the deep South, it is clear that the Muslim majority in the southern border provinces of Thailand has suffered for a long time from wars, riots, and suppression by the Thai authorities. Unjust treatment at the hands of the authorities has been a daily occurrence. Different interpretations of events have always flourished.[39]

Therefore, identity politics and its related discourse lead to related rationalizations of events. Information becomes dispersed and scattered around all corners of societal structures to individuals, groups, as well as network organizations both in urban and in rural areas. Rumors and gossip about the violence, much of it inaccurate or wildly speculative can be heard everywhere from sidewalk tea shops, to local buses, taxis, the cafeterias of public schools, and pondoks, to university campuses and government offices.[40] Opinions are everywhere, but facts are hard to come by.

Fig. 14. Deaths and injuries classified by region, January to June 2005.

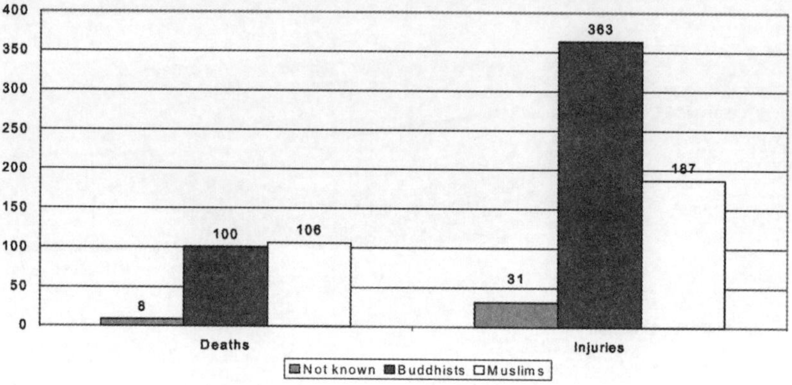

A Quest for Facts

In an attempt to obtain a much clearer understanding about the identities of those attacking civilians in the three provinces since the beginning of 2004, we led an extensive research project on behalf of the NRC. The project involved taking questionnaires to more than a thousand key informants in different communities that had experienced attacks on civilians. These informants came from a wide range of backgrounds, but were personally selected for their high level of local political awareness. The informants were asked to identify the person or persons whom local people knew or believed to behind individual attacks, and to provide descriptive accounts of the events. We received 1,217 responses. The research team then evaluated and analyzed the background information about the circumstances of the incidents to ensure reliability of the data. In order to substantiate their claims about the perpetrators of individual acts of violence, the informants were asked to provide evidence or background information about relevant previous events, the backgrounds of the victims and details about the assailants. For instance, many informants reported that numerous assailants had left markers or warning signs, outside target victims' home. These markers included sand, rice, white clothes, or eggs — symbolic items for burial rites of Muslims. Informants reported that most victims were working for the authorities. Where informants passed judgment concerning the perpetrators without providing any such supporting information, their responses were not used in the study. The 28 April and Tak Bai incidents were not included in this study. When closely investigated and classified, the 1,217 cases of attacks on citizens in 2004 and 2005 comprised three types: 83.4 percent of the attacks (1,015 cases) were attributed to militants or insurgent groups, 15.2 percent of the cases (185 cases) were regarded as criminal or personal conflict cases, and 1.4 percent of the attacks were believed to have been carried out by the authorities. Clearly, militant activities in local communities were widespread, and were believed to account for the overwhelming majority of the attacks.[41]

While it is impossible to ensure the complete reliability of this sort of data, these findings strongly suggest that neither the "bandit theory" (blaming much of the violence on organized criminal gangs), the "personal conflict theory" (which argues that many of the attacks are simply normal crimes, of the kind commonly found throughout Thailand), nor the "conspiracy theory" (different versions of which argue that many of the attacks are being committed by the Thai state itself, or perhaps by external actors such as the CIA), nor the self-explanatory "rogue government officials" theory holds much water. Perhaps some of these theories were more valid in the period before January 2004, but they are now less persuasive.

Does Ideology Matter?

In the face of this evidence, it no longer seems plausible to attribute the violent incidents in the deep South, as Nidhi does, to a spontaneous "peasant rebellion." There are clear patterns of violence in terms of locations, victims, and tactics of operation. In 2004, violent incidents increased twenty-seven–fold compared with the average rate of similar incidents during the previous decade. If identity politics — a consciousness of Patani's glorious ancient kingdom,[42] or the sense of Malay ethnic identity — are the main reasons behind the operations, the question remains: Why has violence surged now, and not earlier? If the government and the authorities have made a great blunder, business as usual for the Thai authorities, why has this led to the greater intensity and momentum of violence at this time? The violent incidents took place in spite of the fact that the Thaksin government had already deployed about twenty thousand soldiers and police officers in the three affected provinces. The violence in the Thai South contains important psychological elements, reflecting attempts to instill and propagate fear. In this sense, the violence conforms to the classic definition of "terrorism," differing from other types of criminal actions because of its political aims and motives, and their far-reaching psychological repercussions beyond the immediate victims or target.[43]

History, though important, does not offer a satisfactory explanation for recent events. Nor do socioeconomic arguments about poverty, or general arguments about the need for the Malay-Muslim minority to be justly treated by the Thai government. The tragic and appalling events of 28 April and the Tak Bak incident should not obscure the central facts: during the eighteen months from January 2004 through June 2005, most of the violent incidents that took place in the three provinces were not killings of Muslims by agents of the Thai state. Based on the known death tolls from those two incidents, and the data gathered from the individual attack surveys, perhaps a few more than two hundred Muslims died at the hands of the Thai authorities during this period.[44] Whatever mistakes the Thaksin government has committed, it cannot be held directly responsible for all of the remaining incidents. Most of these killings fell into two categories: the murders of Buddhists by Muslim militants (the majority of the 388 Buddhist victims), and the murders of fellow Muslims by Muslim militants (the majority of the 282 Muslim victims). Claims that many of these murders are attributable to personal conflicts or criminal activities are not supported by the individual attack survey evidence. Because most of these political murders were isolated cases, in which typically only one or two people were killed at a time, the collective enormity of these unfolding events has been difficult to grasp. During the first half of 2005, Muslim victims of political murders began to exceed Buddhist victims. The growth of this Muslim-on-Muslim violence is one of the most important trends in the data. In the eyes of their Muslim assailants, most of these victims may have been seen as "hypocritical" collaborators with the Thai authorities.

More research is still needed on the structural underpinning of Malay-Muslim grievances against the Thai state, on the politics of identity, and a host of other salient background issues. But this research is unlikely to help much in explaining the post–January 2004 upsurge in violence. The most important questions concern the psychology and motivations of those behind these increasingly vicious attacks. The ideology of the militants is no longer the somewhat romantic and low-key separatism of the past: the latest waves of attacks have had a much more aggressive and ruthless character. It is time to turn to serious studies of the thinking behind the sizeable militant movements currently operating in the three provinces of Pattani, Yala, and Narathiwat. The root causes are no longer the most critical factor: it is the militant movements and their ideological parameters that really matter.

❑

5   ISLAM, RADICALISM, AND VIOLENCE IN SOUTHERN THAILAND

Berjihad di Patani and the 28 April 2004 Attacks

Wattana Sugunnasil

VIOLENCE IN THAILAND'S DEEP SOUTH centers on Muslim unrest, which has been simmering since World War II. Yet what was once a low-level secessionist insurgency has now developed into a full--scale conflict and violent campaign that has claimed hundreds of lives in the three southern border provinces of Pattani, Yala, and Narathiwat. The recent spate of violent attacks is a result of an escalation of campaigns by Muslim militants launched in early 2004. Acts of sporadic violence have given way to an unprecedented and sustained wave of terrible incidents, often involving direct confrontations between security personnel and militants. This amounts to the most serious political violence in recent Thai history. This article emphasizes the need to understand that there have been some significant changes in Muslim separatist politics. Not only have attacks grown increasingly sophisticated, there has also been a radical shift in the discursive practice of separatist groups. The relationship between separatism and Islamism may best be characterized as a shifting one, in a state of flux.

Several factors underscore the dissatisfaction of Muslims in this part of Thailand.[1] First is a widespread perception that local Muslims have not benefited from development programs implemented since 1960s. Second is resentment at government attempts to impose Buddhist social, cultural, and economic domination. Third is a rejection of the secular orientation of the Thai state, which is seen as incompatible with the region's devoutly Muslim ways. Fourth — and probably most important over the last decade — is fear and distrust of the security forces, whose activities in the region are viewed as heavy-handed and repressive.

In the 1970s and 1980s, most separatist violence took the form of orthodox guerrilla warfare, typified by hit-and-run attacks directed against members of the military. Hundreds of militants gave up their arms in the 1980s in response to an amnesty policy. More recently, serious violence has moved into the urban theater, bombs have become more prevalent, and militants have melted into the civilian population. In addition to political violence, old separatist groups have also engaged in criminal activities, including kidnappings and extortion. Generally speaking, these groups have not emphasized indiscriminate violence against civilian and noncombatant targets. However, since 2004, terrorist-type tactics have become prominent. These new forms of violence have been increasingly directed against police officers, government officials (including Muslims), people suspected of being government collaborators and informers, and even against monks and symbols of Buddhist tradition. A sustained campaign of high-profile violence has been carried out, including almost daily killings, and the launching of well-organized raids on army and police depots, in addition to serious bomb attacks in commercial locations of urban areas.

It is tempting to see the current violence in southern Thailand as essentially a continuation of a separatist struggle for self-determination that flared up as soon as Western colonization of Asia began to collapse after World War II. However, the main argument of this article is that the separatist struggle of the 1970s and 1980s, which was initially based on a Malay national liberation struggle (similar to other independence and socialist or nationalist movements elsewhere in Asia), had by the late 1990s and especially in the early 2000s taken on undertones of a radical Islamist ideology. For the first time the discourse of the separatist struggle shifted to a radical Islamist call for a jihad against the Thai state, its local agents, and their Muslim allies.

What gave rise to this unprecedented escalation of violence in the region? To the casual observer, the Thai government's investment and development programs during the past few decades undoubtedly resulted in greatly improved infrastructure, education, and standards of living. These changes were accompanied by the liberalization of Thai politics symbolized by the new "people's constitution" of 1997. This led some observers to argue that the democratization of Thai politics greatly helped the de-radicalization of Malay-Muslim opposition in Thailand.[2] Yet subsequent developments have confounded such optimistic readings.

Development, Democracy, and the Muslim Predicament

State development policies and plans focusing on improving economic conditions in the southern border area began in the late 1950s.[3] These efforts reflected a strategy adopted by the government to improve living conditions among Muslim communities in the border areas, and to lessen deep-rooted political mistrust between the Muslim population and Thai government officials. Moves to show greater sensitivity to the lack of economic and administrative development in the southern border provinces were intended to lessen bitter memories of past discrimination, such as restrictions on the use of the local Malay language and limited access to government jobs and educational opportunities. The authorities hoped that this, in turn, would help reduce popular support for armed separatism. Substantial budgets allocated by the Thai government, coupled with technical support from foreign countries, facilitated infrastructural construction and improvements in the region, especially the construction of important highways. As Srisompob and Panyasak show, the three provinces of Pattani, Yala, and Narathiwat have lagged behind the rest of the South economically, yet were not especially poor by the standards of Thailand as a whole.[4] Nevertheless, Malay Muslims in the three provinces had legitimate grievances in terms of their limited access to educational and employment opportunities, notably in the public sector. In sum, despite decades of economic development and expanded educational opportunities, perceived and real inequalities continue to exist between the three predominantly Muslim provinces and provinces in other parts of Thailand.[5]

An army vehicle parked outside a mosque in Bacho, Narathiwat. The militarization of daily life has been widespread in Thailand's three southern border provinces since January 2004, initially employing martial law provisions. Since July 2005, the security forces have based their operations on a special anti-terrorist emergency law that curtails the rights of suspects.

Another related development that would have a significant impact on Muslim politics can also be observed. By the late 1990s, Muslims were holding unprecedentedly senior posts in Thai politics. Wan Muhammad Nor Matha, a prominent Malay-Muslim politician from Yala, served as the president of Parliament from 1996 to 2001, later becoming deputy prime minister, communications minister, and eventually interior minister during the first Thaksin government. Only a few years earlier, the idea of a Muslim as head of Thailand's local administration and domestic security structures would have been unthinkable. Dr. Surin Pitsuwan, another Muslim from the Upper South, served as foreign minister of Thailand from 1997 to 2001; and during Thaksin's first term (2001–2005) there were fourteen Muslim members of parliament and several Muslim senators.[6] In the deep South, Muslims dominated provincial legislative assemblies, and several southern municipalities had Muslim mayors.[7] In this milieu of increasing political liberalization and institutionalized democracy, Muslims have been able to voice their political grievances more openly and enjoy a much greater degree of religious freedom. Muslim girls and women may now wear the *hijab* in government educational institutions and offices, Muslim names may be officially used, Muslim prayer rooms have been created in public places, and Friday prayers may be held on university campuses.[8]

These constructive developments have no doubt improved the lives of Muslims who are now able to secure greater freedom, more rights, and better opportunities. However, it would certainly be naïve to expect that this enhanced political and social participation would address all the economic, cultural, and political grievances of the Muslim community, especially in the Malay-Muslim–dominated areas of the three southern border provinces.

A parliamentary report also proved problematic for local and national Muslim politicians in that it implicitly linked them with the network of illegal activities, including drug trafficking, cross-border smuggling, organized crime, and the activities of "influential groups."[9] Illegal businesses have thrived with tacit support and help from some senior government officials and even from some elements of separatists. Some violent incidents in the 1990s, including arson and bomb attacks, were believed to have been staged by these groups to either protect or further their vested interests.[10] This is a region where, as one commentator puts it, "bandits, good and rogue police officers, good and rogue soldiers, corrupt officials and remnants of Muslim separatist groups have long associated with, robbed and occasionally killed each other."[11] To make matters worse, Najmuddin Umar — one of the very same constituency MPs mentioned approvingly by Omar — was officially charged with involvement in the insurgency, and accused of being to be one of the "masterminds" behind the recent violence.[12] Najmuddin was acquitted in December 2005. Another problem was that in the face of growing violence during 2004 and 2005, Muslim politicians remained conspicuously silent, so eroding their political legitimacy and support. This cost them dearly in politics: in the 2005 general election, all of the Malay Muslim incumbent MPs who ran in constituencies under the TRT banner in the three provinces were voted out of office.[13]

Moreover, in spite of an increase in political liberalization and a more concrete representative democracy, police harassment and malpractice in the region remain a big problem. Records from the now defunct Southern Border Provinces Administrative Centre (SBPAC) report that 60 percent of harassment and malpractice complaints filed by local Muslims named police officials as the main culprit. The police were seen as more abusive than other government officials.[14] Abuses and brutal acts committed by the authorities continue up to the present as talk of security forces involvement in "disappearances" (the police practice of taking suspects away and making them disappear) and extrajudicial killings has been widespread in Muslim communities in the three provinces. According to one report, since the violence accelerated in early January 2004, at least forty to fifty Muslims have disappeared in the three crisis-hit provinces of Pattani, Narathiwat, and Yala.[15] The most controversial case in this regard was the disappearance of Somchai Neelaphaijit, a well-known and highly respected human rights Muslim lawyer, though not a Southerner.[16] He was reportedly abducted in Bangkok by the police in March 2004 while working to defend four southern Muslims. Among the four was Dr. Waemahadi Wae-dao, a Muslim doctor well known for his grassroots-related activities. Wae had been arrested on charges of planning bomb attacks on Western embassies with the regional terrorist group Jemaah Islamiah (JI), as well as nine individuals suspected in connection with the January 2004 arms raid.[17] Apart from protesting against the alleged torture of the suspects, Somchai was also extremely active in leading a campaign calling for the repeal of martial law in the South. The four Muslims accused of JI links were later acquitted, and Dr. Wae was elected as a new Narathiwat senator in April 2006. But Somchai remains missing, and is presumed dead.[18]

Positive trends toward greater political integration within the national democratic framework have failed to eliminate the economic and social predicaments that southern Muslim communities face. Widespread drug addiction and drug trafficking, unemployment, low educational achievements, poverty, deprivation, social disparity, criminal gangs, and injustice continue seriously to trouble Muslim communities in the region.[19] It is argued here that these failures provide the backdrop — rather than a full explanation — for a discursive shift from a separatist insurgency, toward a more overtly Islamist militancy.

Berjihad di Patani and Cultural Violence

A crucial juncture for political violence in the deep South took place on 28 April 2004, when one hundred and five Muslim militants were killed and seventeen arrested, after launching attacks against security forces at eleven locations in Pattani, Yala, and Songkla. As the International Crisis Group (IGC) notes, "the perpetrators were quite different: young, deeply pious, poorly armed, and willing to die for their cause."[20] According to ICG sources, an Islamic teacher known as Ustadz Soh had assembled a group of at least ten other *ustadzes* in their late thirties and forties, and trained them in Kelantan. Each *ustadz* then recruited between five and twenty men, most of them in their late teens and early twenties, from religious schools. These young militants trained in jungle areas of Songkla and Yala, taking vows of silence, and undergoing ideological indoctrination and spiritual preparation. Early in the morning of 28 April, they launched simultaneous attacks on police stations and checkpoints. For the most part, the militants were armed only with machetes, and their actions were essentially suicidal.[21] In addition to the one hundred and five militants who died in the attacks, one civilian and five members of the security forces also perished. Most media attention focused on the siege at the historic Kru-Ze mosque, where thirty-two militants were killed, many of them at point-blank range.

Since the beginning of 2004, the nature of violence in the deep South has drastically changed following the emergence of radical Muslim militants who have espoused the cause of total war with the Buddhist *kafirs* (infidels or nonbelievers) and brought with them a highly selective interpretation of Islam. This development was most clearly seen in the tragic events of 28 April 2004, which shed some light on the previously overlooked phenomenon of radical Islamist movements in the deep South of Thailand. On that day, a document, written in 2002 in the Malay language's *Yawi* script, entitled *Berjihad di Patani* (The struggle at Patani),[22] was found on the body of one of the militants killed by Thai military forces at Kru-Ze. Although the document apparently originates with the group responsible for the suicide attacks on 28 April, as part of the justification for their actions, its significance arguably extends beyond the light it sheds on this group of Muslim militants. *Berjihad di Patani* is the only authentic and detailed statement of radical Muslim militant views in the deep South currently available.

The discourse of jihad, *shahid* (martyr), and *takfir* (accusing other Muslims of being kafirs or *munafiks,* that is, hypocrites or betrayers of Islam) has come to the fore in the political rhetoric of *Berjihad di Patani*. These Arabic and religious terms, previously regarded as part of the vocabulary of religious elders, are the most visible and radical shift in the language of Muslim and separatist politics. Insofar as its message strikes a sympathetic note in many Muslim minds, the document points to an element in present-day Muslim separatist politics that is potentially very troubling.

To a large extent, what is happening in southern Thailand is not unique. Events there follow more or less similar developments elsewhere, both at the regional level and in other parts of the Muslim world. Two important factors have come to play a major role in the changing discourse and practice of the separatist politics: the influence of Islamic radicalism abroad and the Islamic resurgence and fragmentation of the religious establishment at home.

Berjihad di Patani presents, as then deputy prime minister Wan Muhammad Nor Matha put it, a "very well written" radical worldview with a "persuasive power."[23] Even if the suicide attacks had not been committed by the 28 April groups, *Berjihad di Patani* would still be invaluable for its insights into a mind-set that has probably existed for some time, and that will not be easily eradicated by any measures available to the Thai state. The document is written in a style difficult for nonspecialist readers to understand, but has a tone of unquestionable authority. This authority is invested with a religious power that is reinforced by countless injunctions taken from the Qur'an. The document apparently had two authors, Ismael Jaffar, alias Ismael Yameena or Poh Su, a Kelantan native, and Abdul Wahub Data, imam of Tarpia Tulwatat Mullaniti Islamic boarding school in Yala.[24] Abdul Wahub confessed to writing it and expressed great regret; Poh Su was arrested by the Malaysian authorities but later released without charge.

Accusing the Thai government of oppressing the Muslim population in the South, the authors of *Berjihad di Patani* proclaimed a jihad against the Thai government and those who work with and support it. Without explicitly claiming responsibility for the violence, the document nevertheless provides a rationale for it, and for the attacks that were to follow. It urges Muslims to take up the armed struggle to fight for separatism:

We should be ashamed of ourselves for sitting idly and doing nothing while [Siamese] colonialists trampled our brothers and sisters. The wealth that belongs to us has been sullied. Our rights and freedom have been curbed, and our religion and culture have been violated. Where is our commitment to peace and security for our people? Remember, O *Wira Shuhada* [martyrdom fighters] brothers! Our late parents, brothers, and sisters sacrificed their lives for the land as warriors; they left behind a generation with warrior blood flowing in their veins. Today, let us make a call, so that the warrior blood will flow again and the generation will emerge again, even we have to face pain and sorrow. With the blessings of the martyrs, the blood will flow. On every battlefield, they echo in the heart of every soul with "There is no God but Allah and Mohammed is his Prophet. Allah is the Greatest" in them.[25]

[...]

Sons and daughters of *Patamala*!...Know that in every struggle, there are always sacrifices to be made, especially in the fight for Allah and the Prophet. This is a struggle to liberate us from continuous oppression by the disbelievers and their alliances. They will never be pleased with the presence of Muslims who uphold the teaching of Islam, because they will not feel free to do what they like. Our struggle is also for the liberation of our beloved country, one which is continuously under occupation by heretic imperialists and their alliances. That is why we need the support and sacrifice of the believers. Thus, quickly provide your support according to your capability. Listen to what has been commanded by Allah with regards to the obligation to provide support and sacrifices.[26]

For the authors, Patani[27] is Dar al-Islam (the land of Islam) and it has been invaded by the Siamese or the central Thai government — the infidel state. Therefore it is legitimate to call a jihad of defense against infidel (nonbeliever) or kafir invaders. Drawing a parallel between present separatist struggles and the religious warfare that raged in the time of the Prophet Muhammad in the seventh century C.E., the authors exhort Muslims to wage a jihad and to rise up against the injustices inflicted upon them by the enemies of Allah.

Come, fight in the path of Allah until He grants us victory, which is, either we depart this life as martyrs or we defeat our enemy and the enemy of Allah. Know that the martyr blood flows in every one of us fellow Muslims who believe in Allah and the Prophet, which inherited from our ancestors who had sacrificed their lives in the path of Jihad. This blood is eager to spill onto the land, paint it red, and illuminate the sky at dawn and dusk, from east to west, so it will be known that the Pattani land produces Jihad warriors. Both male and female warriors will shout out "*takbir*" in all directions, while facing and attacking the enemy, *Allahu Akhbar...Allahu Akhbar...Allahu Akhbar* [Allah is the greatest]. Such chanting will arouse life in the weak and pampered. The sound vibrates with anger and vengeance, answering the call of Jihad.[28]

[...]

You must truly believe in Allah's support and have faith that the victory will be ours. March forward and look for the enemy, day and night, in every place and also in your neighbouring countries, and kill them. Let the disbelievers know that Muslims are strong in this world.[29]

The document thus calls upon Muslims to unite in a fight against infidels or kafirs and bring back the great glory of Islam. Other enemies are specifically described:

> My brothers *Wira Shuhada*!...Though it is difficult for the believers to identify who our enemies, the real hypocrites, are, eventually there will be a way in which Allah will guide the believers. The believers can identify them [the hypocrites] easily. Allah has elucidated with clear words to the believers that...those who take and support disbelievers as their leaders with the intention of seeking their favour or to destroy our honourable Islam are hypocrites. They are the most dangerous enemies of Allah. They are our enemies, too, because they live among Muslims.[30]

In other words, the authors view Muslims who do not accept their uncompromising viewpoint as infidels: either the enemies of God, or unbelievers who deserved to die. Those who sacrifice their lives fighting for justice and defending Islam or its ideals hold a special place in Islam and are to be regarded as shahids.

> Let us realize, *Wira Shuhada*, how glorious we will be if we fall as warriors of our land. Brothers, understand! When martyrs are killed, they are not dead but alive next to God. Allah places them to rest temporarily. Allah will place them in the most honourable place. They will continuously receive sustenance from Allah. They will watch and listen to every piece of news to see if their children will follow in their footsteps. My brothers! Are you afraid that you are going to die? Never think that! Know that death will come to each of you when it is destined, even if you try to hide.[31]

The authors pay careful and lengthy attention to the question of martyrdom and the reaping of benefits to be had via jihad. They assert that martyrdom and eternal rewards and blessings are the goals that the

Duncan McCargo

Army encampment at a government school in Narathiwat. A key factor in explaining Muslim dissatisfaction "is [their] fear and distrust of the security forces, whose activities in the region are viewed as heavy-handed and repressive."

Muslim should bear in mind and should form the intent behind participation in jihad. The authors cite as evidence numerous Qur'anic verses discussing the glories to be had in carrying out jihad and reaping its rewards.

Drawing upon classical Islamic ideas and the experience of the recent past to reach the radical conclusion, the authors call for Muslims to take up arms in fulfillment of their religious duty to submit to the will of God. Restoration of Muslim power and prosperity requires a return to Islam, the creation of a more Islamically oriented state and society. To achieve this goal, the authors combine militancy with messianic vision to inspire and mobilize an army of God whose jihad they believe will liberate Muslims. *Berjihad di Patani*, in essence, seeks to cast the separatist struggle in explicitly religious terms. Attacking the Thai government as the oppressor of Islam and some local Muslims as betrayers of Islam, the authors have injected their polemics against the government and other Muslims with traditional Islamist concepts such as jihad, kafir, munafik, and shahid. In the document, jihad is invoked to urge Muslims to take part in war against government of kafirs with the belief that someone who is killed (a shahid) will go directly to paradise. Martyrdom is a powerful theme in the document and the promise of martyrdom is stressed to motivate militant members. It is in this document that the boundary between the militants and others is redrawn along strictly religious lines: nonmilitants are accused of being kafir and munafik (hypocrites or those who betray Islam) and thus can be legitimately killed. "Those who are against the teachings of Allah are not only named as '*Munifikoon*,' they are also cruel. It is a pity to know that those who have intelligence could live happily under control of oppressors."[32] The document reveals the mind-set of the militants and the way they frame their enemies and victims culturally. Using the concept of munafik to justify killing Muslim civilians is a new and significant development in the discourse of struggle in the deep South.[33]

The exact ideological nature of the jihad carried out by the 28 April 2004 attackers remains unclear. The use of magic by the assailants suggests that their thinking was strongly influenced by Sufism. The alleged leader of the group, Ustadz Soh, claimed to have supernatural powers, and trained his recruits to perform *zikir* (reciting Allah's name) and offer special prayers to protect them from knives and bullets.[34] Some recruits were given sacred water that was supposed to make them invisible. Another cell leader ordered magic sand to be sprinkled on roads in Songkla, to prevent military vehicles from traveling to Kru-Ze. Chaiwat Satha-Anand has suggested that the militants' belief in magic offers a partial explanation for the way in which they died.[35] While the tactics used by the militants during many of the 28 April attacks might be seen as suicidal, it would be wrong to equate them with, say, *salafi jihadi* suicide bombers in Indonesia or Iraq — these were people who had been chanting for days on end and drinking magic water, in a vain attempt to make themselves invulnerable. Significantly, however, Ustadz Soh himself did not take part in the attacks, and simply disappeared on 28 April. It appears that he did not have complete faith in the potency of the magical practices he preached. In this sense, the superstitious elements of the 28 April attacks could be seen as tactical rather than ideological, as part of a process of recruitment and indoctrination. In the end, we do not know enough to be sure.

Islamic Radicalism and the Local Politics of Jihad

The discourse of jihad and the practice of takfir are certainly not unique to Thailand's Muslim separatist militants: its leaders have borrowed from other radical Islamist movements that have flourished since the 1990s.

Jihad is a defining concept or belief in Islam, a key element in what it means to be a believer and follower of God's will. Its importance is rooted in the Qu'ran's command to struggle (the literal meaning of the word jihad) in the path of God and in the example of the Prophet Mohammad and his early companions. While jihad is about much more than martyrdom, martyrs who sacrifice their lives to establish or to defend Islamic ideals also hold a special place in Islam. The Qur'an has many passages that support the notion of martyrdom and that comfort those left behind. In the late twentieth and twenty-first centuries, the terms jihad and martyrdom have gained remarkable currency. They are used by Muslims around the world to legitimate their causes and motivate their followers, including those who die for their faith or in the defense of Muslim territory in "just" causes in places ranging from Palestine, to Afghanistan, Bosnia, Kashmir, the Philippines, and southern Thailand. To elaborate on this, a brief excursion into the development of Islamic radicalism is necessary.

When the authors of *Berjihad di Patani* and other militants examine contemporary events, they follow common Islamic practice by citing ancient authorities. Although many non-Muslims would expect believers to refer to the Qur'an and Hadith (Sunnah of the Prophet) for guidance, most would be surprised by the extent to which the ideas of past Muslim theologians, thinkers, and movements still directly impact upon the minds of militants and other Islamic activists and the Muslim world today.[36] Both modern reformers and radical extremists draw, often selectively, on the teachings and examples of early Islamic revivalist thinkers and activist movements to justify their contemporary jihads. Present-day Muslim radicals or militants, including the authors of *Berjihad di Patani*, often link their radical jihadist worldviews to famous earlier interpretations of jihad, for example, that of prominent medieval theologian and legal scholar Ibn Taymiyya, or that of another influential modern thinker, Sayyid Qutb. Arguing that devout Muslims should not accept a ruler as a true leader only because he claims to be a Muslim, in the fourteenth century Ibn Taymiyya asserted the right to revolt against rulers who transgressed or repudiated Islamic law. This doctrine has become the intellectual foundation for Islamic radicalism in modern times.[37] It was a doctrine much favored by modern Islamists in Egypt, especially Sayyid Qutb, the Muslim Brotherhood's influential ideologue who was executed by Egyptian authorities in 1966 for allegedly conspiring to overthrow the government; and later by Muhammad Farag, a member of the radical organization Islamic Jihad, the assassins of Egypt's president Anwar Sadat in 1981. The role played by Qutb, a "godfather and martyr of Islamic radicalism,"[38] in the reassertion of militant jihad and radical Muslim movements around the world should not be underestimated. Qutb, who spent most of his last years being tortured in prison, is recognized today as "a towering figure in the world of modern political Islam."[39] Significantly, Qutb's pioneering and most inspiring work, "Signposts on the Road," widely known as "Milestones," was translated into Thai by Banjong Binkason, a prominent Muslim scholar, and published by Al-Jihad in 1981.[40]

Another radical expression of the new jihadist doctrine and its indebtedness to the past can be found in the writing of Muhammad Farag, a member of the radical organization Islamic Jihad, who articulated its ideology in the pamphlet called "The Neglected Duty."[41] Some of Farag's radical views on jihad can be summarized as follows: devout Muslims should declare a jihad against the governments and countries whose laws were created by infidels; any cooperation with an infidel government that claims to be Muslim constitutes a sin and the punishment for all such rulers is death; the continuous jihad against the infidel state is the highest obligation; armed struggle is the only acceptable form of jihad, but it should be employed only for religious reasons and not for the sake of national of secular motives; and all Muslims must learn about jihad and should not look for excuses to avoid the practice of jihad.[42] And, since jihad is an "individual duty,"[43] it is not necessary for young people to obtain parental permission to take part in jihad. In other words, jihad, an obligation considered since the ninth century to be a collective duty that is satisfied if a sufficient number of Muslims respond to its call, is transformed into an individual duty to be executed by all.[44]

In the works of the Muslim thinkers and activists above, the meaning and practice of jihad, as formulated by classical jurists and kept dormant since the tenth century, are given its most radical and influential articulation.[45] Arguing against classical doctrine and subsequent exhortations by several prominent jurists to endure unjust Muslim rule, they assert that jihad is an urgent imperative that applies to both the relations between Muslims and the unbelieving West, and between Muslims and so-called Muslims who betray the precepts of Islamic supremacy and open the door for foreign corruption. In doing so, their works marked a significant departure from antecedent doctrine and prevalent practice regarding the scope and purpose of jihad.[46] This global emergence of a new radical jihadist's worldview and its mixture with the Malay nationalist ideology of the early separatist movements serve as a backdrop for events surrounding the recent escalation of violence in southern Thailand.

Development of the content and form of Muslim politics in Thailand and elsewhere has been influenced by external events. While Islamic resurgence and militancy were on the rise from the 1970s onwards, attempts to mobilize Muslims all over the world for a jihad in one area of the world such as Palestine or Kashmir were unsuccessful until the 1980s. The Soviet invasion of Afghanistan was a turning point, as it revived the concept of participation in jihad to expel an infidel occupier from a Muslim country as a personal duty for every capable Muslim.[47] The success and experience of *mujahidin* in Afghanistan in the late 1980s undoubtedly helped popularize the radical meaning and practice of jihad in many Muslim societies.[48]

At a regional level, the radicalization of Islamist politics worldwide had given birth to new, more radical Islamist movements and parties in Southeast Asia: whereas the Muslim opposition politics of the 1960s and 1970s in Indonesia, Malaysia, Thailand, and the Philippines was led mostly by secular-educated leaders, the 1980s and 1990s witnessed the emergence of more radical movements whose networks were increasingly expanded and ideologies and discourses more heavily colored by the ideas and values of religion.[49] Even in countries like Singapore, Malaysia, and Indonesia, where Muslim politics had long been moderate, the 1990s saw efforts by jihadi militants to expand their radical networks. In southern Thailand since the 1990s, the rise of Islamic radicalism has helped revitalize a flagging separatist movement, which also received a much needed boost from veteran Afghan mujahidin.[50] The U.S. invasion of Afghanistan and Iraq and the continuing presence of foreign troops in many Muslim societies have further radicalized many Muslims in Thailand and increased their awareness of global Muslim grievances.

From 2001 to 2003, militant groups in Thailand had begun a new round of coordinated attacks using more sophisticated tactics.[51] Local militants fighting for their ethnic and religious autonomy had apparently evolved into something more menacing, as ideas of radical jihad were incorporated into local separatist movements. Admitting that Muslim extremism had taken root in the region, Bhokin Bhalakula, then minister of interior, publicly asserted that "radical ideas brought over by Thai Muslims who had fought in the Afghan War against the Russians in the 1980s have helped provide the ideological basis and inspiration for the ongoing campaign in the South by a new generation of militants."[52] The conflicts were also described by General Sirichai Thanyasiri, then head of the newly established Southern Border Provinces Peace-building Command, as "wars of ideologies" in which the political contest for hearts and minds was paramount.[53]

Along with a set of political and economic grievances,[54] many Malay Muslims in the South felt a sense of malaise,[55] a feeling that their community had slipped, gradually but inevitably, into decline, losing its hold upon religious principles and its pride when confronted with the encroachment of secular modernity. As one informant put it, he was confronted by:

> a world dominated by corrupt politics and a group of elites, secular and religious alike, concerned solely for their personal political and economic interests, rather than spiritual development or other deeply felt religious matters. It is a world soaked in Western culture in dress, music, television, and movies and subjugated to vices and materialistic values.[56]

On the other hand, a new self-confidence and consciousness, partly reinforced by global Islamic resurgence and by conflicts in other Muslim countries such as Afghanistan and Iraq, reflects the pride of Thailand's Malay Muslims in the glories of Islamic civilization, history, literature, philosophy, as well as theology.

The resulting sense of decline and nostalgia raises profound religious and political questions. What has gone wrong? Why have Muslims fallen behind? How are Muslims to respond? For many Muslims, despite all development programs and formal democratization of contemporary Thailand, these questions and issues remained to be addressed. Rhetorical appeals to the power of Islam and the radical concept of jihad have become important elements of separatist politics. Militants could more readily recruit followers by reciting a litany of Muslim grievances against oppression and mistreatment on the part of kafir or Thailand's Buddhist government to justify their violent actions. This rhetoric further enabled them to build more broad-based local support, and to foster a new generation of Muslim militants more attuned to radical notions of Islam and jihad than was previously the case.

Islamic Resurgence and the Fragmentation
of Religious Authority

Militants have also been able to take advantage of the growing religious consciousness within the Muslim community, as the 1980s and 1990s saw a strong Islamic resurgence in Thailand. The primary characteristic of the religious resurgence that swept the Muslim community was not political; rather, it took the form of a growing piety among Muslims who were showing an increasingly strong interest in the ritual demands of their faith and in their religious life. This resurgence can be seen in the growth of mosque attendance, religious education, Muslim radio and television programs, Muslim newspapers and publishing, and a plethora of translated Islamic literature.

An upsurge in manifestations of religiosity and religious awareness could also be seen, ranging from private exercise in personal piety and devotion, involving a detailed observance of the prayers, fasting, and personal morality, to public rituals and behaviors, including a marked increase in the number of women donning the *hijab*, men wearing beards, and in the numbers of Muslims making the haj, or pilgrimage to Mecca. Although the resurgence was for most Muslims a matter of personal religiosity, it nonetheless benefited the radical militants in two important ways: it provided the opportunity for religious symbols and meanings to be increasingly manipulated for political purposes, and simultaneously contributed to the further fragmentation of Muslim religious authority.

Because the resurgence brought Islamic ideas and institutions such as mosques and Islamic schools into public prominence, separatist groups could exploit related political and cultural contestations for the purpose of mobilizing support. While Islamic resurgence is certainly not the same as religious fanaticism, there is a tendency among government officials, academics, and religious leaders to downplay the religiosity of the militants: yet they certainly take their religion seriously, and seek recruits from the ranks of the pious.[57] Some of the militant groups began to work on their ways to recruit new militant members via ustadzes (religious teachers).[58] Although the extent of militant infiltration of the Islamic schooling system is difficult to quantify, evidence seems to indicate that since the mid to late 1990s, an alliance of groups, including former separatists, newly arrived jihadists, and some ustadzes, systematically targeted the education system.[59] The spread of a new radical separatist ideology in the education system, particularly in the private Islamic schools, was far greater than previously suspected. Militant infiltration and recruitment in these schools apparently reflected the activities of numerous politically radical, well-educated ustadzes in their late twenties, thirties, and forties, many of whom had returned from overseas studies in Indonesia, Malaysia, Pakistan, or Arab countries.[60] In the process, the new separatist politics were developing and the political meanings and practice of jihad, as embodied in *Berjihad di Patani*, were to be understood and subsequently used in their most violent forms. The new militants advocated a sustained and relentless violent struggle against the kafirs, broadly construed. The jihad became a focus of attraction, the solution for the Muslim community's ills, and even one of the pillars of Islam.[61]

This assertion has tragic consequences. If jihad is classified as an individual obligation or duty, together with praying and fasting, young Muslims who may be swayed by radical ideology and decide to join militant groups do not need to ask the permission of their parents. In a society where parental authority is often important, this is a significant development. *Berjihad Di Patani* clearly states: "Do not take your fathers, brothers and sisters as leaders if they incline towards disbelieving and rejecting true faith."[62] As a result, parents of many of those militants who were either killed or captured on or after 28 April 2004 were reported to have had no knowledge of their sons' participation in violent activities.[63]

The view of Islam advanced by *Berjihad di Patani* has seriously challenged the authority of the official religious establishment and its leaders, and set the parameters for an ideological contest that is presently being disputed within the Muslim community and beyond. In a "white paper,"[64] intended to clarify the allegedly false or "distorted" teachings of *Berjihad di Patani*, fifteen experts on the Qu'ran, appointed by the Office of the Sheikul-Islam or Chularajmontri, set out to correct the document's misrepresentation of religious issues, and to demonstrate that it was not a religious work, but simply a political pamphlet or militant handbook.[65] The Chularajamontri, who heads the highest Islamic body in Thailand, is officially designated as the country's official Islamic spiritual leader. Although the Chularajamontri and his office are supposed to be nonpolitical, they are widely seen by southern Muslims as instruments of the central Thai state.

In the paper issued by the Chularajamontri's office, the authors of *Berjihad di Patani* are accused of not following the classical prescriptions for addressing questions such as jihad. Instead of making a detailed elaboration of legal arguments or proposing solutions for potential solutions, they argue, the stress should be on moral justification and the underlying ethical values. The white paper argues that the meaning of the word jihad in the Qur'an and the Islamic tradition is not limited to fighting. Military jihad, the white paper asserts, is essentially defensive and subject to rules that lay down that violence should be proportionate, which excludes terrorism and which demands that violence should end when the enemy seeks peace. Moreover, military jihad is only the lesser jihad: the greater jihad is the struggle

May Tan-Mullins

Muslim women examine the destruction in the interior of the historic Kru-Ze mosque, in the aftermath of a Thai military siege that resulted in the deaths of thirty-two militants, many of them at killed at point-blank range.

against one's own failings. This view invalidates much of the *Berjihad di Patani*'s argument.

The fifteen religious experts also attempted to find precedents in the history of Islam for the *Berjihad di Patani*'s way of thinking, and they saw strong similarities with the *kwawarij*, the earliest of the religious sects of Islam, who regarded other non-kwawarij Muslims as kafir and thus enemies of God who had to be killed. The experts viewed this as a ludicrous opinion, and urged readers, Muslim and non-Muslim alike, to regard *Berjihad di Patani* and its doctrine of jihad and the accusations of kafir as equally preposterous and dangerously misleading. In other words, its authors' accusation that other Muslims were kafirs or munafikin was beyond the pale of Islam. Drawing evidence from Qur'an and jurists' opinion, they further emphasized that Islam is a religion of peace, understanding, and tolerance. *Berjihad di Patani* had distorted these profound teachings of Islam and encouraged the practice of intolerance and violence.

Not surprisingly, *Berjihad di Patani* has also drawn strong reactions from other mainstream Muslim religious leaders. A leading member of the Central Islamic Committee of Thailand was quoted as saying:

> *Berjihad Di Patani* is not a Qur'an. It is not even an Islamic textbook, or *keetab*. It is in fact a manual for outcast warriors to mobilize popular support in order to destroy Islam....Whoever possessed or came across copies of the book should burn them right away.[66]

Another member pointed out, "In the Qur'an, a jihad is committed to protect Islam. It is not to harm others in the name of God."[67]

This view of the *Berjihad di Patani* illustrates the potential for religious scriptures and tradition to be interpreted, reinterpreted, and misinterpreted, or "distorted." While Islamic radicalism and militancy should not be conflated — most radicals are not militants — the rise of both phenomena in southern Thailand is distinctly worrying. Nevertheless, the fact that a sizeable number of young men could be readily recruited for the 28 April attacks suggests that within the Muslim community there are people with misgivings about the authority and legitimacy of existing religious organizations. The expansion of Islamic private schools, mass literacy, and almost universal modern school education, and the greater access to higher education among some sections of the Muslim population, have gradually marginalized the traditional role and authority of religious leaders or *ulama*. This has given rise to a newly prominent role for ustadzes, most of whom do not espouse radical Islamist ideologies, but at least a few of whom clearly do.

Further, the traditional form of Islamic knowledge transmission has been increasingly complemented by a range of media, including books and journals, radio and television, videos, VCDs, and the internet. There is now in effect an emerging multiplicity of authoritative voices — the traditional religious ulama, radical Islamists, secularly educated Muslim intellectuals and activists, official Islamic elites, militant separatist leaders, among others — all of whom compete to define and to control the practice and meanings of Islam. In other words, Islamic knowledge and practice have become objects of interest for growing numbers of people, at the same time that religious scholars have lost their monopoly on discursive power.[68] The resulting fragmentation of religious authority illustrated the emergence of competing claims over cultural authority of religion, particularly as many Muslims with no religious training took it upon themselves to decide upon the meanings and practices of Islam. The works of Muslim think-ers and activists like Qutb and Farag, both of whom had no formal religious training, have nonetheless influenced and inspired many militants in the Muslim world and beyond. During the 1990s, Osama bin Laden, one of the world's leading Muslim fundamentalists, had is-sued several fatwas (legal edicts or religious rulings), calling for a jihad against the United States and its allies, even though he had no author-ity to issue a fatwa, let alone declare jihad.[69] Yet, during the U.S. invasion of Afghanistan in 2002, some Muslim students in the deep South, like their counterparts elsewhere, spoke of their admiration for bin Laden, seeing him as a Muslim leader, a hero, and *mujahid* (fighter). The fact that bin Laden also quoted the struggle of Muslims in Pattani in one of his fatwas was, they argued, indicative of his con-cern with the fate of Muslims worldwide.[70] The authors of *Berjihad di Patani* similarly advanced "distorted" notions of jihad that appear to have captured the imaginations of many Muslim youths who died in the doomed attacks on 28 April. Importantly, most of the militants who perished in the Kru-Ze mosque were reportedly buried as shahids.[71] Nevertheless, official religious leaders and modernist Islamic scholars, while pointing out how the authors of *Berjihad di Patani* and Muslim militants have strayed from the correct path, have never issued a fatwa condemning the 28 April attacks, or any subsequent attacks with reli-gious overtones. In many ways, this controversy and its subsequent ambiguity can be seen as a symptom of the reigning confusion about where moderate Muslims should stand on the link between Islam and politics of violence.

In these cases, two features stand out. First, Muslims are increas-ingly unclear about the political use of Islam; second, they lack a credible and acceptable institutionalized central control of religious authority. Muslims in the South tend to regard the Office of the Sheikul-Islam or Chularajamontri as an inherently co-opted religious bureau-cracy. Although an overwhelming majority of Thai Muslims are Southerners, there has never been a Chularajmontri from the deep South. This and other differences make it difficult for the Office to command much legitimacy and credibility in the region. Overall, this fragmentation and delegitimation make the competing interpreta-tions, claims, and accusations of groups, movements, and organizations within the Muslim community difficult, if not impossi-ble, to assess and evaluate, even for Muslims themselves. The existence of difference and fragmentation within the Muslim community, publicly a nonissue but privately acknowledged to be an issue by many educated Muslims, has yet to give rise to open debate over the status of ideological, cultural, and organizational cleavages within the community. Unfortunately, internal divisions may have serious consequences, given the apparent weakness of the established religious authorities both at local and national levels in dealing with the violence in southern Thailand.[72] Altogether, the internal divisions, the ambivalence of the Muslim establishments in the South and the absence of a legitimate fatwa from official Islamic authorities were sources of frustration to the Thai government in the wake of the escalating violence in the region since 2004.[73] In this respect, the rise of new Muslim militant separatist movements was not an isolated phenomenon, something appearing out of a social and cultural vacuum, but reflected the confusion and fragmentation already present in the Muslim community.

Concluding Remarks

Politics and violent struggle over the definition of religious symbols and meanings are most evident in the politics of jihad in the deep South, where conflicts with state authorities, debates on the proper understanding of Islam and peace, and disputes over the Islamic conception of jihad have all intersected — and where violence, killing, and dying have become both new forms of cultural discourse and political practice. This phenomenon of Islamic radicalization in the deep South is part of something much deeper and bigger. Despite its importance, however, Islamic radicalism is little understood by outsiders, particularly by state security officials, academics, and the general public.

The images and words of Muslim militants in the violence on and after 28 April 2004 seem to embody jihad: a concept with multiple meanings, used and abused throughout Islamic history, and deeply influenced by social and political contexts. The meanings and practices of jihad may become increasingly politicized and seriously destabilizing where ethnic tensions, mistrust, corrupt politics, and social disintegration have undermined the established social and political structures and created a desire for radical change. In southern Thailand, the goals of the militant groups have never been in doubt; they certainly intended to strike fear into the hearts of their opponents and enemies in order to win political autonomy. The moral justification of power for these jihadist militant movements, however, was not couched in political terms, but was based on Islamic religious sources of authority and religious principles. By appealing to deeply ingrained religious beliefs and daily lived religious, social, and political discourses, Muslim militants succeeded in motivating their members and creating for them a religious environment that provides moral sanction for their actions.

Whether the current level of militant activity in the Thai South could turn into a mass-based Islamist movement or even a regional jihad is beyond the purview of this article. Yet focusing too much on the logistical connections of southern Muslim militants with external like-minded organizations at the regional level, trying to establish the extent to which they form part of a regional network, could prove futile.[74] Whether or not such connections exist, the importance of radical Islamist ideologies and a new articulation of jihad have become increasingly de-territorialized in this modern globalized world — a world in which ideas, symbols, meanings, and images are more freely and widely circulated and dispersed than ever.

In many respects, separatist militants seem to have successfully grafted the concept of radical jihad onto the old, relatively secular, Malay nationalist independence struggle. In fact, a closer look at the articulation of some of the most influential Muslim thinkers and activists discussed earlier, one can easily understand the appeal of the radical jihad to separatist militants in the deep South, and given the changing of and deepening interaction between international, regional, and domestic settings, it takes no great leap of one's imagination to apply such radical articulation and interpretation of jihad to the local situation of Thailand's Muslim-dominated southernmost provinces. This was exactly the approach of the authors of *Berjihad di Patani*.

As a result, what started as a post–World War II secessionist struggle for independence led by various groups of secular, ethnic, socialist, and nationalist ideologues[75] and became much more self-consciously Islamic during the 1980s has been transformed into a radical-style jihad against Thailand's Buddhist-dominated state. Judging from what happened on 28 April 2004, where over a hundred Muslim assailants were killed, including thirty-two of them in the historic Kru-Ze mosque, it is difficult to overestimate the power of this new discursive shift and practice of jihad politics that captured the imagination, hopes, aspirations, and intentions of the many Muslims who died that day and in the days, weeks, and months of violence that have ensued.

Given the lack of sufficient demographic data about those involved in violent activities, it is impossible to say that jihadist Muslim militants are to blame for all the southern violence.[76] Nevertheless, the religious and cultural dimensions of violence in the region must not be over-looked, because these give the violence its unprecedented intensity and deadly character. A brief look at some statistics is in order.

The death toll from political violence in the three provinces of Pattani, Yala, and Narathiwat from 1979 through 2003 was 233. From January 2004 to June 2005, however, the number increased to 917, including 106 who died after attacking security forces on 28 April, and 85 who died at the hands of military during and after the Tak Bai protest on 25 October. Of the 917 who died, 726 of the deaths remain officially unaccounted for. In other words, the death toll from January 2004 to June 2005 increased almost fourfold beyond the number of deaths throughout the two earlier decades.

What is remarkable about this increase is that, during the same period, the deaths of local Muslims also increased dramatically: from 53 killed during the past three decades to 294 between January 2004 and June 2005, a staggering increase of more than five times in less than two years. While the role of security officials in these incidents cannot be ruled out, a recent study based on a very extensive perception survey indicates that, of the more than one thousand violent incidents in the three provinces classified as "individual violent attacks" committed between January 2004 and May 2005, more than 80 percent were believed by local informants to have been committed by militant groups.[77] These sobering figures indicate the militants' intent and practice: their targets are no longer just kafirs; now they attack civilian and local Muslims[78] who they believe are government collaborators and informers — or in *Berjihad di Patani*'s term, "munafik." Government officials, liberal academics, and moderate Muslim scholars in Thai society tend to assume that political, social, and economic causes underpin the current militancy, and that if these causes are properly addressed, the problem will go away. If the roots of the problem are to some extent ideological, however, it would be naive to expect political gestures and other measures for social and economic improvement to change the hearts of radical militants and their supporters. Attempts to deal with the violence in the deep South as if it were divorced from its intellectual, cultural, and religious foundations must be viewed with great caution.

Notwithstanding socioeconomic and political development programs, the government's counter-violence policy and measures must take the religious and ideological aspects of violence into serious consideration and adopt appropriate measures. They must also be based on an in-depth understanding of the religious justifications of radical Islamist militancy and the development of appropriate responses.

In the local Thai press and other media, Muslim militants are most often seen as mindless terrorists or religious fanatics and anti-Buddhist militants, longing for the past. They are almost always evaluated in harshly negative terms with little or no effort made to seriously comprehend the discontents and the thinking and ideological justification that have provided their support. The success of radical militant groups in the recruitment, posting, and ideological maintenance of sleeper members, with few defectors, demonstrates the deep ideological nature of the phenomenon. Like it or not, people do not undertake violent militant actions without compelling reasons. To ignore the inspiration, mind-sets, and motivations of the militants, is to put up an insurmountable barrier to understanding them.[79]

Studying the activities of militant groups is inevitably very challenging during a low-intensity conflict such as the current struggle in the Thai South. Nevertheless, more and better information about the dynamics and threats of contemporary Muslim separatist politics is urgently needed for academics, government officials, and even for the general public, in order to frame wise and appropriate responses.

ACKNOWLEDGMENTS: This is an extended and updated version of a paper presented at the Ninth International Conference of Thai Studies, at Northern Illinois University, DeKalb, Ill., 3–5 April 2005. This article is part of an ongoing research project, and some issues raised and discussed here certainly deserve further in-depth study. The author welcomes all comments and suggestions.

❏

6 VOICES FROM PATTANI

Fears, Suspicion, and Confusion

May Tan-Mullins

"Bombs or no bombs, life goes on....." — Khun J, Pattani Province

D URING MY TWO-YEAR STAY IN PATTANI, from 2003 to 2004, I met people from many walks of life, including *tok imams* (religious teachers), Muslims returning from studies overseas, academics, fisherfolk, and locals from various ethnic and religious groups. This article will focus on their reactions toward the situation in the South. Due to the sensitivity of the issues involved, my informants will remain anonymous.

On Islam

In the South, overseas scholars who have graduated and returned from religious institutions in the Middle East are often viewed as possible sources for the spread of militancy in the region. One overseas scholar I met during my visits to southern villages I'll call "Ba-A." Ba-A lives and works in a village near the Thai-Malaysian border.[1] In September 2003 he completed a three-year master's degree program at the Yala Islamic College in Egypt, graduating with good grades. The Egyptian government sponsored his scholarship. When I asked him what he would do with his newly gained Islamic knowledge and education, he indicated he would try to do more good for his village and country. When asked his views about the violence in the deep South, he answered:

> Fighting is useless....The government is the main problem. They always see us as terrorists, just because we are not Thai-Buddhist but Muslims. How can we fit into a country when our rights to practice an alternative religion are violated? Maybe we should change the government and the idea of a national religion.

Ba-A's worldview is fatalistic: fighting is futile. He also insisted that it was not true that scholars returning from the Middle East were attempting to introduce a "new school" of Islam to the locals. The new school refers to a more Arabist, modernist form of Islam — one usually much stricter than the syncretic traditional Islam of the Malays. In the early 1990s, Ba-A explained, people were curious and willing to learn new knowledge from these scholars. Donations and funds were then also more abundant, allowing such scholars to start up their own mosques. Today, he says,

> It is unrealistic now to start a mosque to teach people what I have learnt in Egypt, as there are rarely any donations, unless I apply to the Egyptian government. I also don't want to do it as I don't think it will have a lot of people, as some think we are "too Osama Bin Laden." The current situation of anything from Middle East is terrorist also frightens me. I teach now in the *talika* [religious school] in my village, and am happy to talk about the experiences I had in Egypt during coffee time with my friends.

When I asked him what he means by "too Osama Bin Laden," he replied that wearing the white *jubah* and a beard frightens the locals, especially the Thai-Muslims, who consider them "radicals." I verified this myself when I was having tea with a Thai-Muslim friend in Pattani and a man with a full beard, white robe, and turban walked past the front corridor. My friend turned to me, made a face, and cheekily said in Thai: "Muan Osama loei...nakhlua... [just like Osama... scary...]."[2]

Similar sentiments are also present in Malay-Muslim communities, although they are expressed less overtly. I once asked a village headman why he didn't dress like the tok imam in the village: full robe, turban, and beard. He replied, "they are different." In his view, Middle Eastern-style Islam was something removed from the daily realities of village life.

"We are different," he told me. "His religion is for spiritual improvement. My religion is for daily life. That's why he is tok imam and I am a village headman. If I live like him, I cannot make a living."[3]

On Politics

Another important factor behind changing perceptions at the village level is the attitude and policies of the central government, led since 2001 by Prime Minister Thaksin Shinawatra. According to one informant interviewed prior to the 2005 election: "As a Thai, Mr. Thaksin as the prime minister is the best minister for the country. But as a Muslim, I would nevertheless vote for the Democrat Party to ensure stability and avoid Thai Rak Thai getting too much power."[4]

I asked another informant how he would communicate his dissatisfaction with the situation in the South to the government. He replied: "The best way is to vote for the Democrats [the opposition party]. Although they don't have anything better to offer us than Thaksin, it will put a message across to Thaksin that we need more than what is happening now.[5]

Malay-Muslim voters found themselves faced with empty electoral choices. Although the Democrats did not have any concrete plans to address the crisis, voting for them as a form of political expression of displeasure toward the government became a kind of Islamic political act. Voting decisions were closely affiliated with religion and ethnicity, becoming in effect a referendum on the government's handling of the southern violence.

The Tak Bai incident of 25 October 2004, when seventy-eight Muslims who had been arrested by the military suffocated in army trucks, hardened antigovernment attitudes among many Malay Muslims. Another Pattanian local lamented: "Look at Tak Bai, nothing has been done to punish those people. We are really sad that this has happened. Worse is that it happened during *puasa* [fasting month]. Why is the government treating us like this?"[6]

On the Military

Some Malay Muslims found it extremely offensive that Thai soldiers (who are mostly Thai Buddhists) repaired the Kru-Ze mosque, which

Thai soldiers repair the Kru-Ze mosque, which had been seriously damaged when the military laid siege to the historic building on 28 April 2004. Some Malay Muslims found it "extremely offensive" that Thai soldiers (who are mostly Thai Buddhists) were involved in the repair effort. The government of Thaksin Shinawatra allocated 8.5 million baht to renovate the mosque and develop the area immediately around it.

had been seriously damaged on 28 April 2004 when the military laid siege to the historic building and killed the thirty-two militants who had taken refuge there. The government allocated 8.5 million baht to renovate the mosque and develop the area immediately around it, and another 200,000 baht for a community committee to survey of local tourist attractions in order to encourage more visitors. This insensitivity toward the Malay Muslims further frustrated the people of the region. One of the vendors near the mosque explained: "It is not decent for these soldiers, who are not Muslims, to repair our holy sacred mosque. There is no respect for our holy ground and religion. Now it has even became a tourist place for the Thai government. What can be worse?"[7]

The omnipresence of the military in the South only fuels tensions. To most Malay Muslims, the increase in the number of troops deployed in the South resembled the deployment of U.S. troops into Iraq. One informant, a Malay Muslim *tuk tuk* driver, said when passing an army truck full of soldiers: "There are military everywhere, in the town, in the villages. This place is almost like a mini Iraq."[8]

Another Pattanian Muslim concurred: "Look at them; Pattani is almost like Iraq now and we are fighting a war."[9]

Popular perceptions of the military in the South vary according to one's religion and ethnicity. A well-educated Malay-Muslim civil servant said: "Military is not good for us, as they are trained to attack, not to protect."[10]

By contrast, a Thai Buddhist saw the military more favorably: "They are good for us, they are the protectors of the people, while the police do their job to arrest the bad guys."[11] His comments and views are understandable, as Thai Buddhists — including government officials and teachers — are under the protection of the military when traveling to work. Soldiers even accompany Buddhist monks on their morning alms rounds.

On the Militants

Militant Islamic groups and ideas might proliferate in the South due to the above-mentioned factors, but the majority of the Muslim population disagreed with their actions and resented these groups. According to a tok imam in Pattani:

> We actually hate these so-called separatists and terrorists. They gave Islam a bad name and worse, they make things difficult for us, with all these soldiers running around us all the time now. Why should we support them when the method they have adopted is more destructive than constructive for us?[12]

Another tok imam in Saiburi district concurred. He explained that he had organized an informal discussion session after evening prayers to talk about the Islamic ummah in the world and in southern Thailand. According to him, many came to the conclusion that the greatest threat to the southern ummah-hood now was the actions of the so-called terrorists. As nobody in the group knew who the real culprits were, their actions caused intense confusion and frustration. They concluded that the militants were the main threats to the situation in the South, as the tok imam explained in summarizing their discussions:

> Okay, we are worried, as we don't know who the real terrorists are. But if they are real Muslims, and fighting in the name of Islam, they will have the dignity and courage to admit their acts and fight for their cause. Now, we, the tok imams, are on the "watch list" or "blacklist" as the government thinks we are the bad guys. We cannot live our lives like before, and are worried [that] anything we say might be

too dangerous and be branded as "terrorist." How to live a life like this, when we are so scared to speak our minds? Where are our basic rights? The Human Rights Commission wants to look into the Tak Bai incident, the United Nations, too, but nothing has come out of it [sigh].[13]

Another academic based in the Prince of Songkla University (PSU), a Malay Muslim, expressed his fears about the current situation:

At first, I didn't believe that there are militant terrorists in southern Thailand. This is because I am very active in the religious school and as a lecturer too. And nobody tried to "recruit" me. But lately, the media has been reporting on pictures and evidence of militants training in the jungles of the South. I don't like them. Moreover, it is really strange that there are lots of victims in the daily killings who are Muslims, and Muslims don't kill Muslims! But the media just don't report it. Instead, they focus on the so-called "ethnic killings." I don't know what to think anything anymore.[14]

It is true that many media reports have sensationalized drive-by shootings and the murders of Buddhists, especially when monks are killed. In reality, there are Muslim victims, too, but they are not front-page news. These irresponsible reports by journalists have further threatened ethnic relations in the region. A well-known Thai Buddhist businessman in Pattani noted:

Pattani Province is like a fish tank and we are the fishes. The reporters are observing us [in the tank] from outside and see every small move we make. Yet they will only report certain events and happenings, depending on whether they can sell. They come in for a few days, and leave thinking they have grasped the situation, and write about it. They fail to see us as a society, as a whole. In the end, they do more damage to us than helping us.[15]

Media reports have indeed altered the social relations between ethnic groups in the South, especially between Thai Buddhists and the Malay Muslims. One of my favorite food vendors, a Thai Buddhist based near PSU's Pattani campus, lamented:

We [Thai Buddhists and Malay Muslims] can never talk like before or like the way we are doing now. In the past, I had many good Muslim friends and they will come to my place for chats, and we can talk about politics freely. Today, it has changed. They don't come as often, and we cannot hold our conversations as freely. I am worried of offending them, and as a businessman, I don't want to offend anyone, especially the Malay Muslims.[16]

Fear is evident, especially among the Thai Buddhists, who see themselves as a threatened minority in the region. In November 2004, a Chinese Thai-Buddhist friend of mine could not come and join me for dinner and drinks, as his parents refused to let him go out. This was because there had been bombings in Narathiwat (one of them targeted at a Chinese porridge shop) earlier the same day. Another Thai-Buddhist friend of mine, a lecturer at PSU, declared: "I am so scared now, as I am a civil servant. My brother has just bought another two new guns, one for me and one for my parents. Now I sleep with the gun under my pillow when no one is at home."[17]

An officially sponsored ceremony to distribute authoritative versions of the Koran, Narathiwat, 17 May 2005. Thai authorities have tried to rebuild relations with Islamic teachers and imams, in the aftermath of the terrible 2004 Kru-Ze and Tak Bai incidents.

On Conflict Resolution

When asked about how to resolve the conflict, one academic offered an interesting proposal:

> If there are really terrorists, as the reports say, then the best way is to use the Koran. I am not worried about the educated people, but I am most worried about the youths. These youths might be misled by people through money or ideas, and taught to detonate bombs or do drive-by shootings. We should start putting up posters with phrases from the Koran to indicate that killings, generally are wrong in Islam. Hopefully this will help to educate the "lost minds."[18]

Asked the same question, the Thai-Buddhist food vendor was less sanguine: "How would I know, when nobody knows who are the real culprits? Personally, I will move back to Nakorn Sri Thammarat to my parents' place, once my child finishes her sixth-year schooling. I don't want to take any chances."

❏

7 WAR ON ERROR AND THE SOUTHERN FIRE

How Terrorism Analysts Get It Wrong

Michael K. Connors

THE DEEP SOUTHERN PROVINCES OF THAILAND were once part of Patani, a Malay sultanate and a reputed center of Islamic scholarship in Southeast Asia. The region's integration into the Buddhist-Thai nation state in the early twentieth century led to grievances that have bred dissent and open rebellion. Indeed, the history of the South may well be written as a history of differentiated cyclical patterns of Malay resistance and rebellion and state accommodation and pacification. Since the overwhelming majority of the population in the border provinces are Malay-speaking Muslims, the Thai central state arguably has been experienced as a corrupt foreign conqueror whose officials rarely speak the local language or understand local culture. Historically, Thai state officials, whose symbolic capital as guardians of official notions of Thai-ness set them hierarchically apart from the rest of the population, were not only administrators but often agents of Thai-ification through the implementation of culture, education, and language policies.[1]

Duncan McCargo

A military vehicle stands guard at a temple in Panare, Pattani. "Some commentators argue that [Thaksin] government's confrontational and repressive approach to [the surge in violence in the South] might facilitate the emergence of a broad-based secessionist movement in the future."

During Thailand's political liberalization in the 1980s a space opened for Muslim elites to enter the political sphere, and more culturally sensitive policies emerged accompanied by tailored development programs. Even so, the state still issues its predominantly Thai-Buddhist officials in the South with handbooks covering cultural, religious, and language advice in an effort to moderate cultural arrogance.[2] By the early 1990s, militant separatist groups, which had emerged in the 1950s and 1960s and reached their height in the 1970s, were commonly believed to be in terminal decline — a result of accommodative amnesties and development programs.[3] In 2001, however, Thaksin Shinawatra's Thai Rak Thai (TRT) Party won political office, and by 2004 violence allegedly associated with separatism had returned. By the end of 2005, Thailand apparently faced a revived insurgency. Some commentators argue that the government's confrontational and repressive approach to these developments might facilitate the emergence of a broad-based secessionist movement in the future.[4]

Most terrorism analysts watching the South of Thailand are primarily interested in whether the current "insurgency" will transmute into a regional or a "global jihad."[5] Such a development would shift Thailand from a low-key area of interest to the megastar of terrorism studies. This is one of the key themes in *Conflict and Terrorism in Southern Thailand*, whose authors, argue that the current conflict is largely driven by internal factors.[6] Gunaratna et al. raise the possibility that unless the conflict is adequately managed it will be internationalized, as "Muslim brethren" from all over the world join the struggle of southern Muslims against the Thai state (112–14).[7]

This chapter presents an extended critique of *Conflict and Terrorism in Southern Thailand* as a way of addressing more general concerns about the way "terrorism analysts" interpret local conflicts. I argue that it is important to understand *Conflict and Terrorism* as a knowledge product influenced by the "discipline" of terrorism studies. An evaluation of alternative English- and Thai-language sources will show that Gunaratna et al. have discarded a range of explanations about what is happening in the South . in favor of a securitydriven perspective typical of much terrorism analysis. While much of the discussion in this chapter focuses on the shortcomings of *Conflict and Terrorism*, a cautious appraisal of relevant events based on independent research is also offered.

Rohan Gunaratna, the lead author of *Conflict and Terrorism*, heads the International Centre for Political Violence and Terrorism Research at the Institute of Defence and Strategic Studies in Singapore and is also a senior fellow at West Point, the U.S. military academy. He has become the terrorism expert par excellence, based largely on his international best-seller *Inside Al-Qaeda*, his past association with the Rand Corporation and St. Andrews terrorism database, and his ubiquitous presence as a media commentator on terrorism.[8] Despite the fact that his work has been criticized for overreliance on intelligence agency materials and for often making unsubstantiated claims, Gunaratna remains an authoritative international figure.[9] He is feted by governments around the world, delivering keynote addresses on the terrorist threat and response capacity.*Conflict and Terrorism* consists of four substantial chapters, and nearly one hundred pages of appendixes. The opening chapter offers a history of the conflict. The second chapter maps out key events and actors, and offers a discussion of militancy, religion, and possible global linkages. The third chapter contains an overview of insurgent strategy and tactics and a discussion of the government's response. The final chapter consists of security-driven recommendations that are embedded in the framework of Counter Insurgency (CI) and Counter Terrorism (CT). The authors' recommendations address economic and social grievances as a way to undermine support for the insurgents, the "neutralization" of key insurgents, and strategies to win the trust of the local Muslim population. The book concludes that the greatest challenge facing the Thai state is its poor intelligence systems that have left security agencies with "little understanding of the [insurgent] organizational composition, command structure, or the nature and extent of international connections" (102). To overcome this problem the authors recommend the deployment of "a pool of professional undercover agents [who can] imbed themselves into the community and relate to Malay-Muslim communities" (103). This, until the situation has stabilized and new relations of trust have been established between a more responsive state and the local population.

When the book was released in Thailand in mid-2005, it flew off the bookshelves. The ongoing violence in the South and the failure of the government, media, and academics to provide convincing explanations have left the public hungry for analysis. This book will not satiate that hunger, but as the first book in English on the crisis it will shape understandings of the conflict. This potential influence needs to be countered by an extended critique because the book's potted history of the conflict is awash with errors, both factual and interpretative. These errors are not simply attributable to bad scholarship, though this is surely a factor. More significantly, the research design and methodology of the book makes the authors partisan to intelligence agency perspectives and susceptible to superficial explanations.

The Fraught Study of "Terrorism"

Terrorism studies has its origins in studies of violence in the Middle East and in Western Europe. In decline during the 1990s, the sub-discipline found new impetus after the 11 September 2001 attacks in the United States. What does terrorism studies offer? Over a decade ago, Mike Smith noted that twenty years of terrorism studies had failed to generate much genuine insight into the dynamics of local conflicts. The literature tended toward high-level generalizations around tactical modality and causality that emerged from superficial comparative analysis of incommensurable conflicts (for example, the IRA and the Red Army Faction in West Germany).[10] Smith asked: "So who are the experts on terrorism? Answer, there are no experts, just people who know a little about a lot of small conflicts."[11] This insight is significant, for it implies that so-called experts on terrorism have little to offer relative to conflicts they are unfamiliar with.[12] As will be shown, *Conflict and Terrorism* is a good example of Smith's thesis: for all its pretense about being an up-to-date manual on the violence in South Thailand, the book was produced by authors who seemingly know little about Thailand, but who are equipped with the language of terrorism studies.

Burnett and Whyte, in their more recent review of terrorism studies, or "terrorology," note that during the 1990s a complex interaction of government-sponsored research programs, think tanks, and academics produced a discourse on "new terrorism" that informs post-9/11 commentary. The "new terrorism" (hereafter without quotation marks) thesis claimed to be about a terrorism that dispensed with traditional structures of hierarchy and command, that was prone to use weapons of mass destruction, that was indiscriminate in its targets, and that was pathological and beyond rational engagement.[13] Such ideas have informed much of the contemporary writing on terrorism, leading to a politicized academic literature siding with the U.S.-driven "war on terror" (hereafter without quotation marks). *Conflict and Terrorism* shares some of these traits, although its conclusion that Thailand remains as yet a localized struggle allows it to escape from an overzealous application of the new terrorism thesis. Nevertheless, it is the shadow of the threat of new terrorism that lurks behind the book's examination of international linkages, and explains why the book will interest terrorism analysts (59–68).[14]

Something also needs to be said about the current context in which writings on terrorism are produced. This is a period in which terrorism analysts operate in a tense civilizational, geopolitical, and ideological context that inevitably colors their output. Even if Samuel Huntington's "clash of civilizations" thesis is pure ideological and ethnocentric fury, it has captured the disposition of some terrorism analysts who can but view Islam with suspicion; this is so for the authors of *Conflict and Terrorism* (104). It is also noteworthy that the securitization of U.S. foreign policy, whereby economic liberalization policies have been trumped by pressure to conform to U.S. security policies, has led to greater claims on U.S. allies in the so-called war on terror, leading to a global retreat from human rights and democracy.[15] In the West this has meant highly politicized news reporting, often quoting academics sympathetic to the war on terror. These reports typically conflate local conflicts with "terrorism" and downplay human rights abuses. *Conflict and Terrorism* does raise some concerns about excessive use of force in Thailand, but it tends to see the state as being forced into repressive measures as a result of terrorist strategy (see discussion below on Tak Bai). Furthermore, the intensification of relations between intelligence agencies and universities provides an opportunity for some analysts to conform to state policies and agendas and to downplay issues of "state terror."[16] It is true that many terrorism analysts are legitimately concerned with the

Doll displayed at an army checkpoint on the main Pattani-Narathiwat road, 2005.

root local causes and trigger factors for acts of terrorism, and attempt broad-based analyses that run counter to state interests. Such work shows up the shallow nature of some media and academic commentary.[17] But the pressure to follow state interests and the rewards this subservience brings have increased in the post-9/11 environment, increasing the number of opportunists in the field.[18] This politicized environment has lowered the bar on the standards of analysis and research for some terrorism analysts.

For the well-connected terrorism analyst, research extends to connections with intelligence agencies and access to secret documents — selectively offered, of course. Often welcomed into the corridors of power, s/he is the civilian face of networks of intelligence that have their own agendas to advance. The politically significant function of such opportunists, who identify or work closely with governments, is to take the conclusions of intelligence agencies into the public sphere in modified form, and lend such conclusions legitimacy by virtue of being an apparently independent mouthpiece.[19] Backed with megabucks for research, sought out by police commissioners and security ministers, and courted by media, such analysts feel free to comment on any act of terror anywhere, anytime. This commentary-promiscuity is why they so often get it wrong.

Competing Interpretations

Conflict and Terrorism is not a book about Thailand, but a book of terrorism analysis that uses the South of Thailand as a case study. It sits within the genre of terrorism studies. The book's entire objective is to evaluate Thailand's situation from the perspective of CI and CT and to offer terrorism analysts a "threat matrix" of the insurgency — an evaluation of insurgent intentions, capabilities, and opportunities that are to inform state responses (xii). Carrying out the set task requires the authors to identify insurgents, to make an assessment of their strength, and to engage in profiling groups — to create a knowable adversary. They conclude that Thailand is facing a renewed separatist insurgency directed by definable actors (discussed in next section). This conclusion requires that the authors downplay competing interpretations of what is happening, which may have enriched their analysis, in favor of a line pushed by intelligence agencies — this, despite the authors having characterized Thai intelligence as weak. Below, a number of alternative interpretations, which are not necessarily mutually exclusive, are discussed. These interpretations throw doubt on the seductively parsimonious thesis offered in *Conflict and Terrorism*.

A prevalent interpretation of the conflict in the South is that competing state-criminalized networks are fighting a turf war, and that this has implications for national politics. Prime Minister Thaksin Shinawatra's initial skepticism that the violence in the South was related to a separatist insurgency seems to have been based on his own commissioned intelligence that focused on turf warfare in the South. In a detailed intelligence document that was reportedly commissioned by pro-Thaksin forces in February 2004, a very complicated picture of competing networks is presented, with details of different armed groups connected with local elites in the border provinces.[20] The report presents a picture of mini-fiefdoms controlled by local elites with their own private militias, some connected with formal security forces, and interests.[21] Thaksin's oft-repeated mantra that the violence is the work of bandits or forces out to destabilize the government seems to be drawn, in part, from arguments made in this document.

To complicate the picture, the same report also accuses past leading military figures in the South of inviting separatists to return from exile (in the mid-1990s) in order to carry out attacks that would justify increases in military spending.[22] This conforms to a long-standing suspicion, held by some observers of Thai politics, that during the 1990s remnants of the separatist groups and corrupt military figures shared an interest in fomenting instability.[23] Relatedly, in 2002, *Time Asia* carried an article claiming that "Islamic militants" from Malaysia and elsewhere had trained in a Thai military camp run by rogue military personnel, a claim that Thai military officials denied at the time. Training allegedly included making homemade bombs of the sort that have been used recently in the South.[24] Against these admittedly unconfirmed revelations, the idea that the southern situation consists of a struggle between the Thai state and a Muslim-inspired separatist insurgency seems somewhat simplistic.

A more general understanding sees the violence as being stirred up by leading figures in the black market and drugs trade (with connections to influential politicians), worth billions of baht. These individuals are said to have manipulated alienated youth into grotesque acts of violence to keep the state at bay and ensure the continuation of illicit economic monopolies by incapacitating the state.[25] This argument needs to be put into context. In 2003 the Thaksin government waged a massive "war on drugs" that led to over two thousand deaths and the displacement of drug trafficking networks from the North — some argue, to the South. The arrival of such forces complicated an already tense situation. The role of drug traffickers and illegal cross-border traders enjoys regular airings, as some of the youth who have been arrested in recent times have reported being paid for their actions by forces involved in the illegal trade.[26]

Some interpretations stress internal struggles over state control in the South, after the TRT triumph in the 2001 elections. Duncan McCargo, in a preliminary assessment, draws attention to these factors to put the conflict into a broader perspective: when Prime Minister Thaksin Shinawatra disbanded the Southern Border Provinces Administrative Centre (SBPAC) in 2002, in an effort to assert his own authority and foster his own networks, he effectively declared war on a political settlement that had engaged military and Muslim politicians, and that had incorporated former separatist elements.[27] This opened a Pandora's box that unleashed latent forces, including those alienated by Thaksin's incredible rise to political dominance during his first term in office. The utility of McCargo's approach lies in its recognition that the Thai state is highly conflicted, and that this conflict colors events in the South.

Taking this conflicted nature of the state to the local level, some analysts relate the resumption of violence to disaffected members of the Wadah faction within TRT, who are claimed to have links with insurgent groups.[28] In March 2004 police named key members of this group as suspects for the raid on the Narathiwat army base camp in January 2004.[29]

The members of Wadah first contested elections as a group in 1986. The group was formed on a progressive policy platform to "unite Thai Muslims, protect the interests and rights of Muslims, to promote economic, social, and political development among Muslims, to nurture correct political consciousness, to promote the correct understanding of the Islamic system, and to support the development of democracy with the King as head of state."[30] Unlike most other party factions in Thailand, Wadah appeared to have a genuine constituency among local, community, and religious leaders. Among other things, it sought an extensive change in the Buddhist-centered education system in the South; it wanted to address language issues such as the forced change of names of individuals and villages from the local dialect into Thai; and it sought a more culturally appropriate state-society relationship in the South.[31] Wadah was initially led by Den Tohmeena, the son of the famous Muslim leader Haji Sulong (who is believed to have died at the hands of the police in 1954). Wan Muhammad Nor Matha assumed a central role in Wadah in the late 1990s. Wadah's efforts to raise Malay-Muslim issues in the political arena offered an alternative to armed separatism. As a faction, Wadah, like other political groupings in Thailand, has entered different political parties. It contested the 2001 election as members of the New Aspiration Party (NAP), which subsequently merged with the TRT. In the late 1990s, Den and Wan Nor became estranged, with both men supporting different candidates in the 2001 election. The tensions were heightened when Wan Nor, who held several cabinet posts in the Thaksin government (including the Interior Ministry), appeared unresponsive to Wadah calls for a softer approach to the southern crisis.[32] The division may have emboldened militants, believed to be associated with the Wadah grouping, to come to the fore.[33] There has been no shortage of innuendo about the leading role of Den and his associates in the violence in the South, although such a role has been denied.[34]

By far the most conspiratorial of theories, but one that is encountered in the South, is that international intelligence agencies, supported by elements of the Thai state, are seeking to foment sectarian hatred between Buddhists and Muslims to create a permanent zone of instability, providing a point of entry for intervention, which would provide the major power with further geostrategic leverage in the region.[35] This perspective relates more broadly to understanding the geopolitics of U.S. expansion and the instrumental uses to which the war on terror has been put.[36]

Despite their differences one thing characterizes the above approaches. They each, in some sense, view the conflict as being about elites in competition. For some critics, these elitist approaches share the same mistaken assumption that ordinary people are not behind the events, that their experience of oppression, alienation, and poverty has not motivated them to take action.[37]

Historian Thai Nidhi Aeusrivongse's interesting interpretation puts ordinary people at the center of analysis.[38] He argues that the older, established Muslim elites are too heavily invested in the Thai state and are therefore unlikely to be the source of the current violence. Speaking specifically of the 28 April 2004 uprising, but in a point with more general application, Nidhi argues that a new generation of alienated "small people" have been forced, by the expansion of a raw capitalist economy and resulting displacement, to launch a spontaneous millenarian revolt.[39] In short, he contends, "the Melayu Muslims have chosen to pursue their struggle outside the system."[40] Nidhi's analysis may explain the individual motives of those involved in the uprising, but its weakness lies in the fact that most events in the South of Thailand are highly organized; they are not "spontaneous" and without leadership.[41]

Just how difficult it is to be certain about what is happening in the South becomes clear when one considers the contested nature of the event that is now conventionally understood to mark the escalation of the current conflict: the seizure of arms from the Narathiwat army base on 4 January 2004. Who stole the arms and why remains a mystery. A number of suspects taken into custody after the raid, including an alleged member of the Barisan Revolusi Nasional (BRN), were reportedly tortured and confessed to involvement in the arms seizure.[42] Muslim lawyer Somchai Neelaphaijit sought to highlight their plight, before he disappeared on 12 March 2004. In 1993 Somchai had successfully defended defendants in a case related to the burning of thirty-six schools, attesting to his talent in undoing prosecution cases based on poorly arranged evidence or fabrication — enough to make him a threat in the current context. Despite the questions that surround the 2004 event and the absence of any clear evidence, many, including Gunaratna, Achaya, and Chua, now assume that "Muslim insurgents" were responsible for the raid on the Narathiwat base (22).

There is plenty on the public record to throw this "fact" into doubt. Consider, for example, the following story, recounted in *Urban Guerillas*, a book by Thai journalist Sathian Chanthimathon. The wife of local politician Matawlafi Maesae, reportedly heard her husband's abductors asking him about money that was gained from selling weapons supposedly seized during the Narathiwat raid: "Where is the money you got from selling the weapons? Why didn't you send it?"[43] Police argued that Matawlafi, an ex-soldier, was part of the "terrorist movement" and had played a role in mobilizing youth against the Thai state. They charged that his disappearance was related to internal conflicts in the group that had stolen the weapons. The police didn't report the request by Matawlafi's widow that officials expose the truth about her husband's death, given that many people believed that uniformed individuals were responsible.[44] The implication is that it was people in uniform who were asking Matawlafi for the money — an anecdotal account, though not a confirmation, that it was security forces who stole the weapons to sell on the black market, to GAM insurgents in Aceh one theory has it.[45] True or not, this story illustrates the murkiness surrounding violence in the South. The authors cite English-language newspapers to blame the January raid on separatist militants, but an alternative reading of the same sources shows that this contention is disputed.[46]

The above overview of competing theories and the discussion of the Narathiwat army base raid demonstrates that considerable doubt remains about who is responsible for the violence in 2004 and 2005. Observers must be cautious before rushing to any conclusions in a situation characterized by such murkiness, or what one author has called "grey jihad."[47] Thailand is in the middle not only of an undeclared war but also an intelligence war in the South, where counter-intelligence is often ahead of intelligence.[48]

On Premature Conclusions

The authors present a one-page discussion of some of these alternative interpretations, but they dismiss them by arguing that "there is no doubt that the government has a serious Muslim insurgency at hand" (32). Having surveyed a number of separatist groups believed to present in Thailand, they blame the violence on a well-organized and coordinated movement centered on groups with overlapping membership, some of which, they claim, have penetrated religious schools.[49] While they believe that the insurgency "could very well be the handiwork of a group of free-floating cadres actually owing allegiance to none of the groups," the authors endorse "emerging reports" that two groups in particular, BRN Coordinate and PUSAKA, work in alliance and are advancing plans to establish "Pattani Durassalam" (45–46, 192–94). "Although there is a multiplicity of violent groups," they state, "the vanguard in the current phase of the insurgency is BRN Coordinate [and] BRN Coordinate affiliate, PUSAKA" (104).[50]

There is every reason to be skeptical about this conclusion. For the most part *Conflict and Terrorism* is not so much a research monograph as a description of events, organizations, and individuals based largely on English-language newspapers, some Thai sources, and "intelligence briefs." It reads like a first draft that is crammed with "facts" (e.g., a chronology of events, with few qualifications), but that is short on clear analysis and lines of argumentation. The authors' collation of disparate facts about individuals and their organizational affiliation amounts to something of a police dossier rather than a credible historical record.

A significant problem facing the authors of the book was how to forge a narrative out of newspaper reports. Much of *Conflict and Terrorism* takes on faith that selected news reports are an accurate historical record, but journalists are not historians and cannot be expected to provide a coherent historical narrative. Deadlines, breaking stories, editorial demands, and political pressures all impinge on what is the "first draft of history."[51] As Natasha Hamilton-Hart has argued, terrorism studies do not sufficiently problematize the nature of sources.[52] A number of the more substantial sources cited by the authors use regional English-language newspapers as their primary source — and when terrorism analysts cite terrorism analysts the reader enters an infinite loop of backslapping and counter citation. What begins as a tenuous statement issued to the media becomes, through a process of recitation, a virtual fact. In terrorism analysis the terms "alleged," "reportedly," "said to" sometimes function like an invisible scaffolding supporting the main objective of mounting a case for the prosecution. Since almost everything is "alleged" and nothing proved, in some hands these qualifiers can become a euphemism for "we haven't managed to nail the bastards yet — but they are guilty."

The authors claim to have interviewed numerous people; but only draw on these interviews explicitly several times, and without proper citation. Curiously, on key points footnotes make reference to "intelligence briefs," without accompanying detail such as dates or the kind of person offering the intelligence; nor do the authors assess the reliability of sources. The authors understandably want to protect sources, yet they provide no indication of the status of the intelligence. Moreover, a significant number of footnotes are incomplete, showing an egregious disregard for scholarly standards.

If the research is poor, and its presentation flawed, the resulting findings are not likely to be promising. The most basic flaw of *Conflict and Terrorism* is the rush to judgment, without undertaking adequate research. It is not unreasonable to ask how the authors can be so certain of the key organizational actors in the insurgency (i.e., BRN Coordinate and PUSAKA) when almost everybody else is reluctant to name the insurgent ghost. The explanation may lie in the authors' affinity for the line of argument pushed by sections of the military and police, namely, that politically prominent Muslim politicians linked to identifiable separatist organizations are behind the events.

In the wake of the 4 January 2004 raid, intelligence agencies began circulating documents that were reportedly seized in mid-2003 from the alleged separatist and religious teacher Masae Useng, who appears in *Conflict and Terrorism* as a central figure in the insurgency.[53] The authors cite one newspaper report on this event, but fail to present any substantial details about the documents seized and their relevance — although these are publicly available. The documents are said to show ties between BRN Coordinate and PUSAKA and Muslim politicians in the South of Thailand (connected with the Wadah faction). Among the documents seized was a seven-stage plan to establish the Patani state, commonly referred to as the master plan of the current insurgency.[54] That the plan is not reproduced in *Conflict and Terrorism* is surprising given that so much of the authors' case against BRN Coordinate and PUSAKA rests on the "plan." For the record, the seven stages are these: (1) create consciousness of Malay nationality, Islam, and the Patani homeland; (2) create a mass base; (3) establish front organizations; (4) establish an armed force; (5) create a national ideology; (6) prepare for struggle; and (7) insurrection-revolution.[55] Recent reports in the

Thai press claim that the insurgency has reached stage six or seven, with the insurgents having penetrated political, educational, and religious organizations and created a viable cellular structure with thousands of members, along with a sizeable armed force.[56]

Former Fourth Army commander General Kitti Rattanachaya released a book in 2004 that reproduces a number of documents seized during 2003. Kitti's book provides a detailed picture of the organizational structure of the insurgency, international linkages, religious groupings, mass organizations, chains of command, cells in villages, and front organizations.[57] Intelligence from the documents has also been used to launch prosecutions against a number of people.[58] Kitti's principal argument is that a group of separatist politicians and religious leaders integrated into the Thai state during the 1980s and 1990s, but continued to lay the basis for separatism through ideological work and military preparation among youth. This preparation involved infiltration of religious institutions and the creation of youth groups such as PEMUDA, inculcating among youth subverted violent notions of jihad.[59]

Given that the documents purportedly outline the structure of the insurgent groups, and offer insight into operational methods, one would expect the documents to be the centerpiece of the government's response to the crisis, and to be widely discussed in the media. Yet the government, at least publicly, has given scant attention to these documents. The press occasionally alludes to the seven-stage plan but tends to focus on the undeclared nature of the insurgency and the failure of the government to identify the operational hand. The seven-stage plan, and accompanying documents, are clearly contested in their importance and centrality, and might best be seen as weapons in the intelligence wars that have waged within state agencies since the crisis escalated in 2004. Yet the entire conclusion of *Conflict and Terrorism* about "emerging forces" of BRN Coordinate and PUSAKA rests on the very few English-language reports that have mentioned the seven-stage plan. In short, documents whose existence has been sporadically reported in the press and whose authenticity has not been established form the basis for the authors' conclusion.[60]

This superficiality also extends to the treatment of BRN Coordinate, a breakaway group from BRN that the authors identify as being behind the insurgency. Their organizational review of Barisan Revolusi Nasional is largely historical and relies in part on separatist websites without any accompanying qualification.[61] Given the authors' claim that BRN Coordinate is central to the current insurgency it is surprising that they provide little in the way of details except to say that it was recently established (162).[62] Thai-language sources state that BRN Coordinate was formed in 1979, and they present it as a more reformist-oriented grouping centered on Muslim politicians (some say Wadah) who integrated into the Thai state in the 1980s and 1990s.[63] Their interests were served by the 1980s political settlement that took shape in the SBPAC. The authors of *Conflict and Terrorism* simply do not have enough background to interpret the significance or context of the intelligence charges against BRN Coordinate and PUSAKA.

The authors portray PUSAKA as a secretive organization, citing a *Strait Times* article to the effect that "it was during a raid in 2002–2003 on Masae's premises [Useng] that Thai authorities found out about the group from some documents" (44). The organization is actually a public foundation registered in 1994.[64] It has received public monies for its stated purpose of assisting curriculum development in *tadika* (basically informal schools for teaching ethics to young Muslim children), a fact that the authors later acknowledge, without that fact being allowed to get in the way of the presentation of PUSAKA as a shadowy ideological movement driven by militant separatists at the forefront of "ideological indoctrination" of children (191). To further demonize PUSAKA the authors cite a range of reports that contain comments about the organization's "insidious" use of drug addicts, its recruitment of orphans, and its nurturing of radicals within schools under its influence. Allegation is heaped upon allegation, but the sources for the authors' claims are only newspaper reports that offer hearsay or draw solely from intelligence sources. At times the cited sources say nothing. For example, the authors write, "Thai authorities also believe that PUSAKA was the underground movement that instigated the 28 April attack" (192). The cited source for this makes no mention of PUSAKA.[65] The authors suggest that PUSAKA recruits students from the tadikas, whereas intelligence sources tend to see its recruitment of teachers as the key to its role in the insurgency, with recruitment of youth happening at a later stage. When sources don't say what the authors want them to say, the authors are adept at conjuring an organization's manifesto out of thin air: "It is not very clear what PUSAKA's ideology is. However, as Najmuddin [Umar] is the founder and is known for his separatist views, it can be deduced that PUSAKA aims to achieve an independent Islamic Pattani state" (193). Actually,

PUSAKA's publicly stated objectives are these: Islamic studies; educational support to orphans and other charitable works; promoting good norms and customs; and working for the public good.[66] Najmuddin was acquitted of charges of sedition and supporting separatism in mid-December 2005.[67]

Given the limits of their research and the abandon with which they source news reports, one can only assume that the authors rely completely on informants and intelligence briefs/briefings to stick various pieces of the puzzle together and draw the conclusion that BRN Coordinate and PUSAKA are key players in the insurgency. Yet the reader has to take this on faith, for the authors provide few details to support their claim.[68]

Having failed to deal with alternative interpretations, and having relied on fairly thin sources, the authors are not in a position to advance their chosen interpretation. They may offer some interesting details, but they simply do not know enough about Thai politics, insurgent groups, border politics, and the conflicted nature of the state to be able to put forth their explanation credibly. Any position on the South is as yet in the shadow of speculation. And it is this shadow of speculation, this willingness to say that we do not yet really know, that *Conflict and Terrorism* lacks. While the situation demands cautious appraisal, qualified speculation, and intense scrutiny, *Conflict and Terrorism* is gung ho.

On Translation

One of the book's strongest points is its translation into English of the *Berjihad di Patani*, the booklet that was reportedly found on the bodies of some of those killed in the 28 April 2004 uprising.[69] Largely composed of a call for unity and struggle through violence for the resurrection of the Patani state, the booklet justifies violence against the colonizers (Thais), hypocrites, and collaborators. In Thailand the booklet has been invoked as evidence of the distorted religious nature of the conflict: indicating an "Islamization" of the conflict and conjuring images of fanatical militants motivated by a distorted version of the Koran to surrender their lives in the name of jihad against the infidels.[70]

For this author, the claimed origins of *Berjihad di Patani* bring into question its authenticity. Gunaratna et al. claim that Muslims from the South of Thailand paid two thousand Malaysian ringgit to one of the booklet's authors, a Muslim from Kelantan Malaysia, to cooperate in writing the text. He was later reported to be surprised about the uses to which it had been put (vi). It seems suspicious that a key ideological text would be written by a hired gun. If this claim is true, then it shows that forces seeking other objectives were using religion for their own purposes, opening the possibility for a consideration of the alternative interpretations discussed above. Gunaratna et al. state that the booklet had a Thai coauthor as well, Imam Abdul Wahab Data, who confessed to involvement in the 28 April events (54).[71] The authors neglect to note that Wahab Data claimed that the group behind the April events was led by Ustadz Soh, whom he described as being principally interested in money not religion.[72] Nor do they cite the report in *The Nation* that explained that Imam Abdul Wahab Data had joined the Ustad Help Ustad Project, which "uses Islamic teachers who have turned their back on separatism and insurgency to convert militants and rogue teachers."[73] Even an amateur sleuth would be asking questions about the alleged authors of the booklet. What does it mean to have a key insurgent text written by a hired gun and a man who now works to convert "rogue militants"? Fickle fanatics, indeed.

The authors' commentary on the booklet is surprisingly brief given the importance they attach to it. While they state that the booklet has affinities with "jihadi indoctrination" — citing passages that equate jihad with bloodletting — they also argue that their analysis of the text (which is cursory) demonstrates that the text is "devoid of international jihadist ideology," which they seem to equate with pan-Islamic ideology (10, 58). Instead, Gunaratna et al. argue that *Berjihad di Patani* is essentially nationalist in orientation (91).

When Gunaratna et al. quote directly from the text, the result is often misinterpretation. For instance, they claim that *Berjihad di Patani* "sought to employ Islam primarily for the preservation of material possessions — wealth, freedom, peace and security — and then religion" (9). To back up this assertion they quote the following passage from the booklet:

> [E]very possession that belongs to an individual legally belongs to that individual. These include housing estates, material possessions, financial wealth, children and wives, and cultural traditions, and the most important thing of all, is the religion. Thus let us work together to protect all these, even if it costs us our life. (9)

My reading of this passage is that the booklet describes religion "as the most important thing of all," not as a secondary thing as Gunaratna

et al. seem to claim Such erroneous exegesis highlights the poor interpretative skills of the authors.

On Facts and Interpretation

Most books have some errors, but few books that aspire to such authority contain as many as this one. The mistakes are both historical
and contemporary. The authors' positioning within terrorism studies
(knowing a little about lots of conflicts) might explain the flippant attitude to historical context and facts: the authors have nothing more
than a casual acquaintance with the history and modern-day politics of
Thailand and presumably assume that their readers are not well informed either. Below, some errors are presented.

One example demonstrates the authors' ignorance of one of the
most important events in southern history: they mistakenly describe
Haji Sulong, an important southern Muslim leader of the twentieth
century, as the leader of the "Dusun Nyiur incident" in April 1948.[74] He
was, in fact, in jail at the time (5). At times inaccuracy slides into preju-
dice: the authors speak of the threat potential of Islam, writing, "The
presence of a significant Muslim community in the rest of the kingdom, including Bangkok…has the potential to disperse the threat
beyond its current epicenter in the south" (104). This failure to differ-
entiate between militant violent politics and the Islamic faith in
Thailand reveals nothing but prejudicial ignorance.[75] Topping the list
of errors is the claim that Thai Rak Thai MP Wan Muhammad Nor Matha
lost his seat in the 2005 elections, which saw TRT lose all of its seats in
the border provinces (88). He did not; in fact he retained his seat as a
party list MP (based on total national vote of the party). That the authors are mistaken about the status of Wan Nor, one of Thailand's
leading Muslim politicians and a key, though controversial, member of
the Wadah, illustrates their failure to do the basic background work.
Negligence becomes absurdity when the authors claim that the 1993
bombing in the Hat Yai railway station was directed at non-Muslim citizens since, they claimed, "few Muslims use this train station" (36). Hat
Yai railway station is a gateway into the border provinces; it is the last
major stop before Malaysia and many of its passengers are Muslims.

On the question of the authors' understanding of current Thai policy in the South (which they seek to influence), it is worth noting that
they fail to grasp the government's zoning policy. Initiated in November 2004, this policy assigns red, yellow, or green color codes to
villages according to the level of insurgent presence and informs state

approaches to each village. In February 2005 Thaksin made an on-the-run remark that red zone villages (those with alleged core insurgent presence) should be denied funding. The authors mistakenly attribute the "zoning" of villages to these comments (89). Thaksin's mooted linking of zones and budgets was abandoned, but the zoning policy continues.[76]

The book is full of other alarming assertions. A particularly disturbing one concerns the Tak Bai protest of October 2004 during which seven demonstrators were shot and seventy-eight died as they were transported to an army base after being arrested by the military. The protest was organized in response to the arrest of villagers who had given, under duress, their state-supplied "self-defense" weapons to "militants." The authors argue, with no supporting evidence other than deduction, that the Tak Bai protest, was part of the insurgents' agitprop tactics to force security forces into repressive measures in order to create anti-state feeling (77).[77]

This factual and interpretive negligence, and there are more instances, demonstrates a lack of local knowledge. This liability has not, however, hindered the authors from acting as advisors to Thai authorities on the "conflict trajectory," and declaring confidently that with appropriate application of CI and CT security can be returned to the South in two years, and stability in five years (xi). Yet, if the most basic of facts are beyond the authors, how far can they be trusted to offer an understanding of the current situation, which is characterized by contradiction, inconsistency, and counterintelligence?

On the Right to Conclude

When people with little knowledge about Thailand — but with self-proclaimed expertise in matters of terrorism — put pen to paper, the product is a book like *Conflict and Terrorism*. Even though the authors try to appreciate local nuance, circumstance, and specificity, they lack the local knowledge that might have assisted their passage through contradictory information. Their position within terrorism studies also slants them toward an uncritical acceptance of police and intelligence reports, accessed either through the English-language press or through briefings.

This article has explored how a security-driven perspective has led the authors to construct a narrative that consists of clearly defined actors and intentions, when neither the evidence nor the authors' research methodology is adequate to this task. The authors describe their work as "an initial attempt," offering "preliminary findings," and yet the book reads as if it were a definitive analysis (x). There is little caution, qualification, or problematization of sources in evidence. Where *Conflict and Terrorism* reaches firm conclusions and assigns organizational responsibility for the violence, this article contends that it is too early to say with certainty who is responsible for the events of 2004–2005; no force has accepted responsibility for the insurgency and interpretations of the violence are hotly contested. *Conflict and Terrorism in Southern Thailand* should not become the standard reference for the current southern insurgency.[78] If it does, then authors and readers who use it as such will be importing a mass of inaccuracies, preconceptions, simplifications, and uncorroborated claims into their own attempt to work out what is happening. There may well be a renewed separatist insurgency in Thailand, but this is not the book that can explain its structure, objective, and modus operandi with any integrity.

To conclude, this chapter has sought to respond to "war on terror" intellectuals — who wittingly or unwittingly serve state security perspectives — with a considered approach to evidence and analysis. Many more books like *Conflict and Terrorism*, about different places and struggles, require extended critique. Area-specialists and in-country scholars around the world are in a strong position to temper the security-driven perspective of war on terror scholarship with sober facts and an appreciation of local nuance. Should such a concerted effort be made in the name of a "war on error," propagandistic use of bad and self-serving scholarship by state security agencies would be subject to greater scrutiny.

ACKNOWLEDGMENTS: Thanks to Duncan McCargo and Tom Fenton for their suggestions and editorial work. Comments from an anonymous reviewer were wonderfully frank and engaging. I've tried to accommodate criticisms made by that reviewer, while keeping true to my own perspective.

❏

POSTSCRIPT

No End in Sight?

Duncan McCargo

EVEN BY THAILAND'S STANDARDS, 2006 was a year of extraordinary political turmoil and confusion. National politics now overshadowed the crisis in the South. Despite having been elected with a landslide majority in February 2005, Prime Minister Thaksin Shinawatra was in serious trouble less than a year later. Cornered by his opponents in the face of a growing public outcry and mass street demonstrations over the January sale of his family business, Shin Corp., to Singapore's Temasek Holdings, Thaksin was forced to dissolve parliament and announce a snap election for 2 April 2006.[1] When the Democrats and other opposition parties decided to boycott the election, the country experienced a farcical situation: Thai Rak Thai (TRT) candidates competed with unknown opposition parties in essentially fake contests, and in many constituencies spoiled ballots and "no" votes outnumbered those cast for actual candidates. In the South and in Bangkok, numerous races had to be rerun three weeks later. Thaksin announced that he was stepping down from the premiership, but never formally resigned. Following royal advice issued while Thaksin was abroad, the courts invalidated the April elections.

Politics was largely put aside during the month of June, when celebrations of the revered King's sixty years on the throne dominated the national agenda. Meanwhile, Thaksin's top legal advisors deserted the government. Rumors of a military coup were rife, and both the TRT and Democrat parties faced legal cases that might have led to their dissolution. Throughout this period, tensions between Thaksin supporters and the palace network were very evident, illustrated by incidents such as a bomb planted outside the home of Privy Council president Prem Tinsulanond on 9 March, and a high-profile speech by Prem at the Chulachomklao Military Academy on 14 July, at which he reminded soldiers that their primary loyalty was to the crown, rather than to the government of the day. Nevertheless, on 21 July the King signed a royal decree approving a 15 October date for new elections.

In the southern border provinces, political turmoil in Bangkok received mixed reactions. On the one hand, Thaksin had few supporters in the area, and his discomfiture was greeted with a certain schadenfreude. At the same time, the overwhelming focus on national events, elections, and the daily twists and turns in the Thaksin saga served to divert media and official attention from the continuing crisis in the South. During the early part of 2006, the government tried to argue that its security policies were having a positive effect in reducing the number and intensity of violent incidents. Yet these claims soon proved unsustainable. Casualty figures for the whole of 2004 and 2005 confirmed the trends discussed by Srisompob and Panyasak[2] — more Muslims had been killed in the conflict to date than Buddhists (607 versus 538, with another thirty deaths of people whose religion was not known), though more Buddhists than Muslims had been injured.[3] The clear trend was toward increasing levels of Muslim-on-Muslim violence. While late 2005 did see a drop in the number of incidents — perhaps partly because of severe flooding that paralyzed much activity in the three provinces — there was a resurgence of violence in the first half of 2006. A dreadful hostage-taking episode at a school in Kuching Ruepo, Rangae, Narathiwat on 19 May brought home the continuing alienation of many Malay Muslims: infuriated by the arrest of two villagers, a group of local women seized two female teachers and slapped them about; another group of around ten men then beat them with sticks, leaving one teacher in a coma from which she seemed unlikely ever to recover.[4] Less than a month later, forty bombs exploded on a single morning across the three provinces, many of them inside government buildings — though casualties were very light. On 24 July, a

Thai-language teacher was shot dead in front of his students at a government school in Rusoh, Narathiwat. On the morning of 31 August, bombs went off at twenty-two banks across the province of Yala, the first large-scale attack on the institutions of Thai capitalism. In May 2006, the governor of Pattani had asserted that only forty-three armed men were responsible for the violence in the area.[5] Yet subsequent events made clear that the militants retained the capacity to carry out coordinated, complex, and bold attacks, undermining claims that the authorities were closing in on a shrinking band of troublemakers. Incidents such as the attack on the two female teachers inflamed hostile sentiments toward Malay Muslims in the rest of Thailand, creating a gulf of incomprehension and popular fury. Attempts by some Malay-Muslim leaders to explain such incidents with reference to long-standing local grievances cut little ice.

Against the background of continuing daily killings, electoral politics in the region were very fraught. Where TRT candidates faced no rival, election laws stipulated they needed to secure a minimum 20 percent of the vote to secure election — yet many of them struggled to achieve this modest level of support. In the 2 April election, several veteran Muslim politicians were humiliated. Former minister Aripen Utarasint gained less than 20 percent of the vote in his long-standing Narathiwat constituency; rather than risk a second round of humiliation, he asked his political secretary to contest the rerun in his place. Veteran Pattani MP Wairote Phiphitphakdee fared even worse, gaining just over 11 percent of the vote in the 2 April poll, and failing a second time in the 23 April rerun. Results such as these showed that Malay-Muslim politicians who had thrown in their lot with the unpopular TRT government had become essentially unelectable, unable to win even in unopposed races. The alienation of the Wadah group of politicians from their electorate illustrated the difficulty of reverting from armed struggle to political struggle in the southern border provinces.

In response to the widespread feeling that Wadah had betrayed the Malay-Muslim population, various moves were made to create a new Muslim party in Thailand. Yet the establishment of such a party was fraught with complications. Was the aim simply to represent Malay Muslims, as a way of mainstreaming their political demands? Or was the party really intended to provide a voice for the very diverse aspirations of Muslims all over Thailand? Could a new political organization that openly termed itself a Muslim party operate effectively in the Thai context? More darkly, was the creation of a Muslim party simply a ploy by figures associated with TRT?[6] Since TRT's existing candidates in the region must now be considered unelectable, the party could exercise the option of simply cutting them loose (though possibly continuing to present them as its candidates) and invest instead in supporting alternative parliamentary candidates, backed by a "nominee" party controlled ultimately by TRT. In June 2006, a new political party was established led by Sombat Tassanaprasert, initially known as the Thai Muslim Party; it quickly changed its name to the Thai Peace Party. In a clear attempt to distance itself from the existing political order, the Thai Peace Party announced that it would not be fielding any former MPs or ministers as parliamentary candidates, and created its own advisory council of Islamic scholars.[7] But the party was openly backed by a controversial figure, Phichet Satirachaval, secretary-general of the Islamic Council of Thailand. A convert to Islam and former deputy transport minister with close links to Thai Rak Thai, Phichet had been banned from politics for five years by the Constitution Court in August 2002, on charges of assets concealment. He was widely believed to have established the new party as a way of ingratiating himself with Thaksin and Thai Rak Thai and ultimately returning to ministerial office. While claiming to be a "bottom up" movement from ordinary Muslims, the new party was perceived by many in the South as part of a Bangkok-devised scheme to manage and manipulate the political representation of the three provinces.

On 5 June 2006, the National Reconciliation Commission (NRC) finally published its 132-page report. In fact, the report had been essentially finished for more than two months, but Anand had been reluctant to submit the recommendations to a caretaker government. When it became clear that new elections would not be held until late 2006, the NRC had no choice but to hand over the report to a government whose prime minister had clearly long since lost all interest. Thaksin commented that his eyes were too sore to read the report, while caretaker deputy premier Chidchai Vanasatidya also claimed not to have read it — a particularly implausible assertion, since as an NRC member, Chidchai shared responsibility for the contents.[8] The NRC report followed a medical model, in offering a diagnosis and prognosis for the southern violence, before suggesting some therapeutic measures.[9] In its diagnosis, the NRC argued that religion was not the cause of the violence, but just one factor invoked by those who sought to legitimize their actions.[10] The prognosis offered was somewhat pessimistic — unless action was taken, there was likely to be more violence, more civilian casualties and explosions, and a deterioration in the economic situation of the border provinces. Important recommendations included an "unarmed army," a special unit to defuse tense situations by nonviolent means; the adoption of Pattani Malay as a working language in the deep South; and the creation of a new agency to oversee the administration of the area, to be known as the Peaceful Strategic Operation Center for Southern Border Provinces — in effect, reestablishing the positive features of the old Southern Border Provinces Administrative Center (SBPAC).[11] Other measures included creating a regional development council, a fund for reconciliation and healing, devising procedures to deal quickly with complaints against government officials in the region, and promoting dialogue with militant groups. The report's primary author, Chaiwat Satha-Anand, argued at a workshop in Bangkok that the NRC had found the Thai state in a critical condition in the South, with a diminished capacity to govern, and a range of groups seeking to produce ungovernability for different purposes.[12] Most fundamentally, the NRC had found evidence of failed communities in the area, communities no longer able to provide basic protection for their members, or even for hostages such as Khru Juliang, the teacher from Narathiwat.

Though broadly welcomed in the pages of Thailand's English-language press, the report pleased few other commentators. For those with a conservative, security-oriented perspective, the NRC was simply too conciliatory and made too many concessions to the militants. Privy Council president Prem Tinsulanond[13] criticized the proposal to make Pattani Malay a working language, insisting that Thai was the only national language.[14] NRC members tried in vain to explain that a "working language" was something entirely different from an "official language," but this subtle distinction was lost on many Thais, for whom any such change would represent the thin end of the wedge. The proposal for an "unarmed army" was ridiculed in the popular Thai press. And for those who had seen the SBPAC as part of the problem, resurrecting it in new clothes was no real solution.

Barun, the pseudonymous author of an important book on the Southern conflict, published a critique of the NRC report which appeared as part of a special section on the topic in the April–June 2006 issue of *Fa Diao Kan*.[15] He began by arguing that the report — taken together with the more open academic debate about the meanings of "Malayness" during a conference held at Prince of Songkla University's College of Islamic Studies on 11 and 12 May 2006 — offered the possibility of a "better perspective and more comprehensive view of the South."[16] He also concluded that the therapies proposed by the NRC were good ones, especially the nine core proposals for advancing reconciliation.[17] Yet many of Barun's other comments were much harsher, especially when he argued: "If the NRC denies that religion has anything to do with violence, we will be wasting a lot more time before we see any way out."[18] He highlighted the failure of Islamic leaders to take a public stance against the violence on religious grounds, and argued that dealing with deep-rooted political violence using the criminal justice system would not work in the long run. Barun suggested that the misguided teachings of Islam had to be tackled head-on. Barun's views resembled those of some commentators who felt that the NRC was unwilling to talk directly about the real nature and origins of the southern violence, and that the Commission's rhetoric about injustice and reconciliation glossed over the unpleasant fact that most of the violence was being committed by Muslims.

For others, however, the NRC report simply did not go far enough. Many NRC members had been deeply disappointed that NRC chairman Anand Panyarachun had ruled proposals for a political solution to the problems of the South off-limits. One member explained that Anand and deputy chairman Prawase Wasi had tested the waters back in April 2005 with a proposal for a "Pattani Metropolitan Authority," and backed off when they met with hostile reaction from the press.[19] All talk of autonomy or a "special administrative zone" in the South was subsequently off-limits for discussion, even at closed-door NRC meetings. Privately, most educated Malay Muslims wanted to see some form of regional autonomy for the three provinces, but were reluctant to express this view in public for fear of being labeled "separatist," or of wanting to question Thailand's constitutional status as a unitary state: Article 1 of the Thai constitution states: "Thailand is one and indivisible kingdom [sic]." Some NRC members had hoped that Anand and Prawase — whose loyalty to the monarchy and the Thai state was utterly unimpeachable — might have assisted them by articulating such proposals. Some apparently believed that Anand was acting on instructions "from above" to ensure that these ideas did not find their way into the Commission's report.[20] The failure of the NRC report to make a bold proposal for reforming the mode of governance in the three provinces meant that there was little prospect of undercutting the militant movement through a political offensive. From this perspective, the NRC report had simply failed the test; its proposals were worthy, but too dull to have any real impact.

Nation journalist Supalak Ganjanakhundee, coauthor of an invaluable book on the conflict,[21] accused the NRC of making insufficiently bold recommendations.[22] The proposed new administrative body fell far short of a special set of governance arrangements for the three provinces, and lacked sufficient local participation. He criticized the NRC for tailoring its proposals to what the Thaksin government might find acceptable, arguing that the Commission should have staked out a much stronger position in the long-term interests of solving the southern crisis. The Thaksin government might not be around for much longer, but the problem of the South was a long-term one — they should have gone ahead with the boldest proposals they could. The NRC should have been ready to lead Thai society, rather than "realistically" accepting the limitations of ill-informed public opinion about the South. He also criticized the NRC for failing to "name the problem" by engaging directly with the militant movements behind the violence. In addition, Supalak argued that the NRC had not made much effort to reveal the truth about controversial events in the South; though the NRC had made public earlier government reports on Kru-Ze and Tak Bai, it had failed to present new information concerning the Saba Yoi killings on 28 April 2004, or the question of "disappearances" at the hands of the authorities. Nor had the NRC done a good job of disseminating its message; Thais in other parts of the country continued to post hostile messages about southern Muslims on websites, apparently completely untouched by the NRC's work, which they continued to see as a way of "pleasing Muslims" rather than addressing a deep-rooted problem. The NRC needed to engage in a much more effective media campaign, using events such as public hearings to communicate its findings. The Issara News Center — an NRC-backed initiative to promote alternative understandings of the southern crisis in the media — lacked the capacity to influence the mood of wider Thai society.[23] Supalak wrote as someone broadly sympathetic to the NRC's aims, but disappointed by the Commission's outcomes.

Chaiwat argued that the way the NRC report was misread and misunderstood was revealing about the nature of Thai society.[24] He suggested that many of the misunderstandings of the proposals could be traced back to criticism in the popular press, notably a column in *Thai Rath* newspaper dated 8 June, which had expressed unease at the proposal to make Malay an official language, and argued that an "unarmed army" would play into the hands of bad guys.[25] International commentators who did not read Thai tended to assume that the NRC report had been quite well received, not grasping that the much less sophisticated vernacular press largely determines the news agenda in Thailand, while the English-medium *Bangkok Post* and *The Nation* are only bit-players. The popular press was deeply mistrustful of the NRC's conciliatory approach toward the Malay-Muslim community in the South. Chaiwat insisted that the NRC report had been framed by the prevailing political realities and constraints, including what he termed the "history and agonies of the chair himself" — the difficult balancing act that Anand was required to perform. Fundamentally, the public reaction to the report illustrated the extent to which most Thais remained unable to grasp the idea that Siam had acted as a colonial state, and were unable to understand the degree of difference between the Malay Muslims of the southern border provinces and the rest of Thailand.

By 2006, there was a clear divide between two broad-brush approaches to the southern conflict. For most government officials and for the popular media, the conflict remained essentially a security problem, which could best be addressed by refusing to concede ground, employing tough legal measures such as the 2005 emergency decree, and emphasizing a policy of apprehending ringleaders and front-line troublemakers. For most members of the NRC and a small number of academics, journalists, activists, and public intellectuals, the southern conflict was essentially a political problem requiring political solutions: new governance arrangements, new approaches to issues such as rights and justice, better understandings of Islam, and, above all, recognition of the distinctive history and identity of Malay Muslims. In fact, security approaches to the conflict had conspicuously failed to address the problem, violence was growing more insidious, and "failed communities" were rapidly becoming the norm in the three provinces. Yet despite these obvious failures, advocates of political approaches — including, albeit from a variety of perspectives, all the contributors to this volume — had proven unable to mainstream their views. Indeed, even the NRC actually refrained from spelling out the full political implications of its own findings.

The process of elite debate generated by the NRC report, alongside parallel debates taking place within the Malay-Muslim communities of Pattani, Yala, and Narathiwat, was an unfinished one. Just as the 1997 constitution began life with the much-derided report of the 1994–95

Democratic Development Committee (chaired by NRC vice-chair Prawase Wasi),[26] so the NRC should be seen as laying down markers and creating a network of alliances for the crafting of a more long-term solution to the problems of the South. Such a solution would have to await the emergence of a more reflexive, more compassionate, and more imaginative Thai government than the Thaksin administrations of 2001–04 and 2005–06.

The anachronistic military coup of 19 September 2006 brought Thaksin's government to an untimely end. His deeply divisive leadership had eroded democratic politics and triggered the return of the military. While Thaksin's forced downfall boded ill for the future of Thai politics, it was greeted with great enthusiasm by many Malay Muslims in the southern border provinces. Thaksin's nemesis, coup leader and army commander Sonthi Bonyaratkalin — himself a Muslim — had regularly expressed his frustration with the government's hardline policies in the South in the months prior to the coup. For better or worse, the end of the Thaksin regime signaled a new opportunity to address the worsening violent conflict.

❑

NOTES

Preface

1. Chaiwat 1992: 29.
2. Chaiwat 1992: 29–31.
3. See National Reconciliation Commission 2006a: 28, for a detailed discussion.

Introduction

1. For historical overviews, see Che Man 1990 and Thanet 2004.
2. On political reform, see McCargo 2002; on Thaksin, see McCargo and Ukrist 2005.
3. For the best overview of the recent violence in English, see International Crisis Group 2005.
4. In this issue, we have followed Chaiwat Satha-Anand's preferred spelling of the name of the mosque, Kru-Ze. Variant spellings often used include Kru-ze, Krue Ze, and Kru Se.
5. McCargo and Ukrist 2005.
6. Horstmann 2004, 89.
7. Gunaratna et al. 2005.

Chapter 1

1. Renan 1990, 11.
2. "Truth" management is the term I first used in a keynote address I gave as president of the Social Science Association of Thailand in 1997. This address, *"Sangkhomsat kap kanjatkan 'khwam jing' nai sangkhom thai"* [Social science and "truth" management in Thai society] was later published in *Sangkhomsat Parithat* [Social Science Review]. See Chaiwat 1998. The ways in which a given society manages "truths" vary, reflecting how power works in that society. Thai society manages different "truths" differently. For example, the law of the land could be enforced to silence

"undesirable truths" that come out of a research paper; social pressures could be mounted for a university to recall an advanced degree given to the author of a published thesis that many consider blasphemous to their local heroine; ideas of political reforms could be praised for their sophistication, yet regarded as too idealistic to be put into practice and therefore shelved; or a part of history deemed too ugly to face could be relegated to the realm of silence. In other words, "truth" management reflects how a society selects, presents, neglects, or suppresses certain "truths," which in turn, could reveal much about the realities of that society.

3. Imron 1995, 157. The date of the most serious fighting was identified in this work as 25 April 1948.

4. Surin 1985, 161. Surin stated that the incident occurred on 26–27 April 1948.

5. "Malay Muslim(s)" is my own preferred term. However, where sources cited have used alternative terms, e.g., "Thai Muslims," "Southern Muslims," "local Malay Muslims," "Thai Muslims," "local Patani Muslims," and "the Muslims/ these Muslims," I have retained these usages in my discussions based on these sources.

6. Syukri 2005, 97. Syukri asserted that the Dusun-nyor incident took place on 28 April 1948 and the violence lasted thirty-six hours.

7. Ahmad 2000, 7.

8. Ibid., 49–50.

9. Gillis 1994, cited in Thongchai 1999.

10. Bickford 1999, 269.

11. Ibid., 270–71. Here Bickford is summarizing reasons used by Latin American human rights advocates on this issue. I did not include one of his reasons: it is impossible to ignore the past, because there are so many states producing "new pasts" that "old pasts" could be importantly clouded.

12. Ibid., 271–72.

13. Bickford points out that one of the best works on "monuments of memories" is Linenthal 1995. See ibid., 278n8. The making of holocaust museums engenders numerous problems and debates. See, for example, Henningsen 2001, 198–211. Here Henningsen raised the question why the history of American-German relations has been clouded by the shadow of the holocaust, a European phenomenon, notably after the 1960s. He also observed that while the holocaust museums in the United States are receiving federal financial support, the proposal to build a monument for the memory of African Americans under slavery has never passed through Congress.

14. The pioneering work on monument studies in Thailand was Pibul 1984. Two other interesting works written on the subject by Thai academics in English are Thongchai 1999 and Thak 2001, 64–110. (In the case of Thak 2001, the book is in Thai but Thak's essay is in English.) Thak attempts to consider national narrative by opening up space for differences in terms of ethnicity as in the case of the Chinese or regional/ethnic. In the latter

case, Thak used the Sarit Thanarat Monument in Khon Khaen to connect the province and the Northeast with a modernized Thailand through Sarit, a son of the Northeast who had become a Thai prime minister. The other important work is Reynolds 2000. Reynolds compares the meanings of the Burma's Shwedagon Pagoda with the Thai Democracy Monument, arguing that they are not confined to official nationalist narrative but because both sites have become protest sites, a different type of narratives that reflect the feelings of those who chose to engage in political struggles could challenge and even emerge victorious over the "official versions."

15. Nidhi 1995, 89–124. Thongchai Winichakul wrote in the introduction to this book that the chapter on monuments is "the best in this book" and "most outstanding in terms of its analysis" (22).

16. Ibid., 104.

17. Ibid., 120.

18. Malinee 1998.

19. Ibid., 238

20. The opening ceremony — held on 15 January 1934, after the suppression of the royalist rebellion in 1933, with its stronghold in Korat — was premature, since the monument was still under construction. Saipin 1996, 16.

21. Saipin 1994. This thesis was published as *Kanmuang nai anusawari Thao Suranaree* [The politics of the Thao Suranaree monument] (Bangkok: Matichon, 1995). But after the protest in the "honor war" for the Korat people, the publishers sent a letter to the governor of Korat, dated 28 February 1996, expressing their "sincerity by immediately withdrawing copies of this book from the market." The best record of this incident is Kanchanee 1996.

22. Senate Special Committee 1999, chap. 2, 16.

23. Piyanat 1991, 104–5.

24. Imron 1995, 161.

25. The case of Haji Sulong appears in Chaiwat forthcoming, chap. 4.

26. Syukri 2005, 97.

27. Mahmud 1999, 77.

28. Syukri 2005, 97.

29. Malek 1993, 210–11.

30. Che Man 1990, 67.

31. In Imron 1995, this incident is called "a rebellion" (149) and "a riot" (156–57). Imron also used the term "Narathiwat Rebellion," which differs from others. He is a Muslim but not a Malay Muslim.

32. The term "Pue rae" is an expression in the local dialect in the Pattani area for the word "perang," in common Malay, meaning "war."

33. Rattiya 2001, 163.

34. Ahmad 2000, 7.

35. An interview with Mukta Tapoo, 76. House number 263, Moo 1, Tambon Dusun-nyor, Janae District, Narathiwat. Interviewed by Saronee Duereh.

36. The *Straits Times*, 29–30 April 1948, reported that between two thousand and six thousand Pattani residents had migrated to Malaya. Cited in Che Man 1990, 67.
37. Syukri 2005, 35; Rattiya 2001, 163.
38. Ahmad 2000, 7. Caption under the photograph.
39. Anderson 1992 (1973), esp. chap. 5, Cartoons and monuments: The evolution of political communication under the new order, 174, 179.
40. Malinee 1998, 241–46. A note at the end of the table on p. 246 indicates that the list does not include monuments built without seeking official permission.
41. Nidhi 1995. `
42. Interviewed by Saronee Duereh, my research assistant, 1 November 2005.
43. Le Goff 1992, 1.
44. It would be interesting to compare my methodology with Thak's in "deconstructing" the Sarit Monument visually. The Sarit Monument in Khon Kaen is a bas-relief depicting the field marshal performing different activities in eleven panels. These separate panels are in a diaorama that Thak called "modern pictographs." The panels are read from left to right, showing the connection between the Northeast and the nation through the life and works of Sarit. See Thak 2001, 94–104.
45. An interview with Lieutenant Nares Wongsuwan, Royal Thai Army, Bangkok, 29 May 2001, based on the photograph of the monument, by the author.
46. *Phraratchabanyat awutpun khruangkrasupun wathurabeut dokmaiphleung lae singthiam awutpun 2490: prap prung mai phrom duay kotkrasuang chabap thi 1 pajuban* 1999, 45–46.
47. Nidhi 1995, 96. The Private Black (*ja dam*) monument in Nakhon Si Thammarat is a memorial to the Thai soldiers who died resisting the Japanese landings there during World War II.
48. Author's conversation with a police officer, Provincial Police Station, Muang District, Narathiwat, 9 April 2002.
49. A report from Saronee Duereh, my research assistant, 25 May 2001. Another monument in Thailand does contain the bones of dead people, namely, the World War I Volunteer Soldiers monument in Bangkok, built in 1921. See Malinee 1998, 5.
50. As evident in the 1999–2003 security policy for the Southern Border Provinces, formulated by the National Security Council.
51. Musil 1987, 61–63, cited in Anderson 1998, 46–47.
52. *Phraratchabanyat awutpun khruangkrasupun wathurabeut dokmaiphleung lae singthiam awutpun 2490: prap prung mai phrom duay kotkrasuang chabap thi 1 pajuban* 1999, 5 Clause 1 (a) and (b) indicate that official agencies with these duties are exempted from this law. This means that guns and bullets are standard objects for such agencies.
53. Anderson 1998, 56.
54. Piyanat 1991, 106; and Imron 1995, 161. Imron wrote that the Dusunnyor villagers "were full of acute anger."

55. Parliament Secretariat 1948, 789. Cited in Chalermkiat 1986, 158–59.
56. Anderson 1998, 56.
57. Thompson 1984, 42–72.
58. *Raingan khanakamakan isara taisuan kho thae jing karani hetkan masayit krue se (phakraek)* 2004, 11; and Supalak and Pathan 2004, 187.
59. See for example, *Matichon Daily*, 1 May 2004, and *Post Today*, 3 May 2004. The former is an account of the interview I gave on FM 97.5 radio on 29 April 2004. The latter was the talk I gave at the Thai Senate on the subject on 30 April 2004. Both are in Thai.
60. See for example, a discussion of the militants as "Islamic warriors" in Supalak and Pathan 2004, 183–242.
61. Supara Janchitfah's comment. See Supara 2004, 154.
62. This letter, together with my response, was published in *Sinlapa Watta-natham* [Art and Culture] 25 (9 July 2004): 149–50. The quote was on p. 149. The writer of the letter was Chalermkiat Khunthongpetch, whose master's degree thesis has been recently reprinted. See Chalermkiat 2004. To date, this work is the best study on Haji Sulong available in Thai.
63. Hannah Arendt, "Truth and Politics," in Arendt 1967, 227–64. I discuss her thought and its influence on this research, among others, in chap. 1 of Chaiwat forthcoming.
64. Supalak and Pathan 2004, 67.
65. Pallop 2004, 304. Pallop's best-selling book was printed four times in three months. The publisher advertised at the end of the book that any-one who wants to record his/her distinguished career, as an entrepre-neur, a politician, government official, or similar, in a book, which would normally cost them around 300,000 baht, can approach them and they will publish it for free.
66. Bhiksunee Waramai Kabilsingh 2005, 9. This is based on Waramai's ac-count as a journalist when she traveled to the South in June 1948. It was first published in 1949.
67. Ibid., 161.
68. Khattiya 2004, 167. This is another best-selling book, with four printings in the month of October 2004. Written by a maverick soldier, it is a per-sonal vendetta against a former director general of the Police Bureau. In the book he holds the police accountable for the deterioration of vio-lence in the South, in the context of a conflict between the police and the military that began when a military officer decapitated a police officer in 2003.
69. From the Chinese perspective, the myth of Kru-Ze is the story of Lim Kun Yew, a Chinese girl who came to Pattani to persuade her brother, who had embraced Islam and was involved in the construction of the Kru-Ze mosque, to return to their mother in China. When her brother refused, she committed suicide under a cashew nut tree near the mosque. Before taking her own life, she issued a curse that the construction of the mosque would never be completed. Legend has it that lightning struck the mosque whenever someone tried to complete it. However, some

pointed out that the beams of the mosque showed no sign of having been struck by lightning. (Chaiwat 2005, 65–68.) Khattiya alluded to this idea in his rather wild writing in *Kom...Sae Daeng* (2004, 172 and 179).

70. For example, the number of bombs thrown into the mosque. According to General Pallop, eight grenades were used. (See Pallop 2004, 40.) But according to the *Report of the Independent Fact-finding Commission on the Krue Se Mosque, Pattani Incident,* nine grenades were used (*Raingan khanakamakan isara taisuan kho thae jing karani hetkan masayit krue se [phakraek]* 2004, 18).

71. Chaiwat 2005, 60–77.

72. On 2–3 June 1990, some three thousand Muslims participated in a political campaign to reclaim the mosque, which had begun in July 1989. Some of the leaders made speeches detrimental to the monarchy, and some police officers who tried to apprehend them were assaulted. This led to the arrest of a number of demonstration organizers. See Chaiwat 2005, 62–63.

73. Janjira 2005.

Chapter 2

1. This article focuses on the areas known historically as "Patani." This subregion roughly corresponds to the present-day provinces of Pattani, Yala, and Narathiwat, where more than 80 percent of the population are Malay Muslims. There has also been some violence in neighboring Songkla Province.

2. Pallop 2004, 39–41.

3. International Crisis Group 2005a, 24.

4. Connors 2005.

5. McCargo and Ukrist 2005.

6. The concept of network monarchy is elaborated in more detail in McCargo 2005.

7. Chai-Anan 1997, 56.

8. McCargo and Ukrist 2005, 513–14.

9. See Cartier Bresson 1997; McCargo and Ukrist 2005, chap. 6.

10. Ockey 2004, 183.

11. Liow 2004, 535.

12. *Bangkok Post*, 12 August 2001.

13. Chaiwat 1994, 287.

14. Interview with Dr. Worawit Baru, deputy rector of Prince of Songkla University, Pattani campus, and member of the National Reconciliation Commission, 24 October 2005.

15. Chidchanok 2005, 24.

16. Croissant 2005, 5.

17. *Bangkok Post*, 19 January 1998.

18. Chidchanok 2005b, 19.

19. Ibid., 51.

20. Chidchanok 2005a.
21. Supara 2001.
22. Liow 2004, 542.
23. Philippine National Security Office 2002, 10. This point was based on an interview with Colonel Akanit Maunsawat, representative of the Fourth Region Army commander.
24. *Bangkok Post*, 24 June 2001.
25. *The Nation*, 5 April 2001.
26. *Bangkok Post*, 20 July 2001.
27. Barnes 1993.
28. *Bangkok Post*, 22 July 2001.
29. McCargo and Ukrist 2005, 136, 144.
30. *Bangkok Post*, 11 August 2001.
31. Chidchanok 2005a.
32. Wassana 2004, 2.
33. *The Nation*, 19 March 2002.
34. *Patipatkan Joh Ai-rong.* 2004.
35. I am not seeking to give credence to these interpretations: verifying or discrediting them would require substantial fieldwork-based research. But their existence is extremely significant. The document quotes an extensive network of sources in the southern border provinces, the upper South, and Bangkok.
36. Kavi 2004, 274.
37. *The Nation*, 3 May 2002.
38. Chidchanok n.d: 22.
39. Philippine National Security Office 2002, 8. Citing a 20 August 2002 interview with Somporn.
40. *AP*, 16 July 2002.
41. *The Nation*, 15 March 2005.
42. Surachart 2004, 171.
43. Rung 2005, 133. At the time he published the book, Rung was serving as assistant minister for educational affairs, based at Government House. He was appointed deputy minister of education in March 2005. Would Rung have written this if he had not been told as much by Thaksin himself, or by people around him? It is impossible to be sure, but the Rung book could be seen as a retrospective defense of Thaksin over the closure issue.
44. *Thuk sotsai*, bold in original.
45. *The Nation*, 21 December 2004.
46. *Thai Press Reports*, 31 July 2002.
47. *The Nation*, 19 March 2003.
48. Chidchanok 2005a.
49. Liow 2004, 543.
50. Croissant 2005, 9.
51. Supara 2004, 158.

52. At one point, Thaksin was said to favor appointing Surachart as assistant minister at the Defence Ministry. *The Nation*, 26 March 2003. Surachart played a leading role in drafting TRT's defense policies.
53. *The Nation*, 30 January 2004.
54. Interview with security official, 16 October 2005.
55. *The Nation*, 27 October 2004.
56. *The Nation*, 18 December 2004.
57. *The Nation*, 5 January 2004.
58. National Security Council 1999.
59. Supalak and Don 2004, 302–3.
60. Ibid. 303–4.
61. Ibid. 304–5.
62. Ibid. 305.
63. *The Nation*, 15 March 2004.
64. Wassana 2004, 3.
65. Chaiwat 2004b, 6.
66. Supalak and Don 2004, 306.
67. Ibid. 6–7.
68. Chaiwat 2004b, 4, quoting *Matichon*, 29 April 2004.
69. Ibid. 7–8.
70. Supalak and Don 2004, 306–7.
71. *Bangkok Post*, 20 December 2001.
72. See McCargo 2003, 146–49.
73. *New York Times*, 9 May 1982.
74. Kitti 2004.
75. AFP, 14 January 2004.
76. AFP, 24 February 2004; *The Nation*, 25 February 2004.
77. *Bangkok Post*, 2 November 2004.
78. *The Nation*, 14 October 2004.
79. Xinhua News Agency, 15 October 2004; 17 November 2004.
80. *Bangkok Post*, 17 November 2004.
81. *The Nation*, 17 November 2004.
82. Croissant 2005, 4; *The Nation*, 22 November 2004.
83. *The Nation*, 20 November 2004.
84. *AFP*, 18 November 2004; *AP*, 18 November 2004.
85. *Bangkok Post*, 29 October 2004.
86. "Inside Politics," *Bangkok Post*, 28 October 2004.
87. *Bangkok Post*, 29 October 2004.
88. *The Nation*, 30 October 2004.
89. *Bangkok Post*, 2 November 2004.
90. *Bangkok Post*, 13 March 2005. Somchai, who had been defending suspects from the South arrested on terrorist charges, had openly accused the police of torturing his clients. He was abducted on 12 March 2004; he remains missing, and is presumed dead. For details of the case, see Somchai 2004 and Rengsak 2004.
91. Quoted in *The Nation*, 2 November 2004.
92. *Bangkok Post*, 17 November 2004.

93. *The Nation*, 4 January 2005.
94. Comments made to the author during two visits to the South in February 2005.
95. *The Independent*, 19 November 2004.
96. Not all the cranes bore messages of peace — some contained anti-Muslim slogans. Personal communication, December 2004.
97. *The Nation*, 16 February 2005.
98. *Thai Press Reports*, 24 February 2005.
99. *Thai Press Reports*, 3 March 2005.
100. *The Nation*, 1 March 2003.
101. *Bangkok Post*, 1 March 2005.
102. *The Nation*, 2 March 2005.
103. *AP*, 28 February 2005.
104. *AP*, 1 March 2005.
105. For details and a critique of the emergency legislation, see International Commission of Jurists 2005. See also, International Crisis Group 2005b.
106. *Kansanthana phiset ruang kansang santhisuk nai 3 jangwat chaidaen phaktai* [Special conversation about peace-building in the three southern border provinces], broadcast on 28 July 2005, 20.35 on TV Channel 11.
107. Worawit interview, 24 October 2005. It is ironic that Thaksin was now opposed by much of the NGO-sector leadership, since these same people — including several NRC members — had backed TRT in 2001.
108. These processes are discussed in McCargo and Ukrist 2005, chaps. 3 and 6 respectively.
109. Interview with Phra Maha Thawil Khemkaro, the abbot of Wat Lak Muang in Pattani, conducted by the Issara News Centre, Pattani, posted 23 October 2005 at http://www.tjanews.org/cms/.
110. Author's notes, Anand Panyarachund speaking at conference entitled "Kansang samanchan lae ruam funfu thongthin paktai" [Building reconciliation and joining together to revive the Southern locality], organized by the National Research Council, Prince of Songkla University, and UNDP, JB Hotel Hat Yai, 29 September 2005.
111. Piyanart 2006.
112. Wassana and Abdulloh 2006.
113. His troubles included the news that Grammy, an entertainment company with close ties to Thaksin, was trying to buy a controlling interest in the Matichon newspaper group. This generated such a furious public backlash that Grammy had to back off. Network monarchy was striking back in various ways, leading to public claims that Thaksin was trying to subvert the prerogatives of the palace. The main focus of this controversy was the government's attempts to dismiss anticorruption campaigner and auditor-general Khunying Jaruvan Maintaka, who insisted that the King had appointed her, and that only the King could fire her. For a discussion of these issues, see Pasuk and Chris 2005.

114. Pramuan 2005. Pramuan's book is very conservative, arguing that the Thaksin government has sought to undermine the powers of the throne. The book received a positive endorsement from the palace.

115. This is not to suggest that the various groups criticizing Thaksin by late 2005 had much in common; to a large extent, this was a tactical alliance created by the need to confront a common enemy.

Chapter 3

1. Chaiwat 2004a.
2. Chaiwat 2004b, 2–3; Thanet 2004; Dorairajoo 2004, 466–67.
3. For the best overview of the events, and detailed discussion of the three main incidents in 2004, see International Crisis Group 2005a.
4. For details, see Cumming-Bruce 2005. For detailed local commentary see *Matichon Sutsapda*, 22–28 July 2005.
5. The main advocates of this view are Pasuk Pongphaichit and Chris Baker, in Pasuk and Baker 2004. For a more critical reading, stressing Thaksin's police background and fixation with the military, see McCargo and Ukrist 2005.
6. Economist Intelligence Unit 2003, 15.
7. Elegant (2002) reported, based on information from several intelligence experts, that the plot to bomb Bali, Indonesia, was initiated from a mid-January 2001 meeting in southern Thailand. He also reported that "police officers mentioned at least five terrorist cells involved in this attack, with members from four Southeast Asian countries namely Indonesia, Malaysia, Thailand and the Philippines."
8. *Manager Online*, 20 March 2004.
9. Many local Muslims in the South, however, believed at least initially that the Thai security forces had in some way staged or manufactured the incidents.
10. *Phujatkan*, 30 April 2004.
11. Thaksin, quoted in *Matichon*, 29 April 2004.
12. Chaisit Shinawatra declared: "[T]he majority of the raiders were drug addicts. They can be recognised by black outfits, rosaries, and knapsacks on their backs. Motorcycles were used as vehicles for the attack. Those involved in this unrest should be described as 'forces', and not 'youths.' ...[T]hey are also supported by influential groups associated with drugs." *Phujatkan*, 28 April 2004; *Matichon*, 29 April 2004.
13. *Post Today*, 26 October 2004.
14. Initially Prime Minister Thaksin Shinawatra, accompanied by leading forensic scientist Khunying Dr. Porntip Rojanasunan, referred to this statement, issued by the SBPPC on the night of 25 October 2004. INN News Agency, 26 October 2004.
15. Thaksin's 29 October 2004 national television broadcast, transmitted on all channels at 9.00 p.m.

16. Reports of a statement made to the Senate, evening news, Channel 5, 27 October 2004, and *Phujatkan*, 28 October 2004. Thaksin's 29 October 2004 television broadcast.

17. Thaksin's 29 October 2004 television broadcast.

18. During a seminar for the development of administrative leaders, attended by provincial governors and deputy governors, at the Royal Cliff Beach Resort, Pattaya, on 25 November 2004, General Vinai Pattiyakul, secretary-general of the National Security Council mentioned in his lecture on national security that "Intelligence agencies had discovered the establishment of separatist insurgency network since 2002 but no one dared tell the prime minister because they perceived the separatist movement as belonging to the old generation, and disregarded any suggestion that it could connect with the new generation." *Krungthep Thurakit*, 26 November 2004.

19. General Thammarak stated at the meeting: "[T]he insurgent movement persuaded the youths to join by brainwashing them. Their goal is to seize Narathiwat within one thousand days after the New Year, as well as to replace the flag at Thaksin Rajanives Palace. It is actually the parents' idea to have kids go out and exercise at night in the forest. Therefore, members of the general public are not convinced by the capability of state officers. Two things must be done in this mission, first, generating public confidence, and second, overthrowing the structure of their movement." *Khao Sod*, 14 January 2004.

20. Chetta was not originally considered a candidate for defense minister when Thaksin formed his first government in February 2001. A former army chief, General Chetta was once invited to join the Democrat Party by then secretary-general Sanan Kachornprasat, but subsequently opted to join the TRT Party instead (*Matichon Sutsapda*, 22 January 2001). He disappeared from the arena of national politics until November 2003, when he was named science and technology minister.

21. Former assistant chief-of-staff to the army commander, he replaced former Region 4 Army Commander Pongsak Ekbannasingha, who was transferred to serve at the Office of the Prime Minister on 19 March 2004, together with national police chief Sant Sarutanont. *Manager Online*. http://www.manageronline.co.th/politics/politicsview.asp?newsid (accessed 20 March 2004).

22. Announcement made shortly after the Tak Bai tragedy, covered by Channel 5 TV, 25 October 2004; *Krungthep Thurakit*, 26 October 2004.

23. See McCargo and Ukrist 2005, 121–65. Ukrist was the primary author of this chapter on the military.

24. Religious leaders in the area announced they would not cooperate with the army because General Chaisit had ordered mosques and houses of religious leaders searched by soldiers, who had behaved disrespectfully. These leaders filed a complaint with the prime minister. *Phujatkan*, 16 February 2004.

25. *Matichon*, 14 March 2004.

26. See Pope 2004. Pope cites a figure of 2,849 deaths.

27. Pallop stated during a seminar organized by the Institute of Asian Studies, Chulalongkorn University, on 19 September 2003 that the unrest in the South was organized by a terrorist movement.
28. TRT Party treasurer Sirikorn Maneerin served for several terms as deputy education minister prior to becoming deputy public health minister in February 2004. McCargo and Ukrist 2005, 231.
29. *Bangkok Post*, 16 December 2004.
30. Pisan's ties with Thaksin go back to the late 1980s, when he was an aide to General Wanchai Chitchamnong, then secretary to Prime Minister Chatichai Choonhavan. At the time, Thaksin worked closely with several veteran northern politicians. *Bangkok Post*, 11 November 2004.
31. *Bangkok Post*, 11 November 2004.
32. Ibid.
33. Thaksin interview at the airport before he left for Tak Bai, shown on TV Channel 5 Evening News, 25 October 2004.
34. See McCargo 2005.
35. Associated Press, 28 October 2004.
36. *Bangkok Post*, 19 December 2004.
37. Malaysian Prime Minister Abdullah Amad Badawi denied Thaksin's accusation that Malaysia was used as a military base, harboring insurgents involved in unrest in southern Thailand, and demanded that Thaksin produce evidence to validate his accusations. *Krungthep Thurakit*, 19 December 2004.
38. It is particularly interesting that Sutham made this statement. As a former student leader from the 1970s, he was widely seen as one of Thailand's most progressive politicians, and was very well respected when he served as deputy speaker of Parliament in the mid-1990s under the Palang Dharma banner. On the face of it, Sutham was about the least "hawkish" of Thaksin's ministers. By contrast, Interior Minister Dr. Bhokin Bhalakula stated he had never seen the photographs, none of which have yet been shown in public.
39. *Krungthep Thurakit*, 19 December 2004.
40. Prawase Wasi's proposals deal primarily with general ideas to generate a better understanding of historical roots and religious differences. He called upon the government, and especially the prime minister, to pay serious attention to finding a peaceful solution. See the proposal of Prawase Wasi, "Seven causes of the violence in the South," in Koisin and Supalak 2004, 126–34.
41. One-hundred-and-forty-four academics called for (1) an apology by the prime minister to the families of people killed during the Tak Bai tragedy; (2) the use of peaceful methods to ease the southern violence; and (3) the use of community involvement to solve problems. Cited from "Khosanoe tuataen wichakan ruang kan khae panha paktai" [Proposal to address the problem of the South from 144 academics], submitted by representatives of scholars from many institutions at a meeting with the prime minister, 14 November 2004.

42. In March 2004, the Human Rights Commission submitted a proposal to the government calling for the use of legislative and peaceful methods to solve the problems in the three southern border provinces. *Matichon*, 26 December 2004.
43. Deputy Prime Minister Chaturon's team included Dr. Chaiwat Sathaanand and representatives from the Community Development Institute; Prince of Songkla University, Pattani; the National Economic and Social Development Board; and the National Security Council.
44. The 66/2004 policy, a nonviolent peace-building strategy for the three southernmost provinces. For details see *Manager Online,* http://www.manageronline.co.th/politicsview.asp?newsid=4766565529703 (accessed 20 March 2004).
45. The team traveled to the South and had several discussions with villagers, religious leaders, and Imams, and with representatives from pondoh schools and the private sector (e.g., chambers of commerce and the fisheries association). They also met the three governors of the three provinces, the Fourth Region Army commander, commanders of the provincial police in the three provinces, district chiefs, assistant district chiefs, and finally, from the political sector, representatives from the House of Representatives and the Senate.
46. *The Nation*, 10 April 2004.
47. *Matichon Sutsapda*, 16 April 2004.
48. Information given to the author by some scholars who met the prime minister on 14 November 2004.
49. Thanyaporn 2004.
50. *Fah Diao Kan*, October-December 2004, 152–53.
51. *The Nation*, 11 December 2004.
52. Head of the Investigation Commission Pichet Sunthorn, and Dr. Charan Malulim, advisor to the prime minister for Islamic affairs, both urged the government to present the Tak Bai report quickly. The government tried to delay the report's publication, however, by summoning the Commission for a meeting with the prime minister. *Krungthep Thurakit*, 21 December 2004.
53. The Commission declared that the decision to throw eight hand grenades into the Kru-Ze mosque was unnecessary. A more appropriate course of action would have been to surround the mosque and engage in negotiation, rather than resorting to violence. *Matichon*, 5 August 2004.
54. *Phujatkan*, 29 December 2004.
55. McCargo and Ukrist 2005, 143–46.
56. Pallop 2004. The book's subtitle, "The General McArthur of Thailand," is indicative of Pallop's somewhat inflated self-image.
57. The three officers were Fourth Army commander Lieutenant-General Pisan Wattanawongkiri, Deputy Fourth Army commander Major-General Sinchai Nutsathit, and Fifth Infantry Division commander Major-General Chalermchai Wirunphet.
58. *Phujatkan*, 29 December 2004.

59. The Wadah faction was a long-standing group of Muslim MPs in the deep South, originally founded by Den Tohmeenah. The faction was associated with a series of parties, joining Thai Rak Thai when the New Aspiration Party was dissolved in 2002.
60. *The Nation*, 22 February 2005.
61. *Matichon*, 21 February 2005.
62. *The Nation*, 22 February 2005; *Bangkok Post*, 22 February 2005.
63. *The Nation*, 22 February 2005.
64. Ibid.
65. *The Nation*, 1 March 2005.
66. *Matichon*, 1 March 2005.
67. Sanitsuda 2005.
68. *The Nation*, 26 April 2005.
69. General Pravit Wongsuwan retired on 30 September 2005.
70. *Matichon*, 11 May 2005.
71. *Matichon*, 28 September 2005.
72. *Bangkok Post*, 7 June 2005.
73. Chaiwat 2004b, 2–3; Kavi 2004; Surachart 2004.

Chapter 4

1. This politically related violence comprises events in the three southern border provinces of Pattani, Narathiwat, and Yala, including bomb attacks, arson attacks, shootings, raids aimed at seizing arms, and attacks on military installations. We have compiled this data from newspaper reports of events during the period 1993 to 2005, triangulated against the official records of the police and the Office of Narcotics Control Board (ONCB).
2. These figures do not include the 187 deaths in two major incidents: the 28 April 2004 incidents (involving coordinated attacks on various security posts) and the Tak Bai incident of 25 October 2004 (when a demonstration in front of Tak Bai's police station was suppressed by the security forces and dozens of those arrested died, mainly due to suffocation). We exclude these cases because the definition of violence used here applies to attacks on private citizens and government personnel by nonstate actors.
3. Narathiwat comprises twelve districts: Muang, Ra-ngae, Su-ngai Padi, Sungai Kolok, Ruso, Yi-ngo, Waeng, Bacho, Tak Bai, Si Sakhon, Sukhirin, Chanae, and the subdistrict of Cho Ai Rong.
4. Pattani comprises twelve districts: Muang, Kapho, Khok Pho, Mai Kaen, Amphoe Mayo, Nong Chik, Panare, Sai Buri, Thung Yang Dang, Mae Lan, Yarang, and Yaring.
5. Yala comprises seven districts and one subdistrict: Muang, Bannang Sata, Amphoe Betong, Kebang, Raman, Than To, Yala, and King Amphoe Krong Pinang.
6. Crispin 2004, 12–14.
7. Abuza 2003, 153.

8. Che Man 1990, 97–115. For a discussion of earlier and current forms of violence by Che Man, see "Dr. Farish A. Noor interviews the head of the Patane BERSATU movement," Brand New Malaysian website, 16 June 2005. brandmalaysia.com/movabletype/archives/2005/06/dr_farish_a_ noo.html.

9. Detailed discussions and arguments about the underlying causes and motives for increased violence in the deep South can be seen in the magazine *Fa diao kan* 2004, 122–64.

10. Two surveys were carried out by the Department of Political Science, Prince of Songkla University, Pattani, in March 2004 and in February 2005. The target population and sample, people living in Pattani town, were selected through a random-sampling process from official lists of eligible voters. Each sample size was about five hundred. It should be noted here that people of Pattani town are likely to give somewhat different answers from people in rural Pattani, Yala, and Narathiwat, because almost half of the population in town are Buddhists, while approximately 90 percent of population in rural areas are Muslims.

11. This survey was conducted by Assumption University's ABAC KSC (known as ABAC Poll) and Prince of Songkla University's Center for Humanities and Social Sciences Research. The sample comprised 3,279 people aged over eighteen years, living in the three southern border provinces, surveyed between 15 February and 2 March 2005. A press release was issued (see Xinhua News Agency 2005), but the findings about attitudes toward separatism were not made public.

12. U.S. Department of State 2005, 41.

13. Abuza 2005.

14. Officially, the populations of the three provinces are: Narathiwat, 708,241; Yala, 465,446; and Pattani, 634,619. These 2000 census figures need to be treated with some skepticism, since in practice a significant number of these people are actually working in Malaysia at any given time.

15. Prinya et al. 2002, cited in Surat 2003.

16. Official results of the "2000 Household Socio-economic Survey," National Statistics Office, cited in *Pocket Thailand in Figures 2003* 2003, 203–05.

17. Rasida et al. 2005, 10.

18. Cited in Supara 2004, 81–82.

19. See Kelantan, whose proportion of people living below the poverty line (RM 340 or about 3,400 baht per month) in 2002 was 12 percent, while that of Malaysia nationally was only 5 percent (Leete 2004). It is worth noting that in 2000, only 3.5 percent of people in Songkla were living below the poverty line (879 baht per month) (United Nations Development Program 2003, 143, 145).

20. It is noteworthy that around half of Buddhists in the three southern provinces have only a primary-level education. It should not be overlooked that these provinces include a significant proportion of very poor Buddhists; poverty is not confined to Muslim communities.

21. Higher pay in Malaysia and the dearth of job opportunities in border provinces have been the main reason for these commuting migrants. There is no official figure available for the magnitude of this cross-border migration. However, Dr. Ibrahim Narongraksaket, an academic at the College of Islamic Studies, PSU, Pattani, has suggested that the number of these legal and illegal Muslim migrants may be as high as two hundred thousand.

22. Records of *yaba* (methamphetamines) use in the South are not high when compared with the same records in other regions, particularly in Bangkok and the central region. For instance, indictments of yaba cases in 2004 number 2,964, whereas Bangkok had 10,962 cases. Statistical records of the Office of Narcotics Control Board (ONCB), Ministry of Justice.

23. Statistical records of the ONCB, Ministry of Justice. The kind of psychotropic drug most frequently used in the deep South is alprazolam.

24. Lieutenant General Pisan Wattanawongkiri, commander of the Fourth Army Region, claimed that the young Muslim protesters appeared "drunk, without any smell of alcohol." This condition allegedly produced a confrontational, irrational hostility that resulted in the attacks on authorities and the subsequent tragic crackdown. *Thai Rath,* 26 October 2004.

25. *Raingan khong khanakamakanisara sop kho thaejing karani phu sia chiwit nai hetkan amphoe tak bai jangwat narathiwat mua wan thi 25 tulakhom 2547* 2004, 36. Eight of the detainees tested positive for metamphetamines, one for ephedrine, one for Benzo, and two for marijuana. Of those who died, one tested positive for ephedrine and one for morphine. One of the injured demonstrators tested positive for morphine.

26. *Raingan khanakamakan isara taisuan kho thae jing karani hetkan masayit krue se (phakraek)* 2004, 20.

27. Information from a presentation on the southern situation by an official from the ONCB, 20 December 2004. According to an interview with the same informant, methamphetamines (yaba) are used by some young Muslims in the three southern border provinces, but usage of this kind of drug is not as widespread as it is in the central and northeastern regions.

28. To be classified as above the poverty-line, 70 percent of people in a given community should have an annual individual income of more than 20,000 baht (roughly US$500). Data about poor communities comes from the Ministry of Interior, 2004. The GIS database has been developed at the Center for Humanities and Social Sciences Research, Faculty of Humanities and Social Sciences, Prince of Songkla University, Pattani, under the direction of Srisompob Jitpiromsri.

29. *The Nation,* 28 October 2005.

30. Chaiwat statement cited in Piyanat 2003, 34.

31. Piyanat 2003, 36–37.

32. Nidhi 2004.

33. Prawase 2004.

34. Maslan 2004. Dr. Ismail Lutfi Japakiya, a well-known Islamic scholar at Yala Islamic College, also emphasizes that Islam and peace are indivisible; they are identical twins and two sides of the same coin. See Ismail Lutfi Japakiya Japakiya 2004, 19.

35. Ahmad Omar Chakapia 2004.

36. *Fa diao kan* 2004, 105.

37. Under this policy, individual provincial governors are required to exercise centralized control over a wide range of governmental agencies.

38. As part of the provincial strategic planning of Pattani, Yala, and Narathiwat, designed in 2003 under the Governor CEO project, the plan aimed to increase export products of halal food by 15 to 30 percent and so boost the value of border trade up to 10 percent. Planning goals included making the cluster of southern Muslim provinces a major center of the halal food industry, developing border trade, and making the southern provinces a center of international Islamic studies.

39. Thongchai Winichakul (2004) examines the new imagery of Pattani's history, which has been constructed by both local people of the three southern provinces and Thai state over the past century. This is an example of different realities in the construction of reality through history.

40. One extreme example of a conspiracy theory concerned the dramatic raid on a military barracks that took place on 4 January 2004. Rumor had it that the raid had been fabricated by the soldiers themselves, who had previously sold all their weapons and needed to stage an attack to cover this up. Rumors to this effect had spread to all three provinces within a week of the raid itself.

41. Srisompob 2005.

42. As explained in the Preface, the term "Patani" refers to the historical Patani kingdom, which covered the whole present three southernmost provinces, before the Siamese integration in the early twentieth century. The Romanized spelling of the word is fraught with political meaning: with two "t"'s, it refers to the modern Thai province of Pattani, whereas writing the name with one "t" evokes a deeper, pre-Siamese history.

43. Hoffman 1998, 43.

44. This figure does not take into account those Muslims said to have "disappeared" during this period. Gaining an accurate sense of these numbers is not easy.

Chapter 5

1. For discussions of the historical background to the conflict, see Surin 1985; Che Man 1990; and Thanet 2004.

2. See, for example, Suria 1998, cited in Omar 2005, 12.

3. Nantawan 1976.

4. See Srisompob and Panyasak 2006.

5. For a fuller discussion, see ibid.

6. Omar 2005, 11.

7. Ahmad 1997, 313, cited in Omar 2005, 11.
8. Prince of Songkla University, Pattani, was the first to build a mosque on its campus in the late 1990s.
9. Parliament Secretariat Office 1999.
10. McCargo 2006.
11. Kavi 2004.
12. In March 2004, Narathiwat MPs Ariphen Uttrasin and Najmuddin Umar, and prominent Pattani senator Den Tohmeena, all Muslims, were accused of involvement in the 4 January 2004 military camp raid. Only Najmuddin subsequently faced charges, however. He had been implicated by an informant, the reliability of whose testimony has been questioned. Najmuddin was close to Masae Useng, an alleged Barisan Revolution National member and secretary of Najmuddin's Pasuka (*tadika* or kindergarten religious school association) before Useng fled to Malaysia (International Crisis Group 2005, 19–20). Najmuddin's trial for treason opened in October 2005, but was immediately adjourned. On his acquittal, see *The Nation* 2005c.
13. *Thai Rath*, 8 February 2005.
14. Parliament Secretariat Office 1999, 4–5.
15. Davis 2004a.
16. Somchai's disappearance created an uproar within the Muslim community, particularly in the deep South. One popular Muslim restaurant in Pattani still displays a poster asking about his whereabouts.
17. For details of the case, see Somchai Homlaor 2004.
18. *The Nation*, 9 July 2005.
19. For local narratives on negative impacts of development projects, see also Piya Kittaworn et al. 2005.
20. International Crisis Group 2005a, 21.
21. Five assault rifles and a grenade launcher were used by the large group of militants who retreated inside the Kru-Ze mosque.
22. The document, which was translated into Thai and English, provides the best available evidence regarding the radically religious ideology of Muslim militant groups in the deep South. The following discussion of *Berjihad di Patani* is based upon both the Thai and English versions. For a full translation of the latter, see Gunaratna et al. 2005, 118–45.
23. *The Nation*, 2 June 2004.
24. Gunaratna et al. 2005, 59.
25. Ibid., 120.
26. Ibid., 130.
27. The term "Patani" as used in *Berjihad di Patani* apparently refers to the historical Patani kingdom, which covered the whole present three southernmost provinces, before the Siamese integration in the early twentieth century.
28. Gunaratna et al. 2005, 123.
29. Ibid., 139.
30. Ibid., 125.
31. Ibid., 122.

32. Ibid., 126.
33. The importance of this development has been confirmed in interviews with young Muslims in Pattani and Narathiwat, and with older exiled leaders in Kelantan. Personal communication, 24 October 2005.
34. International Crisis Group 2005a, 22.
35. See Chaiwat 2006.
36. Esposito 2002.
37. Marin-Guzman 2003.
38. Esposito 2002, 56.
39. Bouzid 1998.
40. Banjong Binkason 1981.
41. Jansen 1986.
42. Marin-Guzman 2003.
43. There is a difference between the classical view, which regards jihad as only a collective duty and not a pillar of Islam and the view of the modern jihadists, for whom jihad is both a pillar of the faith and a personal duty (Roy 2004, 295).
44. Albertini 2003.
45. Euben 2001.
46. See also, Esposito 2002, 26–70.
47. In his famous work "Join the Caravan," Azzam, the key Islamist who was a leading Afghan anti-Soviet *mujahidin* and mentor of Osama bin Laden, states that jihad comes just after *iman* (faith), which makes it a pillar of Islam, but maintains the difference between "offensive" jihad, which is *kifaya* (collective), and "defensive" jihad, which is *ayn* (compulsory for individuals). However, he considers de facto that contemporary jihad are all defensive (Roy 2004, 295).
48. Gunaratna 2002.
49. Noor 2003; Hefner 2002; van Bruinessen 2002.
50. In 1995, a new Muslim separatist group in the deep South, the Islamic Mujahidin Movement of Patani (GMIP), emerged. Founded by local Afghan veterans, GMIP was reported to have distributed leaflets calling for jihad and support of Osama bin Laden in 2001 (International Crisis Group 2005, 13).
    GMIP's Malaysian cousin, Kumpulan Mujahidin Malaysia (KMM) was also set up by Afghan veterans in 1995.
51. International Crisis Group 2005a, 15–16.
52. *The Nation*, 8 June 2004.
53. Davis 2004b.
54. The economically driven and western-oriented development of today's Thailand, with its sexual services, alcohol consumption, and drug abuse, poses serious affronts to Islamic teachings and sensibilities.
55. Interviews were conducted with seven Muslims in their 20s and 30s for opinions regarding problems and prospects confronting their community in July 2004. Their comments and ideas suggest a rather pervasive sense of malaise and alienation among many, if not most, of their peers.
56. Conversation in July 2004 in Pattani.

57. Investigations and reports following the 28 April attacks revealed that, far from being petty criminals and drug addicts, a large proportion of the youths killed had passed through the private Islamic schools and most were regarded by their families and communities as devout, promising youths (Kavi 2004).

58. The role of such teachers as "the recruiting sergeants and field commanders of *jihad*" in the radicalization of large numbers of the region's Muslim youth has been such that, as one commentator puts it (Davis 2004b): "The Royal Thai Army's (RTA) Southern 4th Army command now refers to the unrest as the 'Ustaz rebellion.'"

59. Davis 2004b; International Crisis Group 2005a, 18–19, 21.

60. Kavi 2004; Davis 2004b.

61. "O Believers! Migrate or fight in the path of Allah with your wealth and your life. It is known that firstly, based on Surat Al-Baqarah, verse 216, it is clear that fighting to uphold the truth is a compulsory obligation, *fardu ain*, that every one must fulfill" (Gunaratna et al. 2005, 134).

62. Ibid., 137.

63. See, for example, Phumibutra 2004.

64. This Thai-language paper entitled "Chijaeng khotaejing kanbit buen kham son satsana itsalam nai ekasan *Berjihad di Patani* [Facts about the distortion of Islamic teachings in the document *Berjihad di Patani*] was commissioned by the Sheikul Islam, or the Chularatjamontri's Office. It was distributed to mosques and religious schools throughout the country in early December 2004.

65. Some publicly denounced the author of *Berjihad di Patani*, saying he was not an Islamic scholar with a true understanding of the Qur'an (*The Nation*, 3 June 2004).

66. *Bangkok Post*, 11 June 2004. Ironically, in one incident copies of the Sheikul-Islam's white paper were burned instead. The incident was aired on February 2005 on a late-night news program of the Nation channel, but was
    not publicized in newspapers. (Personal communication with a colleague in Bangkok who watched the program, which was broadcast only around Bangkok and its vicinity.)

67. *Bangkok Post*, 16 June 2004.

68. Echoing the continuing disintegration of the *ulama*'s monopoly or exclusive jurisdiction over religious matters, Maududi (1969) argues, "Nobody can... claim in Islam to enjoy spiritual monopoly, and the 'Mullah' or 'Alim' is not a titular head claiming any inherent and exclusive rights of interpreting religious laws and doctrines. On the contrary, just as anybody may become a judge or a lawyer or a doctor by properly qualifying for those professions, similarly whosoever devotes his time and energy to the study of the Qur'an and the Sunnah and becomes well-versed in Islamic learning is entitled to speak as an expert in matters pertaining to Islam" (Mandeville 2001, 79). This analogy is actually rather misleading, since there are standard criteria for entering the legal and medical professions, but no such clearcut criteria for becoming an ulama.

69. A passage from his "farewell massage" after 11 September 2001 is particularly revealing. It reads: "The *jihad* (fighting in the way of Allah) has become *fard-ain* (obligatory) upon each and every Muslim. We advise the Muslim youth not to fall victim to the words of some scholars who are misleading the *ummah* (Muslim community at large) by stating that *jihad* is still *fard-kifayah*. The time has come when all the Muslims of the world, especially the youth should unite" (Albertini 2003).

70. Personal communication with a Muslim colleague who is a lecturer at a college in Yala.

71. Another source reported that Muslims killed by security forces over the past year, including the protesters who died in the Tak Bai incident, were buried as Muslim martyrs (*The Nation*, 22 November 2004). These protestors were entirely different from the 28 April militants — seventy-eight of whom died
    after being suffocated in army trucks following their arrest. The same source also quoted one leading local Muslim as saying: "It is believed that for every martyr, a thousand more will replace him."

72. Echoing this problem, one leading and highly respected ulama in the deep South shared his concerns with the NRC as follows: "Presently nobody [in the Muslim community] seems to listen to anybody anymore" (Personal communication with NRC member, September 2005).

73. High-ranking security authorities kept repeating their calls for Islamic organizations to issue a fatwa to all Muslims that killing others is against the principles of Islam (*Bangkok Post*, September 2004; *Thai Rath*, 26 April 2005), but to no avail.

74. See, for example, International Crisis Group 2005a.

75. Surin 1985; Che Man 1990.

76. Other than the persistent allegations of extrajudicial killings (*The Nation*, 31 July 2005), the southern violence has also been described by former interior minister Chidchai Vanasatidya as a mixture of Islamic radicalism and local "influential groups" involved in illegal activities (*The Nation*, 16 June 2005).

77. Srisompob and Panyasak 2006.

78. "Local" Muslims means Muslims in the three southern provinces, as opposed to officials sent from elsewhere, who happen to be Muslim.

79. Alas, such a refusal is rather common among peace-building advocates, subscribers to conspiracy theories, and liberal academics and commentators in today's Thailand.

Chapter 6

1. Personal interview, Pattani Province, in Pattani Malay, 18 August 2004. Note: the footnotes that follow are all personal interviews in Pattani Province.

2. In Thai, 16 November 2004.
3. In Pattani Malay, 2 February 2003.
4. In Thai, 14 November 2004.
5. In English and Thai, 17 November 2004.
6. In Pattani Malay, 12 December 2004.
7. In Pattani Malay, 14 December 2004.
8. In Pattani Malay, 16 December 2004.
9. In Pattani Malay, 12 December 2004.
10. In Thai, 3 November 2004.
11. In Pattani Malay, 5 November 2004.
12. In Pattani Malay, 2 June 2004.
13. In Pattani Malay, 14 November 2004.
14. In English and Pattani Malay, 11 November 2004.
15. In Thai, 12 November 2004.
16. In Thai, 13 November 2004.
17. In Thai, 6 May 2004.
18. In English, 11 November 2004.

Chapter 7

1. See Connors forthcoming.
2. See Interior Ministry 2002. The manual promotes an understanding of cultural diversity and acceptance of different ways of life, and criticizes past state cultural assimilation policies. Information on the ethnic/religious composition of the Thai bureaucracy in the South is not readily available. While decentralization policies will inevitably lead to a greater number of Muslims in local bodies, the central bureaucracy in provincial centers is likely to remain heavily Thai Buddhist for some time to come. Nimu Makajeh, deputy head of the Yala Provincial Islamic Council, in a speech to the Thai military, noted that 90 percent of the bureaucracy in the deep south are Thai Buddhists. This figure cannot currently be confirmed, but its importance perhaps lies more in the perception that it is true. Nimu Makajeh, unpublished speech made in Bangkok on the 9 July 2005. Notes sighted by author.
3. Acts of violence still occurred but were mostly seen as linked to bandits.
4. See Ukrist 2005, 8–13, 8.
5. See, for example, Abuza 2005. One influential commentator, whose reports circulate through web-based discussions groups and email lists is B. Raman, who writes regularly for the South Asia Analysis Group. His paper, Raman 2005, draws significant links between Bangladeshi and Pakistani "jihadis" and Thai "jihadis" working in cell structures.
6. Gunaratna et al. 2005. Page references in parentheses in the body of this article are to this volume.
7. The border linkages between Malaysia and Thailand and their people's, historically preceding the nation-state, are not considered here as evidence of "internationalization," although they have considerable impact on bilateral relations.

8. Gunaratna 2002.

9. See, for instance, Byman 2003, 139–163, which describes *Inside Al Qaeda* as one of the most disappointing books on the subject. Byman draws attention to a number of shortcomings that are worth listing here, since they establish that Gunaratna has a track record for unsubstantiated claims, intelligence reliance and allegations. "Although it [Inside Al Qaeda] often overwhelms the reader in detail, many of its key claims, such as bin Laden's supposed involvement in the assassination of his mentor and partner, Abdullah Azzam, are unsupported. In addition, it often relies on intelligence reporting without so much as a hint of whether the material is from an interview, a document, or a media leak (Gunaratna 2002, 23). Other claims advanced by Gunaratna deserve additional substantiation: a figure attributed to the CIA without further sourcing that terrorist groups have infiltrated one-fifth of Islamic NGOs" (142).

10. Smith 1995, 225–40, 230–231.

11. Ibid., 231.

12. For a critical study of terrorism studies, see Hamilton-Hart 2005: 303–325. Terrorism studies is as varied a discipline as any, and my particular critique focuses on those practitioners who embrace security driven agendas and fail to take a more rounded, historically based approach to local problems.

13. Burnett and Whyte 2005, 1–18, 4–5.

14. That the authors should be so restrained is interesting, despite occasional glimpses in the press and among some commentators of various international linkages. At the time of writing both the U.S. government and the Thai government are emphatic that the struggle remains local.

15. Specifically on Thailand, see Connors 2006.

16. The U.S. government has established the Pat Roberts Intelligence Scholars Program to financially support over one hundred students for two years; in return, the students, who are to have area expertise and foreign language skills, undertake an internship with the CIA. See Democracy Now 2005. Burnett and White (2005, 10) note that "The RAND-St Andrews Chronology of International Terrorist Incidents" specifically excludes acts of state terror but includes popular protests in its chronology.

17. For instance a more rounded and historical approach regarding Thailand is attempted in Liow 2004, 531–48.

18. For a broader discussion of "new terrorism" and a discussion of key figures see the discussion on terrorology in Burnett and Whyte 2005, 1–18.

19. A point made forcefully in Hamilton-Hart 2005, 320.

20. *Patipatkan Joh Airong* 2004. I thank Marc Askew for providing this document. This 97-page document has no author or date of publication. The title page for this document has been removed. For convenience the section heading on page 2, *Patipatkan Joh Ai-rong,* is used. It may well be the title of the document.

21. Ibid., 33–88.

22. Ibid., 26. The document argues that the BRN Coordinate emerged after the state had infiltrated the old separatist networks using them for their own purposes (35).
23. The intelligence dossier *Patipatkan Joh Ai-rong* (2004, 22–23) also provides extensive discussion of this, including the role of Thai rangers (*thahan phran*) in killings and raids.
24. Perrin 2002.
25. On illegal business in the South, see *Matichon* 2002.
26. Before the breakout of violence in 2004 earlier reports argued for the connection between youth gangs and illegal traders. See *Khom chat leuk* 2002, 2; and *Matichon* 2003. For a discussion on drug networks and the violence in the Muslim press, see Muhammad Laichuri 2005, 8–9.
27. See McCargo (2006) for an extensive discussion of how this engagement had worked. As described by the International Crisis Group, "The SBPAC was initially established [1981] to quell the communist insurgency in the southern provinces but was also effective in managing separatist violence. Attached to the interior ministry and serving as an interface between the south and Bangkok, it formulated political, social, economic and security policies to ameliorate the conflict. Its director was the deputy interior minister but it had local board members, and many of its staff were local ethnic Malays. Non-Malay staff were given language training." See International Crisis Group 2005.
28. Daungyewa Utarasint notes that Wadah is a word of Arabic origin meaning unity. See Daungyewa 2005. When the group was first formed it also used a Thai equivalent (*ekkaphap*) to name itself.
29. *The Nation* 2004. The accused included Pattani Senator Den Tohmeena, and TRT MPs Ariphen Utarasin and Najmuddin Umar.
30. Phichai c.1986, 59.
31. Ibid., 58. Daungyewa (2005) discusses Wadah's programmatic position on a range of issues. These include Friday being declared an official holiday, and a form of limited autonomy based on a Bangkok or Pattaya model.
32. *Matichon Sutsapda* 2004, 11.
33. Intelligence sources claim that Wadah associates continued to support the military training of youth (ibid).
34. In a book defending his family's role in Thai politics, Den speaks of multiple dimensions to the crisis, but also of interest groups creating incidents and framing people, including himself. See Den 2004. The loose translation of the title of Den's book was assisted by the publishers. Den also figures prominently in *Patipatkan Joh Airong* 2004.
35. On an alleged CIA extended presence in the South, beyond the joint US-Thai Counter Terrorism Intelligence Centre, see *Focus pak tai* 2004. This lists over a dozen alleged CIA operatives and provides work history and past zones of activity. See also, "Krai lae thammai jeung tonkan kokanrai nai paktai" [Who (and why) needs terrorism in the South?] available on the Tohmeenah Foundation's website http://www.tohmeena.com.

36. See Glassman 2004, 3–28.
37. See the booklet by the Workers Democracy Group 2005.
38. Nidhi 2005.
39. On 27–28 April 2004 over a hundred "militants" staged attacks on a number of state facilities. Although lightly armed (mostly with knives) the military response was to kill them.
40. Nidhi 2005.
41. For an account that shares Nidhi's attempt at contextualizing individual involvement in the 28 April events, but that argues that participants were vulnerable to manipulation by unnamed outsiders, see Ba-run 2005, 49–56. "Ba-run" (pseud.) is a former separatist who has acted as a mediator between militants and the military in the past.
42. See Asian Human Rights Commission 2004.
43. Cited in Sathian 2005, 59.
44. Ibid.
45. See the comments made by Maj-General Kattiya Sawatdipol on arms seized on a Thai trawler headed to Aceh in *The Nation* 2004b.
46. One of the few witnesses to the raid was killed in August, see *The Nation* 2004f. This same report notes that a number of mass surrenders by so-called militants are occurring because they fear their names are on blacklists, for reasons unknown, and they fear that they might be targeted. Furthermore, a number of those arrested in relation to the raid of 4 January claim to have been tortured into making confessions. In mid-July 2004 police dropped charges against twenty-six alleged militants involved in the 4 January raid. See *The Nation* 2004d and *The Nation* 2004e.
47. Ba-run 2005. The qualifying term "grey" indicates a cautious approach to understanding the relationship between religion and the insurgency in the South.
48. To that end note that Thailand and the United States already have a joint Counter-Terrorism Intelligence Centre and that the United States is assisting the Thai government in intelligence training. See *Phujatkan* 2004.
49. The groups include Barisan Revolusi Nasional (BRN) and its offshoots, the Pattani United Liberation Organization (PULO) and PULO's offshoots, Gerakan Mujahideen Islam Pattani (GMIP), United Front for the Independence of Pattani (BERSATU), and the Centre of Tadika Narathiwat Foundation, otherwise known as PUSAKA.
50. In Thailand it is clearly understood that reference to BRN Coordinate and PUSAKA is at the same time reference to some Wadah-linked politicians close to the governing party, Thai Rak Thai, and also associates of senator Den Dohmeena. This grouping lost most of its parliamentary seats in the 2005 election, due to affiliation with TRT, but it still remains influential.
51. Take for example the reliance on media reports about the arrest of suspected JI members in 2003, on suspicion of plotting attacks during the APEC summit in Bangkok (Gunaratna et al. 2005, 60–61). The authors

give details of the charges to suggest the presence of JI cells, although the words "apparently" and "reportedly" act as qualifiers. The charges against the Thai JI suspects were dropped in mid-2005 for lack of evidence.

52. Hamilton-Hart 2005, 308–10.
53. See *Thai Post* 2004. See also *Matichon* 2004a and *Matichon* 2004b for full details of the documents and accompanying intelligence analysis. Intelligence continues to leak reports to the media on the activities of Masae. He is "reportedly" behind a militant "youth" group, "Permuda," that is said to be behind some of the daily attacks. See *Banmuang* 2005.
54. Supalak and Pathan 2004, 164–65.
55. See Kitti 2004, 119–21. 127. Virtually all of the groups (e.g., Pemuda, PUSAKA, and BRN Coordinate) discussed in Kitti's book have been mentioned in subsequent media reporting. The book also reproduces an alleged strategy document that focuses on psychological operations to divide Buddhists and Muslims by subversion of teachings about the nation, religion, and the homeland. The document also argues for frequent killings in order to destroy public faith in the state to provide for public safety (120–21). Different versions of the plan have been discussed in the Thai media. One explanation of the seven-point plan focuses on operational measures: (1) Military training overseas; (2) Mobilization toward alienation and ill-feeling of the people toward state officials; (3) Use of religious schools for indoctrination of youth to believe that they are not Thai; (4) Creation of division among the military and police; (5) Destruction of military and police security [intelligence] in order to seize weapons; (6) Carrying out separatist activities from Songkla to Kalentan, Malaysia; and (7) Final stage is to establish the Pattani republic. See *Matichon Weekly* 2004.
56. See, for example, *Phujatkan* 2004. An informant from the Southern Border Provinces Peace-Building Command told *Matichon* in mid-November 2005 that insurgents were still intent on implementing the seven-stage plan and estimated that of the 1,650 villages in the three border provinces, 825 hosted around three or four core militants, suggesting a total of one to two thousand militants, supported by around ten thousand sympathizers. See *Matichon* 2005, 15.
57. Kitti 2004. Kitti's book is by far the most detailed to date, offering detailed organization charts, a history of groups, and current structure of the alleged insurgency. See pages 85–87 for graphic representations. An extended discussion of the documents can be found in Supalak and Don 2004.
58. See *The Nation* 2004e and *Krungthep thurakit* 2005.
59. Kitti 2004, 126–28. This analysis follows that offered by "secret documents" reported in *Matichon Weekly*, that discusses the continuing commitment to separatism of some Wadah members. See *Matichon sapda* 2004, 11.
60. The authors cite brief English-language newspaper reports in relation to the documents. As to the authenticity of the documents seized in 2003, I

am in no position to say. It is worth noting however that in *Patipatkan Joh Airong* (2004, 60) mention is made of the so-called 1000-day plan to establish the Patani state in 2005, supposedly the final stage of the seven-stage plan, being doctored by those forces allied against TRT and Wadah.

61. See, for example, the authors' discussion of BRN (Gunaratna et al. 2005, 33–36) and their use of an alleged BRN website: http:// www.geocities. com/brn_supremecommand/index.html.

62. The other groups they mention as having recently split from BRN or having formed factions also date back several decades. A more detailed discussion of BRN Coordinate is available in International Crisis Group 2005, passim.

63. Chidchonok 2005a, 10–12. *Patipatkan Joh Airong* (2004, 35–36) reports that BRN Coordinate was established after other organizations had been infiltrated by statist elements. The value of these reports is no less and no more than those reports that appear in newspapers.

64. See *Khom chat luk* 2004, 2.

65. *The Nation* 2004c.

66. See *Matichon* 2004a.

67. See *The Nation* 2004e, 2005c. The press carries occasional stories of arrests of "militants," but rarely follows up the story. Disappearances and death are not uncommonly related to court cases. For example, in March 2005 eight religious teachers were charged with sedition and membership in BRN. The lawyer representing them noted: "Despite the recent deaths of three key witnesses who stood by them, we still have enough witnesses to prove our case." See *The Nation* 2005a.

68. The authors sometimes refer to informants in the body of the text with no subsequent referencing. At times the information source is simply footnoted as "intelligence brief" with no further details.

69. It is useful to have this text in translation from its original Malay version in Arabic script (Yawi). For the sake of consistency we are using the Berjihad di Patani spelling throughout this book.

70. See, for instance, comments made by Chavalit Yongchaiyut as reported in *Khom chat luk* 2004b.

71. See *The Nation* 2004g.

72. The press (see ibid.) reported Soh as the leader of the mysterious Talekat Hikmahtullah Abadan (Direction from God Towards Invincibility).

73. *The Nation* 2004h.

74. Actually the authors return to this event and attribute the leadership to another person, without realizing they are writing about the same event using a different transliteration, naming it the "Duson Nyor Revolt" (Gunaratna et al. 2005, 26). For the same event the authors have created two different leaders, two different names, and a different estimation of the numbers killed. Their confusion is understandable as there is a contested history relating to the "rebellion" and the numbers killed, but no source cites Haji Sulong as the leader, and no one thinks the two events they record are separate events. See Chaiwat 2006.

75. See Scupin (1998, 229–58) for a more nuanced understanding of the differentiated Muslim population in Thailand.
76. *Matichon* 2005a, 13.
77. They also mistakenly speak about fifty hooded armed protestors at Tak Bai. For an English-language summary of a government appointed committee's report into the events, see, *The Nation* 2005b.
78. A better starting point is International Crisis Group (2005a), which properly cites interviews, is better researched, and draws on a larger range of Thai sources.

Postscript

1. For the best academic discussion of these developments, see Kasian 2006.
2. Srisompob and Panyasak 2006.
3. Srisompob Jitpiromsri, personal communication 12 July 2006.
4. The second teacher escaped with minor injuries; for her account of what took place, see Amornrat 2006. http://www.nationmultimedia.com/2006/05/20/headlines/headlines_30004508.php
5. Interview with Pattani governor Panu Uthairat, 25 May 2006.
6. These and other questions were extensively debated at a seminar organized by Dr Wowaridh Baru at Prince of Songkla University, Pattani, on 15 June, entitled "Thung wela phak Muslim Thai?" [Is it time for a Thai Muslim party?].
7. Wolff 2006.
8. Avudh 2006.
9. National Reconciliation Commission 2006b.
10. National Reconciliation Commission 2006b: 4.
11. National Reconciliation Commission 2006a: 59–99.
12. Chaiwat comments at Bangkok workshop, 12 July 2006.
13. Some commentators privately speculate that Anand and Prem enjoy a degree of unspoken rivalry.
14. *The Nation*, 26 June 2006.
15. See also the four other responses to the NRC report in this issue.
16. Barun 2006: 107. The May workshop, organized by the Midnight University, featured presentations by leading Thai academics Nidhi Aeusrivongse and Kasian Tejapira.
17. Barun 2006: 111.
18. Ba-run 2006: 110.
19. Interview with NRC member, 21 May 2006.
20. This point draws on several interviews and conversations with NRC members. It is also equally possible to argue that Anand received no actual instructions "from above," but sought nevertheless to ensure that the NRC report accorded with the known or assumed preferences of the palace.
21. Supalak and Don 2004.

22. Supalak 2006b. Supalak also made another, much milder set of comments on the report, published in *Fa Diao Kan* (2006a).
23. On the Issara News Center, see Supara 2005. The Center's output may be viewed at www.tjanews.org
24. Chaiwat comments at Bangkok seminar, 12 July 2006.
25. The column, known as "Samnak khao hua khiao" [Green headed news office] was written by "Mae lukjan" [pseud.]
26. On the background to the 1997 constitution, see McCargo 2002.

❑

REFERENCES

Abuza, Zachary. 2003. *Militant Islam in Southeast Asia: Crucible of terror.* Boulder, Colorado: Lynne Reinner.

Abuza, Zachary. 2005. The conspiracy of silence: Who is behind the escalating insurgency in southern Thailand? *Terrorism Monitor* 3 (9): May. Available at: http://www.jamestown.org.

Ahmad Omar Chakapia. 2004. Interviewed in *Raignan kan samruat tassanakati khong prachachon lae naksuksa tor satanakan changwat chaidaen tai* [Report on the survey of peoples' and students' opinions toward the situation in the southern border provinces]. National Human Rights Commission and Prince of Songkla University, Pattani Campus, 2 July.

Ahmad Omar Chapakia. 1997. *Politik Thai Dan Reaksi Masyyarakat Islam Di Selatan Thai, 1932–1994* (Thai politics and the reaction of the Muslim community in South Thailand, 1932–1994). PhD diss., Jabatan Sejarah, Universiti Malaya.

Ahmad Somboon Bualuang. 2000. Dusun-nyor ra kua kabot? [Was Dusun-nyor a rebellion?]. *Thang nam* [Islamic Guidance Post], October.

Albertini, Tamara. 2003. The seductiveness of certainty: The destruction of Islam's intellectual legacy by the fundamentalists. *Philosophy East and West* 53 (4): 455–71.

Amornrat Khemkhao 2006. I will not go back to that school: Sirinart. *The Nation*, 20 May.

Anderson, Benedict R. O'G. 1992 (1973). *Language and Power: Exploring Political Cultures in Indonesia.* Ithaca and London: Cornell University Press.

Anderson, Benedict. 1998. *The Spectre of Comparisons: Nationalism, Southeast Asia and the World.* London: Verso.

Arendt, Hannah. 1993 (1967). Truth and Politics. In *Between Past and Future: Eight Exercises in Political Thought.* 227–64. New York: Penguin Books.

Asian Human Rights Commission. 2004. Thailand: Severe torture victims still in custody while police torturers remain in posts. Available at http://www. ahrchk.net/ua/mainfile.php/2004/753/.

Avudh Panananda. 2006. NRC report could be left on shelf. *The Nation,* 21 June.

Banjong Binkason. 1981. *Hon tang su lak chai* [Milestones along the path]. Bangkok: Al-Jihad.

Banmuang. 2005. Masae Useng triam puan tai: lai thai phut [Masae Useng prepares for southern unrest: Drive out Thai Buddhists]. 1 October.

Barnes, William. 1993. Backlash from Muslims feared. *South China Morning Post,* 27 September 1993.

Barun (pseud.). 2005. *Yihat si tao: khrai sang khrai liang fai tai* [Grey Jihad: Who creates and nurtures the southern fire?]. Bangkok: Samnakphim Sarika.

Barun (pseud.) 2006. Mong prawatisat duay ta nua [Seeing history through Northern eyes]. *Fa Diao Kan,* 4 (2): 107–111.

Bhiksunee Waramai Kabilsingh. 2005. *Dusun-nyor 2491 thung tak bai wipyok* [(From) Dusun-nyor 1948 to Tak Bai misery]. Bangkok: Ruam Duay Chuay Kan.

Bickford, Louis. 1999. Memory and truth-telling in Latin America. In *Memory, truth-telling and the pursuit of justice: A conference on the legacies of the Marcos dictatorship. A conference report.* Manila: Office of Research and Publications, Ateneo de Manila University, 20–22 September.

Bouzid, Ahmed. 1998. Man, society and knowledge in the Islamist discourse of Sayyid Qutb. PhD diss. Virginia Polytechnic Institute and State University.

Burnett, Jonny and Dave Whyte. 2005. Embedded expertise and the new terrorism. *Journal for Crime, Conflict and the Media* 1 (4): 1–18.

Byman, Daniel L. 2003. Al-Qaeda as an adversary: Do we understand our enemy? *World Politics* 56 (1): 139–63.

Cartier-Bresson, Jean. 1997. Corruption networks, transaction security and illegal social exchange. *Political Studies* 45:463–76.

Chai-Anan Samudavanija. 1997. Old soldiers never die: They are just by-passed. In *Political change in Thailand: Democracy and participation*. Ed. Kevin Hewison. 42–57. London: Routledge.

Chaiwat Satha-Anand. 1992. Pattani in the 1980s: academic literature and political stories. *Sojourn*, 7 (1):1–38.

Chaiwat Satha-Anand. 1994. *Hijab* and moments of legitimation: Islamic resurgence in Thailand. In *Asian visions of authority: Religion and the modern states of East and Southeast Asia.* Ed. Charles F. Keyes, Laurel Kenkall, and Helen Hardacre. 279–300. Honolulu: University of Hawaii Press.

Chaiwat Satha-Anand. 1998. *Sangkhomsat kap kapkanjatkan "khwam jing" nai sangkhom thai* [Social science and "truth" management in Thai society]. *Sangkhomsat Parithat* [Social Science Review] 19 (2):44–55.

Chaiwat Satha-Anand. 2004a. A new dimension to unrest. *Bangkok Post*, 17 October.

Chaiwat Satha-Anand. 2004b. Fostering "authoritarian democracy" with violence: The effect of violent solutions to southern violence in Thailand. Keynote lecture, Fifth National Conference of the Thai Political Science Association, 1–2 December.

Chaiwat Satha-Anand. 2005. *The life of this world: Negotiated Muslim lives in Thai society.* Singapore: Marshall Cavendish.

Chaiwat Satha-Anand. 2006. The silence of the bullet monument: Violence and "truth" management, Dusun-nyor 1948 and "Kru-Ze" 2004. *Critical Asian Studies* 38 (1): 11–37.

Chaiwat Satha-Anand. Forthcoming. *Khwam runraeng kap kanjatkan "khwamjing"*: pattani nai rop kung satawat [Violence and "truth" management: Half a century of Pattani]. Bangkok: Thammasat University Press.

Chalermkiat Khunthongpetch. 1986. *Kantotan nayobai rathaban nai si jangwat phak tai khong prathet thai doy kannam khong Haji Sulong Abdul Kadir, 2482–2497* [Resistance against government's policies in the four southern provinces, Thailand, under the leadership of Haji Sulong Abdul Kadir, 1939–1954]. Master's thesis, Silpakorn University, Southeast Asian Studies, History Department.

Chalermkiat Khunthongpetch. 2004. *Haji Sulong Abdun Kadir: kabot ru wiraburut haeng si jangwat phak tai* [Haji Sulong Abdul Kadir: A rebel...or a hero of the four southern provinces]. Bangkok: Matichon. In Thai.

Che Man, W.K. 1990. *Muslim separatism: The Moros of southern Philippines and the Malay of southern Thailand.* Singapore: Oxford University Press.

Chidchanok Rahimmula. 2005a. Oral presentation at workshop "Understanding conflicts and violence in southern Thailand: Global and local nexus." Faculty of Humanities and Social Sciences, Prince of Songkla University, Pattani, Thailand, 26 February.

Chidchanok Rahimmula. 2005b. Wikhritkan chaidaen tai [Southern border crisis]. In *Khwamru kap kankaepanha khwam khatyaeng: karani wikritkan chaidaen phak tai* [Knowledge and solving conflict problems: The case of the Southern border crisis]. Ed. Uthai Dulyakasem and Lertchai Sirichai. 5–63. Bangkok: Centre for Humanities, Walailak University; Asia Foundation; and William and Flora Hewlett Foundation.

Chidchanok Rahimmula. n.d. Peace resolution: A case study of separatist and terrorist movements in southern border provinces of Thailand. Faculty of Humanities and Social Sciences, Prince of Songkla University, Pattani, Thailand. http://www.geocities.com/bluesing2001/media/ peace resolution. htm.

Connors, Michael K. 2006. Thailand and the United States of America: Beyond hegemony? In *Bush and Asia: The US's evolving relationships with East Asia*. Ed. Mark Beeson. London: Routledge.

Connors, Michael K. Forthcoming (new ed.) *Democracy and National Identity in Thailand.* Copenhagen: NIAS Press.

Connors, Michael. 2005. Thailand: The facts and frictions of ruling. In *Southeast Asian Affairs 2005*. 365–84. Singapore: ISEAS.

Crispin, Shawn W. 2004. Thailand's war zone. *Far Eastern Economic Review*, 11 March.

Croissant, Aurel. 2005. Unrest in southern Thailand: Contours, causes and consequences since 2001. *Contemporary Southeast Asia* 27 (1): 21–43.

Cumming-Bruce, Nick. 2005. Thai shift of power by decree draws fire. *International Herald Tribune*, 19 July.

Daungyewa Utarasint. 2005. Wadah: The Muslim faction in Thai political party. Paper presented to the Ninth International Thai Studies Conference, 3–6 April 2005, Northern Illinois University DeKalb, Ill.

Davis, Anthony. 2004a. Thailand's southern predicament. *Jane's Islamic Affairs Analyst*. 1 April.

Davis, Anthony. 2004b. School system forms the frontline in Thailand's southern unrest. *Jane's Intelligence Review.* 1 November.

Democracy Now. 2005. The intelligence-university complex: CIA secretly supports scholarships. *Democracy Now.* 3 August. Available at http://www. democracynow.org/article.pl?sid=05/08/03/1420209.

Den Tohmeena. 2004. *Leut nua chai chua fai* [My family (flesh) is not behind the southern fires]. Bangkok: Samnakngan Working Experience.

Dorairajoo, Saroja. 2004. Violence in the South of Thailand. *Inter-Asia Cultural Studies* 5 (3): 465–71.

Economist Intelligence Unit. 2003. *Thailand country report.* February.

Elegant, Simon. 2002. Unmasking terror. *Time,* 18 November.

Esposito, John L. 2002. *Unholy war: Terror in the name of Islam.* New York: Oxford University Press.

Euben, Roxanne L. 2001. Killing (for) politics: *Jihad,* martyrdom, and political action. In *Islam: Critical concepts in sociology.* 368–98. Vol. II. Ed. Bryan S. Turner. London: Routledge.

Fa diao kan [The Same Sky]. Bangkok. 2004. July–September.

Focus pak tai. 2004. CIA-palangngan-muslim=korkanrai [CIA-power--Muslims= terrorism]. 30 January–6 February.

Gillis, John, ed. 1994. *Commemorations: The politics of national identity.* Princeton, N.J.: Princeton University Press.

Glassman, Jim. 2004. The "war on terrorism" comes to Southeast Asia. *Journal of Contemporary Asia* 35 (1): 3–28.

Gunaratna, Rohan, Arabida Acharya, and Sabrina Chua. 2005. *Conflict and terrorism in southern Thailand.* Singapore: Marshall Cavendish Academic.

Gunaratna, Rohan. 2002. *Inside Al Qaeda: Global network of terror.* London: C. Hurst.

Hamilton-Hart, Natasha. 2005. Terrorism in Southeast Asia: Expert analysis, myopia and fantasy. *The Pacific Review* 18 (3): 303–26.

Hefner, Robert W. 2002. Islam and Asian security. In *Strategic Asia 2002–03: Asian aftershocks.* Ed. Richard J. Ellings and Aaron L. Friedberg. Seattle: National Bureau of Asian Research.

Henningsen, Manfred. 2001. The place of the holocaust in the American economy of evil. In *The German-American encounter: Conflict and cooperation between two cultures, 1800–2000.* Ed. Frank Trommler and Elliott Shore. New York and Oxford: Berghahn Books.

Hoffman, Bruce. 1998. *Inside Terrorism.* New York: Columbia University Press.

Horstmann, Alexander. 2004. Ethnohistorical perspectives on Buddhist-Muslim relations and coexistence in southern Thailand: From shared cosmos to the emergence of hatred? *Sojourn* 18 (1): 76–99.

Imron Malueleem. 1995. *Wikhro khwamkhatyaeng rawang rathaban thai kap musalim nai prathet: karani suksa klum musalim nai khet jangwat chaidaen phak tai* [Analyzing conflicts between the Thai government and Thai Muslims in the country: A case study of Muslims in the southern border provinces]. Bangkok: Islamic Academy.

Interior Ministry. 2002. *Khu meu kanpatibat rachakan nai jangwat chaidaen paktai* [Manual for the conduct of officials in the southern border provinces]. Bangkok, Krasuang mahathai.

International Commission of Jurists. 2005. More power, less accountability: Thailand's new emergency decree. August. http://www.icj.org.

International Crisis Group. 2005a. *Southern Thailand: Insurgency, not jihad. Asia Report* 98 (May). http://www.crisisgroup.org.

International Crisis Group. 2005b. *Thailand's emergency decree: No solution, Asia Report* 105 (November). www.crisisgroup.org.

Ismail Lutfi Japakiya. 2004. *Islam sasana haeng santipab* [Islam is a peaceful religion]. Pattani: Yala Islamic College.

Janjira Sombatpoonsirii. 2005. Ruang lao heng khwamkhlua [Narratives of fear]. *Matichon Daily*, 4 October.

Jansen, Johannes J.G. 1986. *The neglected duty: The creed of Sadat's assassins and Islamic resurgence in the Middle East*. New York: Collier Macmillan.

Kanchanee La-ongsri. 1996. *Karani nangsue ruang kanmuang nai anusawari Thao Suranaree, songkhram saksi khong chao Korat* [The case of the politics of the Tao Suranaree Monument: The honor war of the Korat people]. *Thammasat University Journal* 22 (3) (September–December): 20–79.

Kasian Tejapira. 2006. Toppling Thaksin. *New Left Review* 39 (May–June): 5–37

Kavi Chongkittavorn. 2004. Thailand: International terrorism and the Muslim South. In *Southeast Asian Affairs 2004*. 267–75. Singapore: ISEAS.

Kavi Chongkittavorn. 2004. Time to acknowledge that "Jihadism" is at work in South. *The Nation*, 17 May 2004.

Khattiya Swasdipol. 2004. *Khom...Sae Daeng* [General Daeng's blade]. Part IV. Bangkok: Ya Yi-eng.

Khom chat luk. 2002. Hetdai...Mujahidin pak tai jeung kla tawsu amnat rat? [For what reason do the southern mujahidin dare to challenge state power?] 9 July.

Khom chat luk. 2004a. PUSAKA: pae tua mai khong sathannakan tai [PUSAKA: A new scapegoat of the South]. 10 February.

Khom chat luk. 2004b. Wianthien klangwan longok [Light waving rite brings relief]. 3 June.

Kitti Rattanachaya. 2004. *Jut fai tai tang rat patani* [Igniting the South: Establishing the Patani state]. Bangkok: n.p.

Koisin Anwar and Supalak Ganjanakhundee. 2004. *Khrai jut fai tai* [Who set ablaze the southern fire?] Bangkok: Indochina Publishing.

Krungthep thurakit. 2005. Najmuddin berkhwam raek patiset pen kabot baengyaekdindaen [Najmuddin denies he is a separatist]. 4 October.

Le Goff, Jacques. 1992. *The medieval imagination.* Trans. Arthur Goldhamer. Chicago: University of Chicago Press.

Leete, Richard. 2004. Kelantan's Human Development Progress and Challenges. Kuala Lumpur: UNDP.

Linenthal, Edward. 1995. *Preserving memory: The struggle to create America's holocaust museum.* New York: Penguin Books.

Liow, Joseph C. 2004. The security situation in Southern Thailand: Towards an understanding of domestic and international dimensions. *Studies in Conflict and Terrorism* 27: 531–48.

Mahmud Nik Annuar Nik. 1999. *Sejarah Perjuangan Melayu Patani 1785– 1954.* Bangi: Penerbit Universiti Kebangsaan Malaysia. In Malay.

Malek, Mohd. Zamberi A. 1993. *Umat Islam Patani: Sejarah dan Politik.* Shah Alam: Hizbi. In Malay.

Malinee Koomsupa. 1998. *Nai thang kanmuang khong anusawri prachatipatai nai sangkhom thai* [Political implications of the democracy monument in Thai society]. Master's thesis, Thammasat University, Faculty of Political Science.

Mandeville, Peter. 2001. *Transnational Muslim politics.* London: Routledge.

Marin-Guzman, Roberto. 2003. Fanaticism: A major obstacle in the Muslim Christian dialogue. The case of twentieth century Islamic fundamentalism. *Arab Studies Quarterly* 25 (3): 63–97.

Maslan Mahama. 2004. Sathanakan paktai: arai khu panha, arai khu thang ok? [Southern situation: What is the problem and what is the solution?] *Matichon Sutsapda,* 2 November.

Matichon Sutsapda. 2004. Masterminds? 26 March.

Matichon Sutsapda. 2004. Pomkatyaeng "Den-Wan Noh" klum wadah daek pen siang 3 jangwat chaidaentai luk pen fai [The crux of the conflict: "Den-Wan Noh" (leads to) fragmentation of the Wadah group. The three border provinces burst into flames]. 26 March.

Matichon. 2002. Thurakit meut: Meun lan, tua prae sathanakan fai dai [Shadowy business: Ten thousand million baht. Protagonists behind the southern fire]. 14 July.

Matichon. 2003. Fai tai patuyok mai [Southern fire: The new war]. 29 April.

Matichon. 2004a. Munithi tadika [Tadika foundation]. 31 March.

Matichon. 2004b. Ekkasan lap [Secret documents]. 30 April.

Matichon. 2005a. Thalaengkan kankamnot si muban 3 jangwat chaidaen pak tai khong ko.so.so.so.jo.cho.do [Statement: Zoning [literally "determining color"] villages in the three border provinces in the South of the Southern Border Provinces Peace-Building Command]. 27 February.

Matichon. 2005b. Ko. so. tho. to. Yan chai prab khwamkit chana – dikhwa kha kan [Policy Committee for Peace in the Border Provinces confirm changing ideas is a better way to win than killing each other]. November 11.

Maududi, Abut Ala. 1969. Al-*Jihad* fi Sabeel Allah [*Jihad* in Islam]. Beirut: Dar Lubnan.

McCargo, Duncan, and Ukrist Pathmanad. 2005. *The Thaksinization of Thailand.* Copenhagen: NIAS Press.

McCargo, Duncan, ed. 2002. *Reforming Thai politics.* Copenhagen: NIAS Press.

McCargo, Duncan. 2003. *Media and politics in Pacific Asia.* London: Routledge.

McCargo, Duncan. 2005. Can Thaksin lead Southeast Asia? Only if he first wins over the region's Muslims. *Time,* 7 February.

McCargo, Duncan. 2005. Network monarchy and legitimacy crises in Thailand. *The Pacific Review* 18 (4): 499–519.

McCargo, Duncan. 2006. Thaksin and the resurgence of violence in the Thai South: Network monarchy strikes back? *Critical Asian Studies* 38 (1): 39–71.

Ministry of Interior. 2004. Poverty data.

Muhammad Laichuri, 2005. Tong kamjat khonbongkan [Eliminate the instigators] *Muslimthai,* 15 November–14 December. *The Nation.* 2004a. Southern bombshell: Faction stands by accused MPs. 23 March.

Musil, Robert. 1987. *Posthumous papers of a living author* [Nachlass zu Lebzeiten]. Trans. Peter Wortsman. Hygiene, Colo.: Eridanos Press.

Nantawan Haemindra. 1976. The problems of the Thai-Muslims in the four southern provinces. Part 2. *Journal of Southeast Asian Studies* 7 (2): 85–105.

The Nation. 2004b. January 4th raid: Four suspects offered immunity. 24 April.

The Nation. 2004c. Southern carnage: Kingdom shaken. 29 April.

The Nation. 2004d. Suspect from army raid: I was tortured. 1 June.

The Nation. 2004e. January 4 raid: MP Najmuddin to be tried for treason. 16 July.

The Nation. 2004f. The changing tone of the insurgency in the South. 4 August.

The Nation. 2004g. Imam admits to contact with separatists. 1 September.

The Nation. 2004h. Army protection for Islamic leader. 2 September.

The Nation. 2005a. Southern unrest: 8 religious teachers indicted for treason. 10 March.

The Nation. 2005b. Tak Bai report. 26 April.

The Nation. 2005c. Treason trial: Najmuddin acquitted as witness accounts clash. 16 December.

National Reconciliation Commission (NRC). 2006a. *Raingan kanakhamakan isara phua khwam samanachan haeng chat (kor or sor): ao chana khwam runraeng duay phalang samanachan* [Report of the National Reconciliation Commission: overcoming violence through the power of reconciliation]. Bangkok: NRC.

National Reconciliation Commission (NRC). 2006b. *Report of the National Reconciliation Commission: Overcoming Violence Through the Power of Reconciliation, Executive Summary.* Bangkok: NRC.

National Security Council (NSC). 1999. *National security plan for the southern border provinces, 1999–2003.* Text in Thai, Malay, Jawi script, and English. Bangkok: NSC.

Nidhi Aeusrivongse. 1995. Songkhram anusawri kap rat thai [The battle of monuments and the Thai state]. In his *Rat thai, muang thai, baeprian lae anusawari* [Thai nation, Muang Thai, textbooks and monuments]. Bangkok: Matichon. Originally published in *Silapa wattanatham* [Art and Culture] 11 (3) (January 1990).

Nidhi Aeusrivongse. 2005. Understanding the situation in the South as a "millenarian revolt." *Kyoto Review of Southeast Asia* 6. Available at http://kyoto review.cseas.kyoto-u.ac.jp/issue/issue5/index.html.

Nidhi Auesrivongse. 2004. Mong sathanakan paktai phan wan kabot chaona [Perspective on the southern situation through the spectacle of "peasant rebellions"] *Silpa wattanatham* [Art and Culture] 25 (8), June.

Noor, Farish A. 2003. Blood, sweat and *jihad*: The radicalization of the political discourse of the Pan-Malaysian Islamic Party (PAS) from 1982 onwards. *Contemporary Southeast Asia* 25 (2): 200–33.

Ockey, James. 2004. *Making democracy: leadership, class, gender and political participation in Thailand*, Honolulu: University of Hawaii Press.

Omar Farouk Bajunid. 2005. Islam, nationalism, and the Thai state. In *Dynamic diversity in southern Thailand*. Ed. Wattana Sugunnasil. Chiang Mai: Silkworm.

Pallop Pinmanee. 2004. *Pom phit ru? thi yut Kru-Ze!* [Was I wrong to storm Kru-Ze?]. Bangkok: Good Morning Publishing.

Parliament Secretariat. 1948. *Raingan kanprachum sapha phu thaen ratsadon krang thi 8, (saman)*. [Report of the House of Representatives meeting, No. 8 (Ordinary session). Bangkok. 29 April.

Pasuk Phongpaichit and Chris Baker. 2004. *Thaksin: The business of politics in Thailand*. Chiang Mai: Silkworm Books.

Pasuk Phongpaichit and Chris Baker. 2005. Thailand's malaise under Thaksin. *Far Eastern Economic Review* (September): 44–47.

Patipatkan Joh Ai-rong [Operation Joh Ai-rong]. 2004. Unpublished, anonymously written intelligence dossier, title page missing, undated but internal evidence suggests February or March. 97 pp.

Perrin, Andrew. 2002. Thailand's terror. *Time Asia*, 25 November.

Phichai Kaewsamran, Somjet Nakrae, and Arwit Baru. c. 1986. *Kanleuktang patani phi 2529* [The Pattani elections of 1986]. n.p.: Munithi pheu kansuksa prachathipatai lae kanpattana.

Philippine National Security Office. 2002. The Thai response to Muslim separatism and lessons for the Philippines. Policy and Strategy Office, Office of the President, Republic of the Philippines. September.

Phraratchabanyat awutpun khruangkrasupun wathurabeut dokmaiphleung lae singthiam awutpun 2490: prap prung mai phrom duay kotkrasuang chabap thi 1 pajuban [Guns, bullets, explosives, flares, and similar objects acts, 1947: Amended with Ministerial Order no. 1 to the present]. 1999. Bangkok: Sutra Paisal.

Phujatkan. 2004a. CIA leng thai su phaikornkanrai thum 100 lan baht nun tang rongrian dan kankhao [CIA takes aim at Thai struggle against terrorist danger: Throws one hundred million baht to support the establishment of an intelligence school]. 28 October.

Phujatkan. 2004b. Laa kaennam ek 100 khon puan tai [Hunting down another 100 southern disturbers]. 17 December.

Phumibutra. 2004. *Nung roi hong sop: khwam tai mi chiwit* [106 dead bodies: The living death]. Bangkok: Khean Phaendin.

Pibul Hattakijkosol. 1984. *Anusawari thai: kansuksa nai choeng kanmuang* [Thai monuments: A political study]. Master's thesis, Chulalongkorn University, Faculty of Political Science.

Piya Kittaworn et al. 2005. Voices from the grassroots: Southerners tell stories about victims of development. In *Dynamic diversity in southern Thailand.* Ed. Wattana Sugunnasil. Chiang Mai: Silkworm.

Piyanart Srivalo. 2006. Violence is on the decline: Chidchai. *Nation,* 2 January.

Piyanat Bunnag. 1991. *Naiyobai kan pokkrong khong rathaban thai to chao thai musalim nai jangwat chaidaen phaktai (2475–2516)* [The Thai government's governing policies towards Thai Muslims in the southern border provinces (1932–1973)]. Bangkok: Research Division, Chulalongkorn University.

Piyanat Bunnag. 2003. *Nayobai kan pokkhrong khong ratthaban toe chaothai muslim nai changwat chaidaentai 2475–2516* [Governmental policies toward the Muslim Thais in the southern border provinces, 1932–1973]. Bangkok: Chulalongkorn University Press.

Pocket Thailand in Figures 2003. 2003. Bangkok: Alpha Research.

Pope, Conor. 2004. Thai King voices unease at level of killings in anti-drug campaign. *Irish Times,* 10 January.

Pramuan Ruchanaseri. 2005. *Phra-racha-amnat* [Royal powers]. Self-published. Bangkok.

Prawase Wasi. 2004. Remarks at a seminar on religious ethics and development. *Khrongkan dapban dap muang* [Project on southern peaceful community development], Faculty of Humanities and Social Sciences, Prince of Songkla University, Pattani, 10 August.

Prinya Udomsap et al. 2002. The findings to understand fundamental problems in Pattani, Yala and Narathiwat. Bangkok: National Research Council of Thailand.

Raingan khanakamakan isara taisuan kho thae jing karani hetkan masayit krue se (phakraek) [Report of the Independent Fact-finding Commission on the Kru-Ze mosque incident. (Part I)]. 2004. Bangkok, 26 July.

Raingan khong khanakamaka nisara sop kho thaejing karani phu sia chiwit nai hetkan amphoe tak bai jangwat narathiwat mua wan thi 25 tulakhom 2547 [Report of the independent commission to investigate the deaths in the Tak Bai incident, 25 October 2004]. 2004.

Raman, B. 2005. Terrorism in southern Thailand: An update. No. 1501. South Asia Analysis Group. August. Available at http://saag.org/papers 16/paper 1501.html.

Rasida Raden-amad et al. 2005. *Raingan kansuksawijai khrongsang setthakit 3 jangwat chaidaen phak tai krang thi 1* [Report on study of three border provinces' economic structure, first draft], commissioned research submitted to National Reconciliation Commission, September.

Rattiya Salae. 2001. *Kanpatisamphan rawang sasanik thi prakot nai jangwat Pattani, Yala lae Narathiwat* [Interactions between peoples of different religions in Pattani, Yala and Narathiwat]. Bangkok: Thailand Research Fund.

Renan, Ernest. 1990. What is a nation? In *Nation and Narration*. Ed. Homi K. Bhabha. 8–23. London and New York: Routledge.

Rengsak Kamthon. 2004. *Wiraburut Yutitham Somchai Neelpaichit* [Hero of justice: Somchai Neelpaichit]. Bangkok: Fueng Akson.

Reynolds, Craig J. 2000. *Icons of identity as sites of protest: Burma and Thailand compared*. In *PROSEA Research Papers* 30. Taipei: Academica Sinica.

Roy, Olivier. 2004. *Globalized Islam: The search for a new ummah*. New York: Columbia University Press.

Rung Kaewdaeng. 2005. *Songkhram lae sanitisuk @ chaidaen phak tai* [War and peace at the southern border]. Bangkok: Matichon.

Saipin Kawengarmprasert. 1994. *Phaplaksana Thao Suranaree nai prawattisat thai* [The image of Thao Suranaree in Thai history]. Master's thesis, Thammasat University, Faculty of Liberal Arts (history).

Saipin Kawengarmprasert. 1996. Kan tham witthayaniphon [Writing a thesis]. *Thammsat University Journal* 22 (3). In Thai.

Sanitsuda Ekachai. 2005. The good news is in the spin. *Bangkok Post*, 3 March.

Sathian Janthimathon. 2005. *Jonyut nai muang* [Urban guerillas]. Bangkok: Samnakphim matichon.

Scupin, Raymond. 1998. Muslim accommodation in Thai society. *Journal of Islamic Studies* 9 (2): 229–58.

Senate Special Committee. 1999. *Raingan phijarana khong khanamathikan wisaman suksa 5 jangwat chaidaen phak tai, khu Pattani,*

Yala, Narathiwat, Songkhla lae Satun wuthisapha [A report by the Senate Special Committee on the five southern border provinces: Pattani, Yala, Narathiwat, Songkhla and Satun]. Bangkok: Committee Division, The Senate Secretariat.

Smith, M.L.R. 1995. Holding fire: Strategic theory and the missing military dimension in the academic study of Northern Ireland, in *Terrorism's Laboratory: The Case of Northern Ireland*. Ed. Alan O'Day. Aldershot: Ashgate.

Somchai Homlaor, ed. 2004. *Um thanai Somchai Neelpaichit: bot saton wattanatham amnat niyom nai sangkhom thai* [The disappearance of lawyer Somchai Neelpaichit: An illustration of the authoritarian culture in Thai society]. Bangkok: Thai Working Group on Human Rights Defenders.

Srisompob Jitpiromsri, with Payasak Sobhonvasu. 2006. Unpacking Thailand's southern conflict: The poverty of structural explanations. *Critical Asian Studies* 38 (1): 95–117.

Srisompob Jitpiromsri. 2005. Situation report on southern violence in 2004 and 2005. Commissioned research report submitted to the National Reconciliation Commission, 5 October.

Supalak Ganjanakhundee. 2006a. Kep moradok kor or sor [Preserving the legacy of the NRC]. *Fa Diao Kan*, 4 (2): 125–129.

Supalak Ganjanakhundee. 2006b. Samphat Supalak Ganjanakhundee: kor or sor mai lomlaeo, kae sunplao thaonan eng [Interview with Supalak Ganajanakhundee: the NRC was not a failure, it was just pointless]. , 19 June.

Supalak Ganjanakhundee and Don Pathan (with the Nation Group news team). 2004. *Santhiphap nai plaew phleung* [Peace in flames]. Bangkok: Nation Books.

Supara Janchitfah. 2001. Southern Discomfort. *Bangkok Post*, 12 August.

Supara Janchitfah. 2004. *Kho sanoe phak prachachon to sathanakhan khwamrungraeng nai phaktai* [Proposals from the people's sector on violence in the South]. *Fa Diao Kan* 2 (3) (July–September).

Supara Janchitfah. 2004. *The nets of resistance*. Nonthaburi: Campaign for Alternative Industry Network.

Supara Janchitfah. 2004. *Violence in the mist: Reporting on the presence of pain in southern Thailand*. Bangkok: Kobfai Publishing

Supara Janchitfah. 2005. Balancing the equation. *Bangkok Post*, 21 November.

Surachart Bamrungsuk. 2004. Special interview. *Prachachart Thurakit*, 22–24 November.

Surachart Bumrungsuk. 2004. *Wikrit tai! su kap yuthasat lae panya* [Southern crisis: Fight with strategy and wisdom]. Bangkok: Animate Group.

Surat Horachaikul. 2003. The far South of Thailand in the era of the American empire, 9/11 version, and Thaksin "cash and gung-ho" premiership. *Asian Review* 16: 131–51.

Suria Saniwa bin Wan Mahmood. 1998. De-radicalization of minority dissent: A case study of the Malay-Muslim movement in southern Thailand, 1980– 1994. Master's thesis, University of Malaysia, School of Social Science, Science.

Surin Pitsuwan. 1985. *Islam and Malay nationalism: A case study of the Malay-Muslims of southern Thailand.* Bangkok: Thai Khadi Research Institute, Thammasat University.

Syukri, Ibrahim. 2005. *History of the Malay kingdom of Patani.* Trans. Conner Bailey and John Miskic. Chiang Mai: Silkworm.

Thai Post. 2004. Nuay khoa pluk pi phak tai tua mai paet 7 khandon [Intelligence agency creates a new southern spectre: 7 stages]. 20 January.

Thak Chaloemtiarana. 2001. Towards a more inclusive national narrative: Thai history and the Chinese; Isan and the nation state. In *Lum khotom ngao ko phao phaendin: ruam botkhwam nuang nai wara khroprop 60 phi Charnvit Kasetsiri* [Forgetting one's roots, burning one's land: Essays in honour of Charnvit Kasetsiri's sixtieth birthday]. Ed. Kanchanee La-ongsri and Thanet Apornsuwan. Bangkok: Matichon Publishers.

Thanet Aphornsuvan. 2004. Origins of Malay-Muslim "separatism" in Thailand. *Working Paper* 32. Asia Research Institute, National University of Singapore.

Thanyaporn Kunakornpaiboonsiri. 2004. Web forums host hot debate on the South. *The Nation*, 2 May.

Thompson, John B. 1984. Symbolic violence: language and power in the writings of Pierre Bourdieu. In his *Studies in the Theory of Ideology.* 42–72. Cambridge: Polity Press.

Thongchai Winichakul. 1999. Thai democracy in public memory: Monuments of democracy and their narratives. Keynote lecture presented at the Seventh International Conference on Thai Studies, Amsterdam, the Netherlands, 8 July.

Thongchai Winichakul. 2004. Tales from the frontier [Ruanglao jak chaidaen]. In *Rat pattani nai sriwichai kaokae khwa rat sukhothai nai prawattisat* [The Pattani state in Sriwichaya is older than the Sukhothai state in history]. Ed. Suchit Wongthes. Bangkok: Matichon.

U.S. Department of State. 2005. Office of the Coordinator for Counter-terrorism. *Country Reports on Terrorism, 2004.* April.

Ukrist Pathmanand. 2005. Thaksin's policies go South. *Far Eastern Economic Review,* July/August, 8–13.

United Nations Development Program. 2003. Thailand human development report. Bangkok: UNDP.

van Bruinessen, Martin. 2002. Genealogies of Islamic Radicalism in Indonesia. *South East Asia Research* 10 (2): 117–54.

Wassana Nanuam and Abdulloh Benjaka. 2006. Prem joins the fight to tame rebels. *Bangkok Post,* 8 January.

Wassana Nanuam. 2004. Thai government slow to realize terrorism in the South. NEWSEAN. http://www.newsean.in.th. Undated, perhaps February.

Wolff, Ismail. 2006. Democrats gather to discuss South. *Thai Day*, 11 July.

Workers Democracy Group. 2005. Thammai rat thai kheu tonhet khong khwamrunraeng nai sam jangwat paktai [Why the Thai state is the source of the violence in the three southern provinces]. Bangkok: Workers Democracy Group.

Xinhua News Agency. 2005. 80 percent feeling fearful in Thailand's deep South. 4 March.

❑

CONTRIBUTORS

Michael K. Connors, senior lecturer in politics at La Trobe University, Australia, has published *Democracy and National Identity in Thailand* (Routledge, 2003) and *The New Global Politics of the Asia-Pacific* (co-authored, Routledge, 2004).

Srisompob Jitpiromsri is assistant professor of political science at Prince of Songkla University, Pattani, and a leading analyst of the politics of Thailand's deep South.

Duncan McCargo is professor of Southeast Asian politics at the University of Leeds in England. His books include *Politics and the Press in Thailand* (Routledge, 2000), and *Reforming Thai Politics* (edited, NIAS, 2002).

Ukrist Pathmanand is a senior researcher at the Institute of Asian Studies, Chulalongkorn University, Bangkok. His books include *The Thaksinization of Thailand* (with Duncan McCargo, NIAS, 2005).

Chaiwat Satha-Anand is associate professor of political science at Thammasat University, Bangkok. A prominent National Reconciliation Commission member, he is the author of *The Life of This World: Negotiated Muslim Lives in Thai Society* (Marshall Cavendish, 2005).

Panyasak Sobhonvasu is a Bangkok-based government official.

Wattana Sugunnasil is assistant professor of sociology at Prince of Songkla University, Pattani, Thailand. He is editor of *Dynamic Diversity in Southern Thailand* (Silkworm, 2005).

May Tan-Mullins teaches geography at the National University of Singapore. She is coeditor of *The Naga Challenged: Southeast Asia in the Winds of Change* (Marshall Cavendish, 2005).

INDEX